Adolf Grünbaum

Philosophical Psychopathology

Philosophical Psychopathology

edited by George Graham and G. Lynn Stephens

A Bradford Book
The MIT Press
Cambridge, Massachusetts
London, England

This book was set in Baskerville by Maple-Vail Book Manufacturing Co. and was printed and bound in the United States of America.

First printing, 1994.

Library of Congress Cataloging-in-Publication Data

Philosophical psychopathology / edited by George Graham and G. Lynn Stephens.
    p.   cm.
"A Bradford book."
Includes bibliographical references and index.
ISBN 0–262–07159–2
1. Psychology, Pathological—Philosophy. 2. Psychology and philosophy.
3. Philosophical anthropology. I. Graham, George, 1945–   . II. Stephens, G. Lynn.
RC454.4.P48   1994
616.89′001—dc20   94–31921
                                                              CIP

Contents

Preface

Philosophical psychopathology long antedates the appearance of this book. To name just two examples, in the *Principles of Psychology* (1890) William James saw psychopathology as a source of questions and data to advance philosophical debate. Two hundred years before James, John Locke, in *An Essay Concerning Human Understanding* (1690), offered an elementary discussion of various mental maladies.

Recent years have seen a dramatic increase of new activity in philosophical psychopathology. Work by philosophers on psychopathology has made a major contribution to our understanding of legal and public-policy issues related to psychopathology as well as the metaphysical and scientific assumptions behind psychiatric diagnosis and taxonomy. Few philosophers would now seriously question whether psychopathology can enrich philosophical reflection or help to stimulate and advance philosophical theorizing.

This is all quite straightforward. However, one should not stop here. What is surprising is that there is no book that reveals or tries to reveal the breadth and richness of philosophical reflection on psychopathology, the puzzles and data within psychiatry and related fields that interest or should interest philosophers, and the extent to which a number of contemporary philosophers and philosophically informed psychopathologists are contributing to a rapidly growing literature at the convergence of philosophy and psychopathology. Interdisciplinary activity is part of the contemporary academic zeitgeist, but the intellectual energy at the intersection of philosophy and psychopathology wants notice and advertisement.

To lay our hopes on the table, this book attempts the advertisement, the notice. More specifically, it aims to exhibit the scope of
philosophical inquiry into psychopathology as well as to advance debates on a number of key issues within the field. Of course, editors
must decide what to include within the scope; that is, the *full* scope
cannot be revealed within a single book. We do not here represent a
number of live areas of philosophical psychopathological inquiry,
such as the excellent work that has been done on psychoanalytic
theory and practice, the relation between gender and other cultural
categories and psychopathology, and (except for one chapter) the
public-policy issues surrounding psychiatry and psychiatric ethics.

To generate chapters of the contributing kind, we also had to decide *who* was to contribute. Philosophers like Patricia Churchland,
Daniel Dennett, Adolf Grünbaum, and Kathleen Wilkes have shown
what can be done within philosophical psychopathology. Although
one of these theorists is represented here in a reprint, we decided
that to demonstrate the emergence of interest in philosophical psychopathology and its diffusion across a landscape of issues, other
theorists should be invited to contribute heretofore unpublished
work. We therefore prevailed on individual philosophers to write
original papers exclusively for this book. With one exception, this is
not a collection of previous publications. It gathers arguments and
fresh contributors to philosophical psychopathology.

The idea that one can ask philosophers to produce original papers
and with no initial guarantee of publication (until the *deus ex machina*
of the MIT Press eventually intervened) may itself be a symptom of
mental disorder. We feel flattered that several philosophers were willing to undertake the risk. The only pure reprint is the concluding
chapter by Adolf Grünbaum on the notion of the placebo in medicine and psychiatry, which is included here in part because it com-
plements Edward Erwin's discussion of the effectiveness of
psychotherapy, and in part to show appreciation of Professor Grünbaum, who is the most influential contributor to philosophical psychopathology in recent years.

We wish to thank all our contributors for their willing, patient, and
illuminating work.

Among the many people who helped with the book are James
Fetzer, Owen Flanagan, the several referees for the MIT Press, and

our editors—Teri Mendelsohn and Betty Stanton. We also appreciate invitations to present our ideas about philosophical psychopathology to audiences at the University of North Carolina at Chapel
Hill, Rutgers University, the University of Texas, Wake Forest University, and Washington University.

We dedicate this collection to the memories of Paul Graham
(1954–1993) and Ferdinand Schoeman (1945–1992). Paul, George's
brother, and Ferdy, as he was known to his friends, did not know
each other, but they shared in virtues of courage and compassion.

Philosophical Psychopathology

An Introduction to Philosophical Psychopathology: Its Nature, Scope, and Emergence

George Graham and G. Lynn Stephens

The last decade has witnessed an upsurge of work by philosophers, psychiatrists, neurologists, and psychologists on philosophical issues connected with the study and treatment of mental disorders. Despite this work, however, the philosophical resources of psychopathology have as yet been only lightly exploited. Accordingly, we believe that the most useful way for us to introduce our readers to the emerging field of philosophical psychopathology is to survey the terrain, describing (some of) the work already done and identifying what seem to us to be some of the most promising opportunities for further investigation. In the course of this survey we shall also briefly describe the twelve papers presented in this volume and locate them vis-à-vis other work in the field.

First, though, we owe our readers at least a preliminary account of what we mean by 'philosophical psychopathology'. To give some specific focus to the general observations that follow, we shall begin with three clinical vignettes adapted from the *DSM III Case Book* (Spitzer et al. 1981), a publication designed to illustrate the application of the since revised (and now superseded) system of differential diagnosis in the American Psychiatric Association's *Diagnostic and Statistical Manual* (*DSM* III, 1987).

Case 1: The case of the worthless woman (*Case Book*, no. 17) A 50-year-old widow is admitted to a medical center. She is agitated and unhappy. She suffers from insomnia and has recently lost a good deal of weight. She reports that her neighbors have tried to poison her and that they have cast a spell on her. She admits to being tortured by feelings of guilt. She sometimes hears accusatory voices telling her that she is worthless and does not deserve to live. She has become preoccupied with suicidal thoughts.

The authors of the *Case Book* note that the patient's "pervasive depressed mood with the characteristic associated symptoms of the depressive syndrome (psychomotor agitation, self-reproach, insomnia, and weight loss) suggests a major depressive episode" (p. 29). They also note her delusions of persecution and her verbal hallucinations. They conclude that "in the absence of any specific organic factor to account for the disturbance," the diagnosis is major depression with psychotic features.

Case 2: The case of the housepainter (*Case Book*, no. 29)   A 46-year-old housepainter with a 30-year history of heavy drinking shows some striking deficits of memory. Although his recall of events from the remote past and of general facts is adequate, he has difficulty retaining new information for more than a few minutes. He can accurately repeat a list of numbers immediately after hearing them, but minutes later he does not even recall having been asked to perform the task. When queried whether he knows the name of his physician, he replies, "Certainly. It's Dr. Masters." He then proceeds to relate a long, highly circumstantial story about how he first met Dr. Masters when they served together in the Korean War. The name is incorrect and the story completely untrue.

The housepainter's specific impairment of short-term rather than immediate or long-term memory, together with his history of alcohol abuse, indicate that he suffers from alcohol amnestic disorder. It is not uncommon for those suffering from this disorder to confabulate in response to requests for information that they cannot recall.

Case 3: The case of Frieda (*Case Book*, no. 30)   A 42-year-old woman seeks a psychiatric consultation at the urging of her husband. Her complaints concern various marital difficulties of an unexceptional nature. Independently, her husband reports that she has on a number of occasions suddenly left the house dressed in a very uncharacteristic manner and without saying where she is going. She returns in 12 to 36 hours but refuses to discuss her behavior with her husband. When her physician inquired about these incidents, the patient initially professed to have no knowledge of them. Under hypnosis, however, she provided a vivid account. During her excursions she experienced herself as Frieda, the girlfriend of a soldier who had raped the patient when the patient was an adolescent in Soviet-occupied Poland. As Frieda, she would go to bars and seduce male customers. She would break off these encounters before intercourse, belittling her partner's masculinity.

The *Case Book* discussion notes that sudden, dramatic changes in behavior can occur in a variety of mental disorders, such as schizophrenia and psychogenic fugue. The patient, however, exhibits none of the psychotic symptoms associated with Schizophrenia. Nor are her repeated shifts of identity and complex behavior patterns typical of Psychogenic Fugue. In this case the authors conclude that the appropriate diagnosis is multiple personality disorder.

We want to use these cases to make two points about the scope of the issues we include under the heading 'philosophical psychopathology'. First, our vignettes mention both the particular impairments and disorders exhibited by the patients and the doctors' diagnoses of the patients' conditions. This reflects the double duty done by the term 'psychopathology' in customary usage. It is used to designate both mental disorders themselves—e.g., Frieda's multiple personalities, the housepainter's amnesia, and the "worthless woman's" (hereafter, WW) depression—and also the subfield of medical practice and psychology that studies such disorders.

Psychopathology, in either sense, merits philosophical investigation. Consider Frieda. One might note that she displays distinct personalities and ask what the possibility of such behavior indicates concerning traditional notions of personal identity or unity of consciousness. Does it suggest, for example, that distinct persons can share the same body? Or does it mean that psychological continuity is not necessary for personal identity? Alternatively, one might be primarily concerned with the diagnosis of Frieda's problem. What exactly is meant by a diagnosis of multiple personality disorder? Is it associated with a well-defined syndrome that can be reliably recognized by different diagnosticians? How is multiple personality to be distinguished from familiar sorts of role playing or acting?

Similarly in the other cases, philosophical interest might be aroused by WW's delusions or the housepainter's tendency to confabulate, on the one hand, or by issues connected with the clinical description and treatment of these disturbances, on the other. Pursuing the first option, one might wonder whether epistemological accounts of hypothetico-deductive reasoning shed any light on the formation of delusions or help to explain what is going on in confabulation. Reciprocally, one might hope that the study of delusion or confabulation would reveal something about the constraints governing the generation and testing of hypotheses. Exploring the second sort of concern, one might ask, for example, whether a partially normative notion, such as *delusion* (which seems to presuppose some standard of epistemic evaluation) can figure essentially in a rigorously scientific or naturalistic account of human behavior.

Under the heading of philosophical psychopathology, we include both investigations of philosophical issues arising from consideration of various sorts of mental disorders and investigations of issues raised by theoretical and clinical studies of such disorders. This inclusive approach is reflected in our survey of the field later in this introductory chapter as well as in the contributed chapters offered in this volume. Some chapters focus on particular sorts of deficits or disorders and argue that such disorders have important implications for philosophical questions concerning phenomenal awareness (Van Gulick), the emotions (Bach), and third-person folk-psychological attributions (Gordon and Barker). Others are primarily concerned with problems at the level of theory and clinical practice, including the contributions of Fulford, Erwin, Grünbaum, and Poland, Von Eckardt, and Spaulding. Still others freely mix both sorts of issues, such as the chapters by Flanagan, Garrett, Graham and Stephens, Heil, and Schoeman.

We think that this inclusive approach to philosophical psychopathology is entirely appropriate and, indeed, necessary. Though particular investigations may usefully limit their concerns to one or the other, the two levels of investigation are ultimately reciprocal. Anyone who wants to make something out of multiple personality disorder by arguing, for example, that its possibility has important implications for our understanding of personal identity needs to show a decent concern for the question of whether 'multiple personality disorder' constitutes a well-defined, clinically useful diagnostic category. On the other hand, critical reflection on the particular sort of phenomena encompassed within a diagnostic category such as multiple personality disorder will form a crucial part in the evaluation of its taxonomical adequacy and usefulness.

Our second point concerns the propriety of regarding all three cases described above as cases of psychopathology (in either sense of the term). The cases of WW and Frieda conform closely to the popular prototype of psychopathology. The housepainter's case does not. There are, perhaps, two reasons for this disparity. First, 'psychopathology' suggests the bizarre and patently irrational. Frieda's multiple personalities and WW's delusions and unwarranted self-laceration fit this image. The housepainter's amnesia, by contrast, seems prosaic and unextraordinary. Second, disorders such as multiple personality and depression have often been explained in psychodynamic terms, for example, as resulting from denial, repression, stress, grief, and so on. Though many people would allow that such disorders probably have some organic basis, they are not associated with any specific organic etiology. The housepainter's condition, however, has a ready, if not fully detailed, organic explanation. Even those bereft of any detailed knowledge of neuroanatomy or neurochemistry recognize that his problem results from brain damage caused by excessive consumption of alcohol.

On the other hand, as its inclusion in the *Case Book* indicates, the housepainter's alcohol amnestic disorder does fall within the range of cases with which contemporary psychiatry concerns itself. So too does a wide range of disorders whose manifestations are relatively prosaic and whose organic etiology or neurological substratum is patent. The class of psychopathological disorders, broadly understood, includes everything from agrammatism and visual agnosia to retrograde amnesia and unilateral neglect, regardless of any association with psychodynamics.

The broad sense of psychopathological disorder is the concept adopted and employed here in this book. A particularly commendable feature of interpreting psychopathological disorder broadly is that the broad view matches the synoptic level at which psychiatrists and clinicians actually work (as revealed by inclusion of organic cases in the *Case Book*). A growing body of research (Shallice 1988) indicates the even the most bizarre and exotic mental disorders are intricately connected with relatively prosaic perceptual and cognitive deficits. And, of course, the general relevance of neuroanatomy and neurophysiology for the study of mental disorders is beyond dispute, however contentious the debates concerning specific connections.

1 The Literature of Philosophical Psychopathology: A Rough and Ready Survey

There exists no systematic, detailed survey of the literature relevant to philosophical psychopathology. Our efforts here will not remedy that deficiency. What we offer instead is a brief, highly selective guide to the recent literature: a freehand, not-to-scale map of the field. Undoubtedly, our own interests, biases, and ignorance have resulted in distortions and omissions. But for all its defects, we hope that our survey will give the reader some idea of the lay of the land.

Our survey organizes the territory into three large, overlapping areas. These include applied philosophy of mind, the metaphysics and philosophy of the science of mind, and ethical and experiential dimensions of mental disorders. Within each area we have attempted to identify works that explicitly address themselves to philosophical issues (whatever the disciplinary affiliations of their authors) and works that describe psychopathological phenomena or theoretical problems that seem to us to merit philosophical investigation. We shall also discuss the particular contributions to philosophical psychopathology included in this volume under their appropriate headings.

Psychopathology and Applied Philosophy of Mind

Philosophy of mind has increasingly turned away from the search for clean counterexample-immune analyses of psychological concepts and toward a wide, integrating, empirically informed sort of theorizing (see Graham and Horgan 1994). This empirical, integrating trend is manifest in the attention directed by philosophers to work in such areas as neurobiology, comparative and developmental psychology, and machine information processing, as well as concern with nuts-and-bolts accounts of particular psychological phenomena. These include accounts of perception, cognition, practical reasoning, emotion, and so on.

The model for much current work in philosophy of mind is interactive and cooperative or coevolutionary (see Bechtel 1988, Flanagan 1992, Kitcher 1992). Traditional philosophical conceptions of mental activities are tested against, and refined in light of, empirical findings, while tools of the philosopher's trade are employed in assessing accounts of particular phenomena in the relevant scientific fields.

Psychopathology provides an especially fertile basis for such applied, interactive studies. In this volume the chapters by Van Gulick, Bach, Graham and Stephens, Flanagan, and Fulford readily fall in this category. There remain a great many unexplored or underexploited opportunities. Below we provide a brief guide to what has been done and what is left to do.

Personal identity and self-consciousness
A perennial philosophic puzzle is the issue of personal identity and self-awareness: the sense of "myness" or self that can accompany thought and action. Disturbances of the sense of self occur in a variety of forms of psychopathology. Eagle (1988) provides a good discussion of the general issue within the psychoanalytic tradition. For a philosophical discussion with a similar orientation, see Zemach 1986.

The disturbance of self most widely discussed by philosophers is multiple personality disorder (MPD) (for examples, see Mackie 1985; Wilkes 1981, 1988; Humphrey and Dennett 1991; Braude 1991; and Haksar 1991). Ross (1989) offers an excellent introduction to the clinical literature on MPD. Gillett (1986, 1991) provides a philosophically informed discussion by a neuropsychiatrist. Here Heil, in his chapter, offers an analysis and critique of the merits of explanatory reference to mental partitioning that accommodates its possible occurrence in MPD. Flanagan, also in this volume, asks whether the proper or normal-function contrast to MPD is a simply and singly unified person or someone still quite diffuse and multidimensional in psychological organization.

Various other phenomena, such as verbal hallucinations, thought alienation, depersonalization, and autoscopic experiences, also involve disorders of self and self-awareness. Stephens and Graham (1994a, 1994b) discuss these phenomena and provide bibliographies of relevant clinical literature. Hoffman (1986), Frith (1979, 1987), Frith and Done (1988), and Slade and Bentall (1988) make provocative proposals for understanding the disturbance of self in verbal hallucinations and provide extensive references to the clinical and psychopathological literature. Fulford's "Thought Insertion and Insight: Disease and Illness Paradigms of Psychotic Disorder," in Spitzer, Uehlein, Schwartz, and Mundt 1993, examines thought alienation. On depersonalization Christodoulou 1986 and Roberts 1984 may be consulted. On autoscopic hallucinations Grotstein's "Autoscopic Phenomena," in Friedman and Faguet 1982, merits reading. Several papers in Prigatano and Schacter 1991 discuss disturbances of self-awareness associated with brain damage. Of particular interest are the papers by Bisiach and Geminiani ("Anosognosia Related to Hemiplegia and Hemianopia"), Stuss ("Disturbances of Self-Awareness after Frontal System Damage"), and Kihlstrom and Tobias ("Anosognosia, Consciousness, and the Self").

Harry Frankfurt (1988) has called attention to cases in which persons are moved to act by desires that are manifestly features of their own psychological history or subjectivity but they do not acknowledge the resulting actions as things *they* have *done*. Frankfurt's cases are largely hypothetical. Psychopathology provides a wealth of actual cases, instances of dissociation and disengagement from thoughts and overt deeds. Graham and Stephens, in this volume, apply ideas derived in part from Frankfurt to identify two dimensions in self-awareness: one of subjectivity, the other of experience of mental agency. Reference to these distinguishable dimensions, they argue, should become philosophically more critical with progress in integrating the epistemology of self-consciousness with psychopathological theory and data.

Voluntary action and self-control
Some attention has been paid to what psychopathology has to tell us about the etiology of voluntary action and the mechanisms for self-control and reflexive monitoring of behavior. The literature on

obsessive-compulsive disorder (OCD) is particularly relevant here. Jenike, Baer, and Minichello (1990) offer a good survey of recent work on OCD. Rapaport (1989) provides a theoretical perspective as well as several fascinating case studies. Also of considerable interest in this connection is the literature on Tourette's syndrome and other tic disorders, such as Cohen, Bruun, and Leckman (1990) and Berecz (1992). Hoffman (1986) and Frith (1987) discuss voluntary action in their accounts of verbal hallucination.

Schoeman in his chapter, utilizes some literature on alcoholism (e.g., Fingarette 1988) and compulsive alcohol abuse to sketch a multidimensional account of connections among psychopathology, moral and legal responsibility, and self-control (or the lack thereof). Fulford, also in this volume, considers the role of action and defects of self-control in delusion. Fulford appeals to a species of reasons for action, namely value judgments, in an attempt to undermine the notion that what makes delusions psychopathological is their falsity.

Cognition and practical reasoning
Philosophy has a long-standing theoretical and practical interest in the notion of rationality. Philosophers interested in developing standards for evaluating human inference and decision making have increasingly looked to the growing body of data on human performance (Goldman 1986, 1993a; Stich 1990).

Disorders and dysfunctions of cognitive performance are among the most common manifestations of irrationality and psychopathology. They often serve as foci of irrationality-based accounts of psychopathological phenomena, i.e., accounts that construe irrationality as at least partly constitutive of various forms of psychopathology.

Oltmanns and Maher's collection (1988) provides an excellent overview of current work on *delusions*. Of particular interest are the chapters by Maher ("Anomalous Experience and Delusional Thinking: The Logic of Explanations") and Chapman and Chapman ("The Genesis of Delusions") which discuss delusions in relation to normal cognitive performance, and the chapters by Johnson ("Discriminating the Origin of Information") and Kilstrom and Hoyt ("Hypnosis and the Psychology of Delusions"), which make connections with a variety of topics in cognitive psychology. For more detailed discussions of particular delusional syndromes, such as Capgras's syndrome, Friedman and Faguet 1982, Christodoulou 1986, and Enoch and Trethowen 1991 are useful.

Confabulation receives a brief philosophical discussion in Wilkes 1988. The phenomenon is particularly intriguing when viewed in the light of Calvin's (1989) and Dennett's (1991) stress on the role of "scenario-spinning" and "narratization" in human cognition. Dennett advances a detailed and provocative account of commonsense psychological explanations of behavior as, in effect, confabulatory. Johnson's chapter in Prigatano and Schacter 1991, "Reality Monitoring: Evidence from Confabulation in Organic Brain Disease Patients," provides an up-to-date discussion of confabulation. Also relevant are sections of Berlyne 1972, Joseph 1986, and Kopelman 1987.

Prigatano and Schacter 1991 contains a variety of papers on *anosagnosia*, i.e., failures to recognize or acknowledge deficits such as blindness, amnesia, paralysis, etc. This topic has attracted attention from such philosophers as P. S. Churchland (1983) and Wilkes (1988). Bisiach and Geminiani's chapter in Prigatano and Schacter, "Anosognosia Related to Hemiplegia and Hemianopia," connects the topic with issues concerning ascriptions of propositional attitudes.

Slade and Bentall (1988) provide an extensive review of recent work on *hallucinations*. Johnson's chapter in Oltmanns and Maher 1988 provides a discussion and good bibliography of experimental work on how people discriminate between hallucination and (genuine) perception.

Finally, psychopathologies based on irrationality are especially popular in the literature on *depression*. Aaron Beck (1967, 1976) argues that depression is produced and sustained by depression-specific logical errors, including a "systematic bias against the self," which is activated by stress and anxiety. Similarly, the learned-helplessness theory of depression in its various incarnations (Seligman 1975; Abramson, Seligman, and Teasdale 1978; Abramson, Alloy, and Metalsky 1989) focuses on depressive biases and attributional styles in inferences about personal control over wanted and unwanted events.

It is difficult to say exactly in what way the reasoning of victims of psychopathology is irrational. Hence much of the psychiatric literature on irrationality-based approaches to depression is devoted to comparing and contrasting the "irrational" or "distorted" beliefs and inferences of depressives with the "rational" beliefs and inferences of nondepressed normals. Some theorists argue that depressed individuals often are more realistic and accurate, more rational, in their attitudes than nondepressives. In particular, nondepressives may experience an "illusion of personal control." They may give themselves more credit for controlling circumstances than evidence warrants.

Productive directions for philosophical research include exploring criteria for the irrationality and errors in reasoning characteristic of irrationality-based psychopathology and psychopathological conditions. Alloy and Abramson's "Depressive Realism: Four Theoretical Perspectives" (1988) offers a philosophically informed discussion of depressive/nondepressive cognition and of whether nondepressed (normal) people exhibit more irrationality and error than depressives. Graham (1990) examines whether clinical depression can be distinguished from nonclinical forms of sadness and depression in the terms of whether the depression is reasonable in or warranted by the subject's unhappy personal or social circumstances. Garrett's chapter in this volume examines the rationality/irrationality of a depressive's overall outlook on life and offers a qualified defense of Beck's proposition that depression is irrational. Garrett contends that if we concede that people's outlooks can be self-defeating, Beck is well within the bounds of plausibility to insist that depressive outlooks are unreasonable. This is because depressive outlooks tend to be self-defeating.

Bach, in his chapter, emphasizes the attentional aspects of emotional and affective disorders, particularly the role of management of attention. Attention mismanagement, Bach observes, is often responsible for disordered emotional states or conditions.

Psychopathology and the Science of Mind

A central question in philosophy of mind is whether human behavior, human intelligence, human experience can be understood scientifically. Do the natural sciences provide a model that psychology should emulate, or is psychological explanation a fundamentally different sort of enterprise than explanation in physics or biology?

Recently discussion of these issues has focused on common sense or "folk psychology" (P. M. Churchland 1981, Christensen and Turner 1993). Do our everyday ascriptions of mentalistic properties to ourselves and others presuppose a theory of mind that might be refined, extended, and deepened—or perhaps discarded—in light of scientific investigation? Or do they represent rather the exercise of a sort of skill or know-how that proceeds independently of any theorizing about the mind? The study of psychopathology presents a variety of opportunities for reexamining and advancing the discussion of these issues.

The medical model of mental disorders

Thomas Szasz's *Myth of Mental Illness* (1961) anticipates some of the misgivings that philosophers like Stich and Dennett have about the incorporation of intentionalistic notions in a scientific psychology. He maintains, for instance, that the concepts used in taxonomizing and diagnosing mental disorders have a normative and holistic character that is uncharacteristic of and not capturable within the concepts employed in medical science. Szasz contends that psychiatry is best understood and pursued as an ethical or practical enterprise that deals with problems of living, rather than as a medical specialty devoted to the treatment of disease.

Issues associated with the medical or disease model of mental disorders are examined in connection with particular mental disorders in Herbert Fingarette's *Heavy Drinking* (1988), a study of alcoholism, and Irving Gottesman and D. L. Wolfgram's *Schizophrenic Genesis: The Origins of Madness* (1991). Christopher Boorse (1975, 1976) provides an analytic treatment of the general notion of illness. Ruth Macklin (1981) examines the distinction between mental health and illness. Jerome Wakefield's (1992a, 1992b) papers on the concept of mental disorder may also be consulted.

Carl Hempel's (1965) paper on the fundamentals of taxonomy for psychopathology is a classic discussion of concepts used in a medical model and continues to generate a critical literature, as evidenced by the work of Helge Malmgren (1993) on the semantic foundations of psychiatric classification. K. W. M. Fulford's *Moral Theory and Medical Practice* (1989) argues that the notion of illness is a fundamentally normative or practical notion not only in psychiatry but within medi-

cine generally. He maintains that an understanding of the norma-
tive/practical dimensions of medicine is crucial for understanding
the ways in which biological science contributes to the description
and treatment of human ills. A sketch of Fulford's general approach
and a detailed application to a particular kind of psychiatric symptom, delusions, is found in his chapter.

Philosophy of science and psychiatry
Adolf Grünbaum's *Foundations of Psychoanalysis* (1984) offers a thorough examination of the scientific status of one theoretical approach
to mental disorder. His book is not only a trenchant critique of psychoanalysis but an illustration of the sorts of questions a sophisticated philosophy of science raises concerning any approach to the
description, diagnosis, or treatment of psychopathology. Three chapters in this volume examine such questions. Grünbaum's contribution, reprinted here, examines the concept of a placebo and the role
of placebo studies in assessing the effectiveness of various sorts of
psychotherapeutic interventions. Erwin's chapter, on the effectiveness of psychotherapy, discusses the use of meta-analysis in statistical
studies of the effectiveness of various psychotherapies. The chapter
by Poland, Von Eckardt, and Spaulding extensively critiques the standard nosological system in American psychiatry, represented by the
American Psychiatric Association's *Diagnostic and Statistical Manual of
Mental Disorders* (*DSM* III R, 1987). They argue that the system of
classification neither provides clinicians with adequate guidance for
diagnosis and treatment of mental disorders nor points the way toward an improved scientific understanding of their etiologies.

One issue raised by Poland, Von Eckardt, and Spaulding's critique
of *DSM* III R is what happens when the diagnostic categories of psychiatry fail to reflect our emerging knowledge of neurobiology.
Philosophers interested in questions about how findings in neurobiology might shape our taxonomy of mind or our account of natural
kinds in psychology can find some fascinating data relevant to such
questions in psychopharmacology. Some philosophers seem aware
of the importance of psychopharmacology and surrounding research on the neurochemical explanation of mental illness for such
questions (Stevenson 1977, P. S. Churchland 1986, Graham 1993),
but the philosophical literature still is sparse. To revisit depression,

helpful overviews of the neurobiology and neurochemistry of this disorder may be found in Wilner 1985 and Whybrow, Akiskal, and McKinney 1984.

A rather consistent preoccupation of psychopharmacological theory is whether susceptibility to the same or different chemical treatments critically determines taxonomizing mental illnesses and emotional disorders. If, for instance, two phenomenologically distinct emotional disorders are susceptible to the same chemical treatment, are they best viewed as versions of the same emotional disorder? Both acutely anxious and severely depressed individuals may be treated successfully with certain antidepressants. Some theorists, e.g., Montgomery (1989), suggest that therefore depression and acute anxiety may be the same kind of disorder. Further work is needed to determine how personal/phenomenological descriptions of psychopathology may best coevolve or integrate with subpersonal, neurochemically based taxonomies.

An excellent example of an attempt to integrate neurobiology into an account of the nature of a particular kind of mental disorder, schizophrenia, is found in Gray et al. 1991. And an excellent example of how to integrate data from different levels of inquiry—the neural and cognitive—for disorders and deficits of cognition and consciousness is Shallice 1988.

Psychopathology and folk psychology
Philosophers sympathetic to eliminativist or fictionalist accounts of folk psychology have often suggested that psychopathological phenomena reveal the inadequacies in such folk-psychological notions as consciousness (Dennett 1991) and belief (P. M. Churchland 1981). Bisiach and Geminiani (in Prigatano and Schacter 1991) argue that a careful examination of patients suffering from anosagnosia (denial of deficit or illness) raises questions about common assumptions concerning propositional-attitude ascription. P. S. Churchland (1983, 1986, 1988), Kathleen Wilkes (1984, 1988), and Daniel Dennett (1991; Humphrey and Dennett 1991) draw heavily on psychopathological data in mounting sustained attacks on the coherence and scientific usefulness of the notion of consciousness. Much of their argument rests on the diffuse and disjoint role that consciousness seems to play in psychopathological phenomena such

as MPD, dissociative states, so-called "hidden observer" phenomena, automatism, somnambulism, blindsight, and hypnotic states. Van Gulick, in his chapter, argues to the contrary that studies of pathological conditions such as blindsight and the agnosias suggest that the notion of phenomenal consciousness has an essential explanatory role to play in our accounts of such phenomena. Ran Lahav (1993) offers a similar defense of the scientific integrity of consciousness, as well as of its role in the integration and flexibility of intelligent behavior. According to both Van Gulick and Lahav, reference to consciousness figures importantly in our best analyses of mental disorders and in our best accounts of intelligent behavior generally.

It has also been maintained that folk-psychological ascriptions of propositional attitudes presuppose or presume that the person to whom the attitudes are ascribed is rational in some strong sense of that term. On Dennett's construal, "there is no coherent . . . description" of a person who "falls short of . . . rationality and avows beliefs that either are strongly disconfirmed . . . or are self-contradictory or contradict other avowals he has made" (1978, 20). This matter is highly controversial. If ascription of intentional states does involve such an assumption, however, it would seem to be in conflict with the common observation that persons often believe, desire, and act irrationally. Davidson (1982, 1986) and others have argued that we can reconcile (to some extent) such instances of apparent irrationality with an overall presupposition of rationality by invoking the notion that beliefs and intentions may be partitioned, i.e., functionally isolated or separated within the subject. Heil, in his chapter, examines this strategy and argues that the desired reconciliation can be effected without resorting to partitioning. Heil leaves open the question of whether there may be other grounds for introducing the notion of partitioning (see also Zemach 1986).

Currently a great deal of attention is being devoted to the question of whether our ordinary abilities to explain and predict the behavior of members of our own species are subserved by a theory of mind. Defenders of folk psychology have generally supposed that we use folk psychology in explaining and predicting other's behavior and that our success at this task argues for the general adequacy of folk psychology as a theory of mind (see Horgan and Graham 1991). Opponents of folk psychology, such as Paul Churchland (1981), often accept this so-called "theory-theory" account of the role of folk psychology but dispute its success in filling this role. Goldman (1992, 1993b) and Gordon (1986, 1992), however, argue that the ability to explain and anticipate the behavior of others does not result from the application of a theory of mind but rather depends upon our natural talent or skill at simulating the other's response to a given set of circumstances. Studies of autism have been used to support the theory-theory account of our folk-psychological abilities (Baron-Cohen, Leslie, and Frith 1985; Baron-Cohen 1992; Stich and Nichols 1992). In their chapter Gordon and Barker argue that a simulation account is not only compatible with, but provides a more adequate understanding of, the pathology involved in autism.

Ethical and Experiential Dimensions of Psychopathology

Whatever their exact nature and etiology, the phenomena studied in psychopathology are indeed problems of living. As such they raise two sorts of questions.

The first sort are questions of legal and moral responsibility, such as whether our current conceptions of responsibility offer adequate guidance for understanding and intervening in the lives of those who suffer from various pathological conditions. As we come to appreciate the complexity of such conditions both in the multiplicity of etiological factors and in their ramifications in the subject's life, questions about what we should expect or demand from the subject and from ourselves regarding the subject become pressing and difficult.

Fingarette's *Heavy Drinking* (1988) is a sober explication of these issues concerning alcoholism. The late Ferdinand Schoeman's contribution to this volume advances Fingarette's discussion by examining the implications of our views concerning the responsibility of the alcoholic for his condition for our more general concepts of legal and moral responsibility. Schoeman thinks that there are no iron-clad rules for determining which of the conflicting standards of responsibility should be applied to the alcoholic. Instead, Schoeman recommends highly context-dependent judgment and reasoning about a range of factors, both agential and non-agential, responsible for drinking.

The second practical question raised by psychopathology is how our concept of a good or at least tolerable human life figures in our understanding and treatment of psychopathology. Flanagan here discusses the distresses of MPD and the preferability of what he calls a multiplex self to a multiple self for a decent, satisfying life. The notion of multiplexity here is cousin to Schoeman's notion of responsibility, since, Flanagan contends, ultimately the best or most satisfying fate for a former multiple self depends on context and involves a plurality of interpretations. One might be tempted to think that a multiple personality should become a highly integrated and particularized self. Flanagan urges that we resist the temptation. Fairly diffuse forms of union and self reconstruction can do life's work.

In his chapter Garrett considers whether when, life becomes emotionally and cognitively intolerable, this is necessarily because of a medical or psychiatric problem (such as clinical depression) or because of a more traditionally labeled spiritual condition (such as philosophical despair). No doubt courage is needed to deal with the problems of living (see Geach 1977). Garrett suggests that an optimistic faith is needed as well. He contends that a person unprotected from slipping into despair is less than fully rational.

2   Conclusion

Some introductions to collections of papers summarize the papers. Since the papers here mostly are new, we prefer to let the authors speak for themselves and not to summarize. We judged it best to focus attention on the nature and scope of philosophical psychopathology and briefly to canvass the literature in both philosophy and psychopathology that is most germane to the chapters in the book.

We organized the order of chapters around the following thematic progression: phenomenal awareness in general (Van Gulick), emotional feelings and attitudes in particular (Bach and Garrett), self-consciousness and self-representation (Graham and Stephens, Heil, and Flanagan), representing others (Gordon and Barker), moral agency and responsibility (Schoeman), epistemic agency and delusion (Fulford), and methodological concerns about psychopathological taxonomy (Poland et al.) as well as psychiatric and medical experimentation and treatment (Erwin and Grünbaum). Different sorts of chapter orders may suggest themselves to different readers. Seasoned philosophical psychopathologists will, of course, be selective. We can only trust that no matter the route no chapter will disappoint.

References

Abramson, L. Y., L. B. Alloy, and G. Metalsky. 1989. "Hopelessness Depression: A Theory-Based Subtype of Depression." *Psychological Review* 96:358–372.

Abramson, L. Y., M. E. P. Seligman, and J. Teasdale. 1978. "Learned Helplessness in Humans: Critique and Reformulation." *Journal of Abnormal Psychology* 87:49–74.

Alloy, L. B., and L. Y. Abramson. 1988. "Depressive Realism: Four Theoretical Perspectives." In *Cognitive Processes in Depression*, ed. L. B. Alloy. New York: Guilford.

American Psychiatric Association. 1987. *Diagnostic and Statistical Manual of Mental Disorders*, 3rd ed. Washington, D.C.: American Psychiatric Association.

Baron-Cohen, S. 1992. "The Girl Who Liked to Shout in Church." In *Mental Lives: Case Studies in Cognition*, ed. R. Campbell. Oxford: Blackwell.

Baron-Cohen, S., A. Leslie, and U. Frith. 1985. "Does the Autistic Child Have a Theory of Mind?" *Cognition* 21:37–46.

Bechtel, W. 1988. *Philosophy of Science: An Overview for Cognitive Science*. New Jersey: Erlbaum.

Beck, A. T. 1967. *Depression: Clinical, Experimental, and Theoretical Aspects*. New York: Harper and Row.

Beck, A. T. 1976. *Cognitive Therapy and the Emotional Disorders*. New York: International Universities Press.

Berecz, J. M. 1992. *Understanding Tourette Syndrome, Obsessive Compulsive Disorder, and Related Problems*. New York: Springer.

Berlyne, N. 1972. "Confabulation." *British Journal of Psychiatry* 120:31–39.

Boorse, C. 1975. "On the Distinction between Disease and Illness." *Philosophy and Public Affairs* 5:49–68.

Boorse, C. 1976. "What a Theory of Mental Health Should Be." *Journal of the Theory of Social Behavior* 6:61–84.

An Introduction to Philosophical Psychopathology

Braude, S. F. 1991. *First Person Plural: Multiple Personality and the Philosophy of Mind.* New York: Routledge.

Calvin, W. 1989. *The Cerebral Symphony: Seashore Reflections on the Study of Consciousness.* New York: Bantam.

Christensen, S. M., and D. R. Turner, eds. 1993. *Folk Psychology and the Philosophy of Mind.* New Jersey: Erlbaum.

Christodoulou, G. N., ed. 1986. *The Delusional Misidentification Syndromes.* New York: Biblioteca Psychiatrica, Karger.

Churchland, Patricia S. 1983. "Consciousness: The Transmutation of a Concept." *Pacific Philosophical Quarterly* 64:80–95.

Churchland, Patricia S. 1986. *Neurophilosophy.* Cambridge: MIT Press.

Churchland, Patricia S. 1988. "Reduction and the Neurobiological Basis of Consciousness." In *Consciousness in Contemporary Science*, ed. A. Marcel and E. Bisiach. Oxford: Oxford University Press.

Churchland, Paul M. 1981. "Eliminative Materialism and Propositional Attitudes." *Journal of Philosophy* 78:67–90.

Cohen, D. J., R. D. Bruun, and J. F. Leckman, eds. 1990. *Tourette's Syndrome and Tic Disorders.* New York: Wiley.

Davidson, D. 1982. "Paradoxes of Irrationality." In *Philosophical Essays on Freud*, ed. R. Wolheim and J. Hopkins. Cambridge: Cambridge.

Davidson, D. 1986. "Deception and Division." In *The Multiple Self*, ed. J. Elster. Cambridge: Cambridge University Press.

Dennett, D. C. 1978. *Brainstorms.* Cambridge: MIT Press.

Dennett, D. C. 1991. *Consciousness Explained.* Boston: Little, Brown, and Co.

Eagle, M. 1983. "A Critical Examination of Motivational Explanation in Psychoanalysis." In *Mind and Medicine: Problems of Explanation and Evaluation in Psychiatry and the Biomedical Sciences*, ed. L. Laudan. Berkeley: University of California Press.

Eagle, M. 1988. "Psychoanalysis and the Personal." In *Mind, Psychoanalysis, and Science*, ed. P. Clark and C. Wright. Oxford: Blackwell.

Enoch, D., and W. Trethowen. 1991. *Uncommon Psychiatric Syndromes*, 3rd ed. Oxford: Butterworth and Heinemann.

Fingarette, H. 1972. *The Meaning of Criminal Insanity.* Berkeley: University of California Press.

George Graham and G. Lynn Stephens

Fingarette, H. 1988. *Heavy Drinking: The Myth of Alcoholism as a Disease.* Berkeley: University of California Press.

Flanagan, O. 1992. *Consciousness Reconsidered.* Cambridge: MIT Press.

Frankfurt, H. 1988. *The Importance of What We Care About.* Cambridge: Cambridge University Press.

Friedman, C. H. T., and R. A. Faguet, eds. 1982. *Extraordinary Disorders of Human Behavior.* New York: Plenum.

Frith, C. D. 1979. "Consciousness, Information Processing, and Schizophrenia." *British Journal of Psychiatry* 1324:225–235.

Frith, C. D. 1987. "The Positive and Negative Symptoms of Schizophrenia Reflect Impairments in Perception and Initiation of Action." *Psychological Medicine* 17:631–648.

Frith, C. D., and D. J. Done. 1988. "Towards a Neuropsychology of Schizophrenia." *British Journal of Psychiatry* 153:437–443.

Fulford, K. W. M. 1989. *Moral Theory and Medical Practice.* Cambridge: Cambridge University Press.

Geach, P. 1977. *The Virtues.* Cambridge: Cambridge University Press.

Gillett, G. 1986. "Multiple Personality and the Concept of a Person." *New Ideas in Psychology* 4:173–184.

Gillett, G. 1991. "Multiple Personality and Irrationality." *Philosophical Psychology* 4:103–118.

Goldman, A. 1986. *Epistemology and Cognition.* Cambridge: Harvard University Press.

Goldman, A. 1992. "In Defense of Simulation Theory." *Mind and Language* 7:104–119.

Goldman, A. 1993a. *Philosophical Applications of Cognitive Science.* Colorado: Westview.

Goldman, A. 1993b. "The Psychology of Folk Psychology." *Behavioral and Brain Sciences* 16:15–28.

Gordon, R. 1986. "Folk Psychology and Simulation." *Mind and Language* 1:158–171.

Gordon, R. 1992. "The Simulation Theory: Objections and Misconceptions." *Mind and Language* 7:11–34.

Gottesman, I., and D. L. Wolfgram. 1991. *Schizophrenic Genesis: The Origins of Madness*. New York: Freeman.

Graham, G. 1990. "Melancholic Epistemology." *Synthese* 82:399–422.

Graham, G. 1993. "Why Did Robert Schumann Starve Himself to Death?" In G. Graham, *Philosophy of Mind: An Introduction*. Oxford: Blackwell.

Graham, G., and T. Horgan. 1994. "Southern Fundamentalism and the End of Philosophy." *Philosophical Perspectives*, forthcoming. Paper presented at the sixth SOPHIA Conference at the Universidad de La Laguna.

Gray, J., J. Felton, J. N. P. Rawlins, D. R. Hensley, and A. D. Smith. 1991. "The Neurobiology of Schizophrenia." *Behavioral and Brain Sciences* 14:1–20.

Grünbaum, A. 1984. *The Foundations of Psychoanalysis: A Philosophical Critique*. Berkeley: University of California Press.

Haksar, V. 1991. *Indivisible Selves and Moral Practice*. Edinburg: Edinburg University Press.

Hempel, C. 1965. "Fundamentals of Taxonomy." In *Aspects of Scientific Explanation*. New York: Macmillan.

Hoffman, R. 1986. "Verbal Hallucinations and Language Production Processes in Schizophrenia." *Behavioral and Brain Sciences* 9:503–548. Includes commentary and response.

Horgan, T., and G. Graham. 1991. "In Defense of Southern Fundamentalism." *Philosophical Studies* 62:107–134.

Humphrey, N., and D. C. Dennett. 1991. "Speaking for Ourselves: An Assessment of Multiple Personality Disorder." In *Self and Identity*, ed. D. Kolak and R. Martin. New York: Macmillan.

Jenike, M. A., L. Baer, and W. E. Minichello. 1990. *Obsessive Compulsive Disorders: Theory and Management*. Chicago: Year Book Medical Publishers.

Joseph, R. 1986. "Confabulation and Delusional Denial: Frontal Lobe and Lateralized Influences." *Journal of Clinical Psychology* 42:507–520.

Kitcher, P. 1992. *Freud's Dream: A Complete Interdisciplinary Science of Mind*. Cambridge: MIT Press.

Kopelman, M. D. 1987. "Two Types of Confabulation." *Journal of Neurology, Neurosurgery, and Psychiatry* 50:1482–1487.

Lahav, R. 1993. "What Neuropsychology Tells Us about Consciousness." *Philosophy of Science* 69:67–85.

Mackie, J. L. 1985. "Multiple Personality." In *Persons and Values*, ed. J. L. Mackie and P. Mackie. Oxford: Oxford University Press.

Macklin, R. 1981. "Mental Health and Mental Illness: Some Problems of Definition and Concept Formation." In *Concepts of Health and Diease: Interdisciplinary Perspectives*, ed. A. L. Caplan, H. T. Engelhardt, Jr., and J. J. McCartney. Reading, Mass: Addison-Wesley.

Malmgren, H. 1993. "Psychiatric Classification and Empiricist Theories of Meaning." *Acta Psychiatrica Scandinavia*, suppl. 373:48–64.

Montgomery, S. 1989. "Developments in Antidepressants." In *Depression: An Integrative Approach*, ed. K. Herbst and E. Paykel. Oxford: Heinemann.

Nagel, T. 1979. "Brain Bisection and the Unity of Consciousness." In his *Moral Questions*. Cambridge: Cambridge University Press.

Oltmanns, T. F., and B. Maher, eds. 1988. *Delusional Beliefs*. New York: Wiley.

Parkin, A. J. 1987. *Memory and Amnesia*. Oxford: Blackwell.

Prigatano, G. P., and D. L. Schacter, eds. 1991. *Awareness of Deficit after Brain Injury: Clinical and Theoretical Issues*. Oxford: Oxford University Press.

Rapaport, J. L. 1989. *The Boy Who Couldn't Stop Washing: The Experience and Treatment of Obsessive-Compulsive Disorder*. New York: Penguin.

Roberts, J. K. A. 1984. *Differential Diagnosis in Neuropsychiatry*. New York: Wiley.

Ross, C. A. 1989. *Multiple Personality Disorder: Diagnosis, Clinical Features, and Treatment*. New York: Wiley.

Sadler, J., M. Schwartz, and O. Wiggins, eds. 1993. *Philosophical Perspectives on Psychiatric Diagnostic Classification*. Baltimore: Johns Hopkins University Press.

Seligman, M. E. P. 1975. *Helplessness: On Depression, Development, and Death*. San Francisco: Freeman.

Shallice, T. 1988. *From Neuropsychology to Mental Structure*. Cambridge: Cambridge University Press.

Slade, P. S., and R. P. Bentall. 1988. *Sensory Deception: A Scientific Analysis of Hallucination*. Baltimore: Johns Hopkins University Press.

Spitzer, M., A. Sokol, M. Gibbon, and J. Williams. 1981. *DSM III Case Book*. Washington, D.C.: American Psychiatic Association.

Spitzer, M., F. A. Uehlein, M. A. Schwartz, and C. Mundt, eds., 1993. *Phenomenology, Language, and Schizophrenia*. New York: Springer.

Stephens, G. L., and G. Graham. 1994a. "Voices and Selves." In *Philosophical Perspectives on Psychiatric Diagnostic Classification*, ed. J. Sadler, M. Schwartz, and O. Wiggins. Baltimore: Johns Hopkins University Press.

Stephens, G. L., and G. Graham. 1994b. "Self-Consciousness, Mental Agency, and the Clinical Psychopathology of Thought-Insertion." *Philosophy, Psychiatry, and Psychology* 1:1–10.

Stevenson, L. 1977. "Mind, Brain, and Mental Illness." *Philosophy* 52:27–43.

Stich, S. 1990. *The Fragmentation of Reason: Preface to a Pragmatic Theory of Cognitive Evaluation*. Cambridge: MIT Press.

Stich, S., and S. Nichols. 1992. "Folk Psychology: Simulation or Tacit Theory?" *Mind and Language* 7:35–71.

Szasz, T. 1961. *The Myth of Mental Illness*. New York: Harper and Row.

Wakefield, J. 1992a. "The Concept of Mental Disorder: On the Boundary between Biological Facts and Social Values." *American Psychologist* 47:373–388.

Wakefield, J. 1992b. "Disorder as Harmful Dysfunction: A Conceptual Critique of *DSM*-III-R's Definition of Mental Disorder." *Psychological Review* 99:232–247.

Whybrow, P., H. Akiskal, and W. McKinney. 1984. *Mood Disorders: Toward a New Psychobiology*. New York: Plenum.

Wilkes, K. V. 1981. "Multiple Personality and Personal Identity." *British Journal for Philosophy of Science* 32:331–348.

Wilkes, K. V. 1984. "Is Consciousness Important?" *British Journal for the Philosophy of Science* 35:223–243.

Wilkes, K. V. 1988. *Real People*. Oxford: Oxford.

Wilner, P. 1985. *Depression: A Psychobiological Synthesis*. New York: Wiley.

Zemach, E. 1986. "Unconscious Mind or Conscious Minds." In *Studies in Philosophy of Mind*, ed. P. A. French, T. E. Uehling, and H. K. Wettstein, Midwest Studies in Philosophy, no. 10. Minnesota: University of Minnesota Press.

Deficit Studies and the Function of Phenomenal Consciousness

Robert Van Gulick

Can we ever solve the problem of consciousness? That is, will we ever be able to explain how consciousness arises from the material composition or functional organization of the brain? Optimism about success, at least success in the long run, might seem the natural view for a materialist. Yet forceful pessimism has been voiced by philosophers who consider themselves genuine materialists. Colin McGinn (1989, 1991) has claimed that although consciousness arises from the physical structure of the brain, human beings lack the cognitive capacity to comprehend the nature of the psychophysical link. That link, he claims is cognitively closed to us. Other philosophers have directed their skepticism at the possibility of understanding consciousness in terms of functional organization. Both John Searle (1992) and Ned Block (1978) have argued that functionalism is of little or no use in understanding consciousness; they claim that any functional organization can be instantiated by systems devoid of subjective phenomenal experience, and they reasonably take such experience as the sine qua non of consciousness.

Both forms of pessimism run counter to widely held contemporary views, but McGinn's runs deeper, since he denies that we humans can bridge the psychophysical gap in any way, not merely that we cannot use functionalism to do so. He argues that to solve the mind-body problem, we would need to identify and grasp the nature of some property P that is instantiated by the brain and in virtue of which the brain is the basis of consciousness. We would also require a theory T, referring to P, that explains how conscious states are dependent on brain states. The central thrust of his argument is that neither introspection nor physical investigation and theorizing will ever allow us to identify and comprehend the nature of property P. Insofar as he supposes that these are the only two routes by which we could form the relevant concept, it allegedly follows that we humans will never be able either to grasp the nature of P or to understand the nature of the psychophysical link.

However, it would seem that McGinn's argument turns on posing a false dilemma and allowing too narrow a range of options for concept-formation. Even if he is correct that neither introspection nor physical perception and inference will ever by themselves provide us with an adequate concept of P, it seems that psychophysical theorizing offers an obvious and promising third option. In particular, we have a large and growing body of evidence about the physical brain correlates of conscious experience and about how various brain changes or manipulations produce corresponding changes in conscious experience. Such evidence admitly has not enabled us thus far to solve the mind-body problem, but surely this is the route of investigation and theorizing that seems most likely to provide us with the required concept of property P (Flanagan 1992). As I will show below, evidence about pathologies of consciousness that result from specific types of brain damage should be of special value in attempting to understand how normal consciousness depends on the properly functioning material brain.

Such evidence should also be of value in answering those like Searle and Block who have claimed that functionalism can be of little help in understanding the nature and basis of consciousness. Deficit studies involving pathologies of consciousness may help us understand its functional role in normal cases, for example by revealing the pattern of abilities that are differentially lost and preserved when phenomenal consciousness is absent or disrupted. Functionalism requires that consciousness, like any other aspect of mind, be explained at a number of levels. At the level of macro (or personal) level abilities, we need to understand the contributions that phenomenal consciousness makes to our cognitive and mental economy. That is, what does it do for us, or allow us to do, that we otherwise couldn't? For example, does it allow us to plan and carry out multistep intentional actions? Getting good answers to this question would be one way to understand the functional role of consciousness (or at least its role in humans). But there are other ways as well in which we would need to explain the functional role of consciousness in order to have a fully satisfactory theory. We would have to explain, for example, not only *what* conscious states do for us but also *how* they do what they do, that is, not only what contribution they make but also how they make it. Nonconscious states might be able to make a similar contribution in the context of at least some systems: perhaps nonconscious computational states could enable a robot to construct and carry out multistage plans. But insofar as such nonconscious states differ from our conscious states in the the processes by which they make their equivalent contribution, there is an important respect in which they differ in their functional roles.

Some philosophers might object that functional roles concern only *what* a state does and that all questions of *how* it does what it does concern the underlying realization of the state and are thus not properly part of its functional role. The objection relies on a mistakenly simplisitic view of functional theories and betrays a commitment to what William Lycan (1990) has called "two-levelism," the view that in dealing with psychological systems, there is just one level of mental function and one level of underlying structure. But surely any remotely plausible functional theory of the human mind and brain will need to describe it at many levels of organization and abstraction; macrolevel functional systems will need to be successively decomposed into finer- and finer-grained underlying subsystems, whose components and processes in turn will have to be functionally characterized and explained. At some point the explanatory process will have to terminate at a level that is pretty straightforwardly structural, yet the structure/function distinction is not absolute but always relative to a specified level of abstraction. An adequate functional account of phenomenal consciousness will surely require specifying many levels of functional organization and decomposition mediating the explanatory link between subjective experience and underlying physical brain anatomy or neurophysiology. There is no reason to suppose that only the highest level of this explanatory hierarchy will be relevant to specifying the functional roles that constitute or define something as a conscious mental state. Understanding consciousness functionally will more likely require us to pay attention to processes operating at many different levels of organization. Once we recognize the need for multilevel functional explanations, we can see that McGinn's way of posing the mind-body problem is somewhat misleading. There is not likely to be any single property P that explains how consciousness arises from the brain. McGinn's search for the mysterious property P suggests, though admittedly it does not entail, that there will be a single-stage explanatory link that passes directly from physical brain structure to full-blown phenomenal consciousness. This is indeed unlikely, but the prospects for a multistage theoretical explanation need not be so dim. Perhaps sound arguments can be given to show that even multistage explanations can never bridge the psychophysical gap, but our beliefs about that issue should not be influenced by the bewilderment we feel when we contemplate trying to get from physiology to phenomenology in a single step.

If we want to end up with a multilevel explanation of how consciousness depends on the brain, then our research methods should be ecumenically pluralistic, embracing both bottom-up investigations, which build up from knowledge of physical brain structure, and top-down projects, which begin with observations about the abilities and behaviors of the whole person or animal, as well as theorizing and experimentation about any number of levels of organization in between. The starting point for top-down research should include not only third-person behavioral data but also whatever we can learn from first-person introspection about the nature of conscious mental states. Cartesian views about the infallibility and comprehensiveness of introspection have been justifiably rejected, but there is still much that we can learn from our first-person awareness of our conscious mental life. Even if there is much about consciousness that escapes introspection and even if there are some ways in which first-person observation may mislead us, there is still good reason to include what introspection *seems to reveal* about consciousness among our initial data. Like all "observations," the apparent insights of introspection may be called into question by later discoveries, but at least initially they provide some of the most promising points of entry for investigating consciousness.

From the first-person perspective, one obvious feature of conscious experience is that we generally understand what we are experiencing. For example, when I have a conscious visual experience of my desk and the objects on it, I know that I am seeing a telephone, which is between a desk lamp and a stapler and just a few inches from a computer monitor. Moreover, my understanding of what a telephone is, how it works, and how to use one are all at least implicitly present to me as part of the phenomenal content of the experience. I have elsewhere described conscious phenomenal representations as having a high degree of *semantic transparency*. The extent to which a representation is semantically transparent is a matter of how readily and completely its content or meaning is accessible to the user of the representation. The contents of phenomenal representation are typically very accessible to us in this regard (I add "typically" because, as we will see below, there are some pathological cases in which this not so). When we have a conscious visual experience, we normally know and understand what is being represented to us, and with almost no effort we can make appropriate links to a vast amount of background knowledge. Our abilities in this regard are so vast and their exercise is so automatic and familiar that we normally don't even notice that there is anything remarkable here requiring special explanation. We just take the semantic transparency of experience for granted and regard the understanding that accompanies experience as inevitable. But as we will see, it is not inevitable, and the processes that underlie it are very much in need of explanation.

Let us take as our starting point semantic transparency, a feature of phenomenal experience revealed by introspection, and see what we can learn about it and about the functional organization of phenomenal consciousness in general from pathological cases. At present there is quite a lot of controversy among neuroscientists and neuropsychologists regarding the evidential value and proper way to make use of data about deficit cases, i.e., cases about patients who, as the result of brain damage, have lost or been impaired in one or more of their psychological abilities. In particular, there has been a lively debate about whether it is legitimate to use pooled data from groups of patients classed as suffering a common syndrome or whether one should appeal only to single-case studies, i.e., to data collected from a single impaired patient. Each method has some obvious shortcomings. The use of pooled data assumes that the subjects form a more or less homogeneous population, but it is often well nigh impossible to determine that the subjects have indeed suffered the same damage. If one is in fact dealing with a heterogeneous population, averaging data across the group may produce results that do not reflect the performance of any of the individuals in the group, and interesting effects may get lost in the variation among subjects (Shallice 1988). Single-case studies avoid the need to establish such uniformity in a population, but at the cost of making replicability extremely difficult, since it will always be possible to dismiss apparent failures to replicate as the result of differences in the deficits suffered by the patients in the different studies. Single-case studies thus threaten to produce unfalsifiable results and to evade one of the important quality-control structures of standard scientific practice. They threaten as well to produce an avalanche of unsystematic data that cannot easily be surveyed or put to good theoretical use (Shallice 1988).

Despite such controversy, there seems to be agreement about at least some ways in which deficit data can be validly used to test and inform psychological hypotheses. If single-case studies are conducted carefully with controlled quantitative measures and a battery of baseline tests are standardly employed to determine the patient's overall level of functioning, it should be possible to obtain results that can help delineate the underlying functional architecture of cognition. In particular, evidence of dissociations, that is, of cases in which one function or ability is lost or severely impaired while another is largely or wholly preserved, can be used to show the existence of independent modules or functional units in the underlying organization of cognition. As long as one has confidence in the experimental procedures used to determine performance, dissociation in even a single case suggests that the two abilities depend at least in part on distinct underlying components, though it is possible that the two could depend on a common unit and that the lost ability simply requires a higher level of capacity from the common component that it cannot provide in its impaired state. Thus evidence of double dissociations is of special value: if we can show by distinct single cases both that ability *a* can be preserved while ability *b* is lost *and vice versa*, then we have strong reason to believe that the two abilities indeed depend in part on distinct functional units (Weiskrantz 1988, Shallice 1988).

Thus, to investigate the role of phenomenal consciousness, I would like to consider two sorts of deficit cases that come close to offering a double dissociation: first, cases in which phenomenal consciousness in a given sensory modality has been lost but residual perceptual abilities have been preserved, and second, cases in which phenomenal consciousness is allegedly present in a given sensory mode despite the absence of the sort of understanding that normally accompanies such consciousness. Cases of the first sort involve so-called blindsight, and those of the second concern associative visual agnosia. My hope is to shed some light on the functional role of phenomenal consciousness in two ways: first, to identify its contribution by finding out what patients can and cannot do in its absence, and second, to find out something about how it makes that contribution by considering how those abilities can be lost despite its presence.

Before proceeding, I should note that there is another way in which evidence from deficit studies has sometimes been used that in the present context promises a more or less negative result as a bonus to my main project. I refer to the method of comparing data about functional deficits with known facts about the anatomical sites of patients' brain lesions in order to test claims about functional localization, i.e., to test hypotheses about which physical brain structures carry out specific psychological processes (Von Eckardt Klein 1978). The negative result to which I refer is the finding that there does not seem to be any local brain site that is the seat of phenomenal consciousness; it seems instead to be very much a process whose physical basis is widely distributed across the brain. Below I shall say something about why the functional organization underlying consciousness would lead us to expect it to have a global physical basis in the brain.

1 Blindsight

Let us turn, then, to the now well-known and much discussed phenomenon of blindsight. Blindsighted patients, such as D.B. studied by Lawrence Weiskrantz (1974, 1986), have occipital lobe damage involving lesions in the region of striate cortex known as V1, which is the initial point of reception for inputs from the retina after passage through the lateral geniculate nucleus. Such lesions produce a blind field, or scotoma, such that patients typically report not seeing anything when stimuli are projected to that region of their visual field (though some patients report some limited visual experience of a nonveridical nature in response to very intense stimuli). Despite their apparently sincere reports, indirect measures have shown that blindsighted subjects have preserved perceptual abilities with respect to stimuli presented in the scotoma. For example, if instructed to "just guess" whether a presented stimlus was of a vertical or horizontal grating, subjects are able to respond quite accurately despite their firm denial that they have seen anything at all. The blindsighted subject appears to be perceiving and responding on the basis of visual stimuli despite his absence of any conscious awareness of having seen anything.

There is quite a lot of variation among blindsighted subjects with respect to how much residual visual ability remains, and there is also variation within each patient depending on the nature and intensity of the stimulus to which he or she is exposed. However, all show remarkably accurate discrimination with respect to at least some stimuli projected into their blind field, despite the reported absence of any visual awareness. Weiskrantz's patient D.B. can detect and locate stimuli in his blind field by pointing. He can discriminate quite well the orientation of a grating (horizontal versus vertical), though not quite as well as normal controls. He can discriminate movement to a degree that is again impressive though less than normal controls. And he can also discriminate Xs from Os and squares from diamonds, though experiments conducted by Weiskrantz suggest that D.B.'s abilities in this regard are derived from his sensitivity to orientation rather than to form per se.

Even more surprising residual abilities have been reported in other blindsighted patients. Anthony Marcel (1983) has reported results showing semantic-priming effects from words projected into the blind fields of two subjects. Marcel has also reported results showing form discrimination with respect to objects presented in the blind field as manifested by subject's preparatory adjustments of hand and arm when "forced" to reach for an object that they report no awareness of having seen (Marcel and Wilkins 1982, Marcel 1988). And some residual wavelength sensitivity, though not necessarily full color sensitivity, has also been reported in some other blindsighted subjects (Stoerig and Cowey 1990).

Despite these impressive abilities, it must be remembered that blindsighted subjects are far from normal with respect their residual perceptual abilities. In many cases they report having no relevant perceptual experiences at all, even in cases in which they are able to make correct discriminations more than 90 percent of the time and to function at the level of normal controls. Moreover, when they do report any visual experiences, as sometimes occurs in response to suprathreshold stimuli, their reported experiences are decidely non-veridical (e.g., reporting waves in response to stimuli of high-contrast geometric shapes) and they could not provide the basis for their accurate discriminations.

The residual capacities of blindsighted subjects are normally re-vealed only in forced-choice discriminations, in which they are in-structed to "just guess" about the nature of a stimulus (e.g., present or absent, vertical or horizontal, moving or not moving) despite their sincere avowal that they have not seen anything. A crucial fact about such patients is that they *will not initiate any response* to a stimulus projected to their blind field unless they are instructed to do so, e.g., to make a choice in a forced-choice situation. Indeed, even when instructed to do so, many subjects are reluctant to respond, since they are not aware of having any visual experience.

It is this fact about what blindsight patients do *not do* rather than their surprising residual capacities that is most important for our present concerns. The question is this: since blindsighted subjects are processing visual stimuli and extracting information from these stimuli adequate to accurately guide their responses, why do they have no inclination whatsoever to make use of any of this informa-tion outside the experimental situations that force them to do so? And why even in experimental situations do they have no awareness of using such information but take themselves to be just guessing? A possible answer of interest to our inquiry is that the crucial missing element is phenomenal experience. That is, the relevant informa-tion is being perceptually extracted from the visual input, but it does not get represented in phenomenal form. It would thus seem that information needs to be presented to us phenomenally for it to play a role in the choice, initiation, or direction of intentional action. It is what we are phenomenally aware of that provides the basis for purposive and deliberative behavior. If information has been extracted but is not incorporated into our phenomenal representation of our situation and our relation to it, then that information will not affect how we intentionally act toward that situation.

Why should this be so? Are there any features of phenomenal representation that help to explain why we should need it to bring information to bear on our intentional action? Recall what we noted above about the high degree to which phenomenal representations are semantically transparent; their content is readily accessible and capable of being applied in a wide range of contexts. In the normal case we can rapidly and easily connect an item of phenomenally represented information with a vast store of background knowledge and place it in a context relevant to evaluation, decision, and action. When I am now phenomenally aware of the telephone on my desk, I am aware of it as a telephone and as located at a particular place in my world. I experience it in relation to myself, as a part of a common shared world, as sharing part of a common physical space, and as affording opportunities for me to use it by means of instrumental cause and effect relations. Introspectively, all of this information is experienced as at least implicitly present as part of the phenomenal content of my perceptual state. There is an important sense in which our phenomenal awareness is standardly a form of self-awareness insofar as we experience objects in relation to ourselves. My experience is of a telephone in front of *me* at this very moment causing *my* present visual awareness of it (see Searle 1983). Representing information in this way makes it readily available for applying it toward pursuit of my goals and plans and the guidance of my action.

Cases of blindsight thus lend at least some support to views already suggested by introspection about the contribution phenomenal representations make to our cognitive economy. That is, the evidence from blindsight supports the view that phenomenal experience provides a highly integrative system of representation that allows many different items about our situation, plans, goals, capacities, and selves to be united in a single interconnected structure. Because the information blindsighted patients extract from visual stimuli fails to be incorporated into their phenomenal representation of their world, it remains disconnected from and inaccessible to the action-guiding systems that lie at the core of their personalities. It cannot be brought to bear on any of the self-conscious or deliberate choices or actions that they undertake as persons. However, the information is not totally disconnected from behavior, as is clear from the ways it shows itself in accurate "just guess" responses to experimental forced choices. By responding to the instruction to just guess, the blind-sighted subject in effect surrenders any conscious control of his or her response and gives up any attempt to bring consciously accessible information to bear on it. This suggests that the conscious-choice system that relies on phenomenally represented information is the dominant but not the only structure mediating between stimulus and appropriate response. When it is in play, it dominates the connection, and nothing can have an impact unless it is phenomenally available to that system, but if it can be temporarily set aside, lesser residual connections can bring information to bear on behavior in apt ways.

Having used cases of blindsight to learn something about the functional role of phenomenal consciousness in terms of what contribution it makes, can we say anything about its functional role in the sense of *how* it makes that contribution? That is, how is phenomenal consciousness organized so as to allow it to make the contribution it does, and into what sorts of interactions do phenomenal representations enter so as to allow them to make the contributions they do? The integrative role of phenomenal consciousness requires some way in which phenomenal representations can bring together many items of information in a unified structure. There are at least two ways in which it in fact does just that. First, it embodies specific unities quite directly in its own structure, e.g., representing the unity and continuity of space by the unified continuous manifold of the subjective visual field. It also embodies in its rich network of contentful interconnections the more general encompassing unity of the objective world within which we experience ourselves and our actions as located. It should be noted that even the more specific unities of the sort associated with a unified representation of space require a rich network of interconnections among distinct items of information. We know, for example, that distinct cortical regions are involved in processing retinal inputs to discriminate specific features of the visual stimuli, such as color, motion, shape, orientation, and location. Somehow all these must be brought together into a unified visual awareness of a red vertical cylindrical coffee mug moving from the the lower left to the upper right portion of my visual field.

The question of how all this information, which is locally determined at different regions, gets brought together into a unified percept of a integrated objective scene is referred to as "the binding problem." It is the problem of how all these physically and informationally distinct items get bound together in the appropriate way. Insofar as phenomenal visual experience involves an integrated and unified spatial representation of one's visual field, progress in solving the binding problem is likely to be of direct relevance to understanding the basis of phenomenal consciousness. Current theories about the neurophysiological nature of binding are instructive in this regard. Most of the leading models involve mechanisms by which the spatially distinct neural centers coding for the multiple aspects of the visual scene can somehow be brought into global coordinated interaction or union. There are suggestions that this is accomplished by getting the distinct groups of neurons to fire simultaneously in conjunction with a 40-hertz oscillation or at least to fire synchronously with less than oscillatory regularity. Few at this time believe the binding problem can be solved by having the information from all the distinct processing regions passed onto a single locus that is the site of an executive (or homunculus) whose function is to analyze and integrate all the channels of information. There does not appear to be any such local supersite, or as Daniel Dennett (1991) has put it, there does not seem to be any "Cartesian theater" in the brain where it all comes together. Getting it all together seems to be more a matter of getting the many distinct regions "talking" to each other, rather than of their all talking to an all-knowing head of a hierarchy (Kinsbourne 1988, Van Gulick 1991).

Our consideration of blindsight has thus brought us the sort of multilevel explanation that, I argued above, will be needed to really understand consciousness and answer skeptics, like McGinn, who doubt that we ever will be able to comprehend the psychophysical link. Above I have uncovered at least three levels of interrelated explanations.

First, at the highest level I have suggested an explanatory link between the contribution that phenomenal consciousness seems to make to our cognitive economy and its introspectively accessible phenomenal organization. That is, I have tried to show that phenomenal consciousness is well suited to its integrative role of bringing together information in a unified format that makes it available for open-ended use in the initiation and guidance of intentional action because it has a number of features that are apparent to us introspectively, such as its high degree of semantic transparency and the various unities it embodies in its mode of representation (like the directly represented unity of space and the somewhat more implicitly represented unity of the objective world).

Second, I have discussed how at least some of these introspectable phenomenal features might be explained in terms of underlying functional organization, specifically, how semantic transparency and phenomenal unity might be explained by appeal to the cooperative interactions and rich network of links between distinct units or modules that independently encode much more specific items of information, as in current theories about how to solve the binding problem in visual perception.

And third, I mentioned some current physiological hypotheses about what brain processes (e.g., the 40-hertz oscilliation) might in turn underlie this functional organization and the required network of connections and cooperative interactions and modules.

Much of the theorizing at any of these levels may turn out to be wrong; I am not claiming that the evidence to date justifies claiming that it is surely correct. Nonetheless, theorizing and model building that is multilevel is the sort that I believe in the end will lead us to the correct explanation of phenomenal consciousness and allow us to fully answer those critics, like McGinn, who claim that no such explanation is possible.

Before going on to discuss what we can learn from a second form of psychopathology, visual agnosia, I would like to discuss briefly two objections that have been raised, or might be raised, against what I have said have about blindsight.

I described blindsighted subjects, quite orthodoxly, as not having any phenomenal visual experience yet able to perform at a very high level on some visual discrimination tasks. However, Colin McGinn (1991) has questioned this way of characterizing blindsighted subjects and proposed an alternative view according to which blindsighted subjects have visual experiences but are just not aware of them. The standard reason for denying that the patients have any visual experience is that they report not having any. But the patients' reports are also consistent with McGinn's alternative hypothesis, since if the patients were having visual experiences but were unaware of them, they would, of course, deny having any. McGinn draws a further distinction that is important to understanding his view of blindsight. He distinguishes between phenomenal consciousness and conscious experience per se and regards the former as merely one (surface) component of the latter. He describes phenomenal consciousness as that part of conscious experience that is accessible to introspection and that makes conscious experience into something it feels like to the person to be in that experiential state. To put it in his own terms, McGinn's view is that blindsighted subjects have conscious visual experiences but are introspectively unaware of having those experiences because they enjoy no visual phenomenology.

I suspect that many readers will find this a strange and unintuitive view, as do I. But this is not a sufficient reason for rejecting it; unintuitive views sometimes turn out right. But is there any reason to regard McGinn's alternative as more than a mere possibilty? The key question is whether or not the residual visual processing that goes on in blindsight should be regarded as involving conscious experience. Both the orthodox view and McGinn's alternative agree that visual phenomenology is absent and that some residual processing must occur if we are to account for the subjects' preserved abilities to discriminate visual stimuli, but why should one regard this processing as involving conscious experience, given the negative reports from the subjects. McGinn (1991, 112) argues for his view as follows:

1. Many of the ordinary causal powers of visual consciousness (e.g., abilities to discriminate visual stimuli) are preserved despite the absence of visual phenomenology.

2. It seems evident that in normal cases of sight it is the experience itself that carries the relevant causal powers (we regard our normal discriminative abilities as based on our visual experiences).

3. Thus we should regard the causal powers in the blindsighted sub-jects as also derived from visual experiences (or at least a residual component of visual experiences).

4. Thus the residual visual processes in blindsighted patients involve conscious visual experience (lacking in any phenomenal feel).

In support of this line of argument, McGinn asks rhetorically, "Do blindsight patients not *look* very much as if they are having visual experiences when they make their surprising discriminations?" (1991, 112). Unfortunately for McGinn, the answer to this question is negative: blindsighted patients do *not* look as if they were hav-ing visual experiences. As was noted above and as has been noted elsewhere (Marcel 1988, Van Gulick 1990, and explicitly in response to McGinn, in Dennett 1991), under normal everyday conditions, blindsighted patients do not act at all like sighted persons but act instead like people who are straightforwardly blind, at least with respect to stimuli in their blind fields. Even in experimen-tal contexts they do not volunteer or initiate any responses to stimuli. Rather, they respond only when they are prodded to do so in a forced-choice situation under instructions to just guess; even then they often feel foolish and respond quite reluctantly. This does not seem at all like what we do when we make a normal discrimina-tion based on visual experience, and it seems highly inappropriate to apply any intuitions we may have about the causal role visual experience plays in our normal behavior to such very different cases.

We should also remember that impressive as the residual abilities of blindsighted patients are, they are still quite limited in comparison with the abilities of sighted persons. For example, as I noted above, Weiskrantz finds in D.B. no abilities to discriminate forms except those that are parasitic on orientation discrimination. How, then, can we make sense of McGinn's view with respect to D.B.? Are we to say that he has visual experiences but they do not involve any representation of form? The suggestion seems incoherent. It seems more reasonable here to forego the notion of visual experience and say that there are residual processes in D.B. that are able to extract information about some aspects of visual stimuli (such as orientation) and bring that information to bear on behavior but that are not adequate to give rise to visual experience.

I do not claim to have refuted McGinn's alternative view, but I do not think we need to take it too seriously unless better reasons can be given to support his unorthodox and unintuitive interpretation. His argument above seems, if anything, to point in the opposite direction, given the radical differences in behavior between blindsighted patients and normally sighted persons.

A second apparently similar but in fact quite distinct line of objection also might be raised against my account of blindsight. It is similar to McGinn's objection in suggesting that the causal role I have attributed to phenomenal consciousness is in fact filled by some other mental component but dissimilar in not regarding that other component as part of (or involving) conscious experience. Max Velmans (1991) has recently argued that human information processing is not conscious and that consciousness is, for all practical psychological purposes, epiphenomenal. He regards consciousness as an aftereffect of information processing rather than as a cause or active component of such processing. For Velmans, consciousness is more like the display that appears on my computer screen than like any of the computational goings on that occur in my computer's CPU (central processing unit). What happens in the CPU produces the display, but the display has no effect on the CPU; indeed, the CPU would continue just the same if the monitor were turned off. According to Velmans, the belief that consciousness plays a more active role is an illusion that results from the fact that consciousness generally accompanies, and is produced by, focal attentive processing (FAP). According to Velmans, FAP does all the real work unconsciously, and conscious awareness is merely a regular and slightly delayed afterglow of FAP. The illusion results because we notice the correlation between absence of phenomenal consciousness and the loss of various abilities and mistakenly attribute the loss of the latter to the absence of the former, when in fact it is the absence of their common cause, FAP, that explains why both are missing.

According to this view, the disabilities and limitations of blindsighted patients (e.g., their failure to bring their visual information to bear on their actions) result not from the absence of phenomenal consciousness but from the fact that such information cannot gain access to focal attentive processing. Its failure to register in phenomenal consciousness is merely a secondary effect of its failure to enter FAP.

Velmans presents a lengthy defense of his position, which I have criticised elsewhere (1991), and I do not want to review the details here. The crucial point that bears repeating for present purposes is that Velmans's view, though possible, seems to be an unduly skeptical alternative. For example, in criticizing Bernard Baar's (1988) thesis that consciousness facilitates learning, Velmans argues that all that one can infer from the correlation between consciousness and learning is that focal attentive processing facilitates learning. But in the absence of independent and successful arguments (which, I have argued [1991], are not to be found in Velmans's article), the claim that focal attentive processing does all the work and consciousness is epiphenomenal remains little more than a skeptical hypothesis. It is perhaps consistent with the evidence, but also consistent with the evidence is the thesis that consciousness, when present, does make a difference to processing (including focal attentive processing).

Moreover, the claim that it is focal attentive processsing rather than conscious awareness, that is doing all the work may depend on the mistaken assumption that the two are always distinct. Velmans is quite right to insist that consciousness should be understood to involve awareness and should not be just equated with, or used as an alternative name for, focal attentive processing. But neither should it just be assumed that they are always distinct and that conscious awareness is merely a by-product or side effect of focal attentive processing. The fact that they are so regularly, if less than invariably, connected surely requires explanation, and the only explanation offered by Velmans (that conscious awareness requires a high-level activation of the sort produced by focal attentive processing) is less than convincing. It seems equally or perhaps more plausible to suppose that many of the states of brain activity that constitute focal attentive processing are in fact identical with states of conscious awareness.

Consider in this light Baar's (1988) claim that one of the functions of consciousness is to "broadcast" information throughout the nervous system and make that information widely available, which Velmans (1991) discusses and rejects. On his view, there are focal attentive processes that both enable this information to be broadcast and also cause a conscious awareness of this information, but the conscious awareness plays no role in making the information available throughout the system. As noted above, Velmans views conscious awareness like the output on a computer monitor: all the work goes on in the CPU, some of whose operations the monitor merely reflects. But if we think of conscious awareness as instead involving large-scale higher-order patterns of brain activity spanning many different sensory and representational modalities (i.e., as involving a very rich set of active associative links), then it becomes quite reasonable to think of conscious awareness as identical with (or at least part of) the process by which information is broadcast.

As discussed above, our conscious awareness is typically of a phenomenal world, in the Kantian sense. We do not experience isolated or disconnected items of information. Conscious experience involves rich and highly integrated representations of a world of interrelated objects from the perspective of our location as subjects within that world. Moreover, experience is typically characterized, as in conscious thought, by a connected and orderly flow of such representations that reflects the myriad connections within the represented world. If we consider the sort of pattern of brain activity required as the neural substrate for such representations and their interactions, it seems that it necessarily also has to satisfy the conditions for broadcasting information. Conscious phenomenal representations, because of their highly integrated and multimodal content, require rich associative networks of activation as their basis.

As noted above, many current models of consciousness do not view it as taking place in a special location, on the introspective "monitor" or in some special module, but treat it as involving the occurrence of complex patterns of activation and associative connection across a wide range of more specific modules. Such models are admittedly still speculative, but they are not without theoretical or empirical foundation. And if they are more or less correct, then consciousness does play a causal role in the broadcasting of information and is anything but epiphenomenal.

At this stage of research it is impossible to refute Velmans's alternative, which reminds us that the sort of evidence I have presented about blindsighted patients, though suggestive, is not conclusive in showing that phenomenal consciousness plays a causal role in guiding action. Nonetheless, I do not think we need to be concerned about Velmans's skeptical alternative, any more than we need to be concerned about McGinn's, unless more in the way of successful positive evidence is given to support it. It remains a possible view, but not a terribly plausible one.

2 Visual Agnosia

Now that I have dealt with these two lines of objection, let us go on to consider what we can learn about phenomenal consciousness from cases of associative visual agnosia. The pathology is interesting both in its own right and also because it poses a potential problem for some of what I have said above about the semantic transparency of phenomenal consciousness. Patients suffering from visual agnosia are described as having "normal perception stripped of meaning." As classically described (Farah 1990), they are characterized by three features:

• They are *impaired at recognizing visually presented objects*, both verbally, in terms of their inability to name the objects, and nonverbally, in their inabilities to show that they recognize the object by other means (e.g., by miming how they would use it if the object is a tool).

• They exhibit *normal abilities to recognize objects presented nonvisually*, e.g., they can recognize objects tactilely or auditorily.

• They appear to have *intact visual perception adequate to the recognition task,* as demonstrated, for example, by their abilties to faithfully copy drawings of presented objects and their abilities to match or correctly sort pictures and objects in terms of visual similarity (though they are unable to do so in terms of semantic similarity or similarity of function).

Associative visual agnosia might be taken as an objection to the claims made above about the semantic transparency of phenomenal visual experience. The agnosic seems to be having visual experiences but not to know what he is seeing; his phenomenal representations are far from transparent to him. The agnosic does not have the ability to link his visual experiences with the rest of his background knowledge despite the fact that his perception seems to be adequate for discriminating visual features of the stimulus, such as shape, orientation, color, and size.

Strictly speaking, the existence of visual agnosia is not inconsistent with what I said above, since I was careful to say that phenomenal visual experience is *typically* semantically transparent. The qualifier "typically" was added in part to accommodate nontypical cases like visual agnosia in which the normal connection between visual discrimination and background knowledge has been broken.

Nonetheless, a critic might appeal to visual agnosia to question the general view of phenomenal visual experience offered above. If, as the visual agnosic seems to show, it is possible to dissociate visual experience from comprehension and understanding of what one is seeing, does this not indicate that semantic transparency is not really a fundamental feature of phenomenal experience but merely a sometime accompaniment? And if it is the latter, then how can semantic transparency shed much light on the nature of phenomenal experience itself? Adding the qualifier "typically" may avoid formal contradiction, but does visual agnosia nonetheless undermine the explanatory value of semantic transparency in understanding the nature of phenomenal experience?

I believe that all these possible objections can be answered and that the facts about visual agnosia, if properly understood, support rather than undercut the analysis of phenomenal consciousness given above. My critic claims that the visual agnosic has complete and normal visual experiences yet does not recognize or understand what he is seeing. Thus he concludes that semantic transparency is not a fundamental feature of visual experience and one should not appeal to it, as I did above, to support claims about the likely functional and physical organization of phenomenal consciousness. A two-part reply is in order. First, the visual experiences of agnosics are not in fact all that normal, and second, even if they were, the alleged conclusion would not follow.

Regarding the first point, Martha Farah, in her recent book *Visual Agnosia* (1990), observes that the perceptual abilities of associative agnosics have been significantly overestimated; the data in fact show significant perceptual impairments. Despite their good results on copying and matching tasks, more careful examination shows that their perceptual abilities are far from intact. Even on such tasks their performance seems to be the result of impaired perception enhanced by coping strategies rather than being the product of normal perception. In copying drawings, visual agnosics employ a slow mechanical line by line technique that involves lots of careful back and forth comparison of small line segments in the original drawing with the details of their copy. They also sometimes lose their place in the drawing with confused results and reduplicated features. They do not seem to proceed from an overall sense of what they are copying. One patient, M.S., was unable to distinguish drawings of possible figures from those of impossible figures (Ratcliff and Newcombe 1982). When M.S. was asked to copy both types of drawings, his performance was accurate but equally slow with both, in contrast with normal controls, who are slower in copying drawings of impossible figures than in copying drawings of possible ones. M.S. seemed unable to guide his production by any overall understanding of the figure. Another patient, H.J.A., despite his more or less normal performance on classical tests, was determined to perform poorly on recognizing overlapping figure drawings and on tasks that involve feature integration (Riddoch and Humphreys 1987). For example, he was tested for his ability to identify the presence or absence of an inverted T in a display of upright Ts. Normal subjects can respond much faster if the the Ts are arranged in a circle rather than randomly, especially when no inverted T is present. However, H.J.A. did not show this fast absent response to the circular arrangement, and his reaction time remained dependent on the number of Ts in the display, which suggests an item by item check. Yet another patient, L.H., who performed at a high level on many tasks, nonetheless was greatly impaired on tests involving visual closure, which require perceiving degraded shapes (Levine and Calvanio 1978). L.H. was very poor at discriminating words if they were partially obliterated in ways that extended across letter boundaries.

Further perceptual deficits can be found in Farah's summary of the literature. What is important for present purposes is simply the fact that contrary to traditional accounts, associative visual agnosics are *not perceptually normal*. Thus the claim of my hypothetical critic that such patients can have completely normal visual experience (or at least normal percepts) but lack any comprehension is just not true; their visual percepts are simply not normal.

Moreover, even if associative visual agnosics did not have the perceptual impairments that they do, my critic's conclusion would not follow; i.e., this would not show that semantic transparency is not a fundamental feature of phenomenal experience. Even if such agnosics were not perceptually impaired, their phenomenal visual experience would still be abnormal and incomplete. Understanding what one is seeing, for example, seeing a telephone *as a telephone* is not something that accompanies visual experience; it is a part of one's visual experience. Instead of saying that associative agnosics have normal phenomenal experience without any knowledge, we should rather say that because the knowledge is absent, they lack a major component of normal experience. Even if the agnosic's visual experience were pictorially complete and accurate (which it is not), it would be phenomenally incomplete insofar as recognition of what was being seen and awareness of such recognition were absent from the experience.

The possiblity of such dissociation between the pictorial and conceptual aspects of phenomenal experience is in fact what one would expect on the account of the underlying organization of phenomenal consciousness given above. The semantic transparency of consciousness is not a matter of getting information into a specially privileged format for presentation to the head processor in an information-processing hierarchy; we must resist the seductive lure of the Cartesian-theater metaphor with its omniscient superhomunculus. Semantic transparency results not from getting information to a special place or in a special format but from getting many different centers of content in cooperative contact with each other. Visual agnosia seems to result from some combination of local failures and failures of communication; i.e., it results from the loss of abilities to construct certain specific types of representations (e.g., those involved with grouped and integrative features) and from breakdowns or disconnections of links between the centers where such representations are computed. If phenomenal consciousness does indeed depend on cooperative interaction between many different centers, then one would expect the possibility of pathological cases in which some components of experience are present while others are missing. Thus the sorts of dissociations found in the associative visual agnosic actually tend to support rather than undermine the general account of phenomenal consciousness that I have offered.

Visual agnosia and blindsight are just two of the many pathologies that can help us understand the functional organization and physical basis of phenomenal consciousness. By themselves they are no more than suggestive, nor can they show that the sort of model I have proposed is correct. But I do hope that I have shown that deficit studies can be a powerful source of evidence for constructing and testing such models and for answering the various types of skepticism voiced by McGinn, Block, and Searle.

References

Baars, Bernard. 1988. *A Cognitive Theory of Consciousness.* Cambridge: Cambridge University Press.

Block, Ned. 1978. "Troubles with Functionalism." In *Perception and Cognition: Issues in the Foundations of Psychology,* ed. C. W. Savage, Minnesota Studies in the Philosophy of Science, no. 9. Minneapolis: University of Minnesota Press.

Dennett, Daniel C. 1991. *Consciousness Explained.* Boston: Little Brown.

Farah, Martha. 1990 *Visual Agnosia.* Cambridge: MIT Press.

Flanagan, Owen. 1992. *Consciousness Reconsidered.* Cambridge: MIT Press.

Kinsbourne, Marcel. 1988. "Integrated Field Theory of Consciousness." In *Consciousness in Contemporary Science,* ed. A. J. Marcel and E. Bisiach. Oxford: Clarendon Press.

Levine, D. N., and R. Calvanio. 1978. "A Study of the Visual Defect in Verbal Alexia—Simultanagnosia." *Brain* 101:65–81.

Lycan, William. 1990. "The Continuity of Levels of Nature." In *Mind and Cognition: A Reader,* ed. W. Lycan. Oxford: Basil Blackwell.

Marcel, Anthony J. 1980. "Conscious and Unconscious Recognition of Polysemous Words: Locating the Selective Effects of Prior Verbal Context." In *Attention and Performance,* vol. 8, ed. R. S. Nickerson. Hillsdale, N.J.: Erlbaum.

Marcel, Anthony J. 1983. "Conscious and Unconscious Perception: An Approach to the Relations between Phenomenal Experience and Perceptual Processes." *Cognitive Psychology* 15:238–300.

Marcel, Anthony J. 1988. "Phenomenal Experience and Functionalism." In *Consciousness in Contemporary Science,* ed. A. J. Marcel and E. Bisiach. Oxford: Clarendon Press.

Marcel, Anthony J., and A. J. Wilkins. 1982. "Cortical Blindness: A Problem of Visual Consciousness or of Visual Function?" Paper presented at the Fifth International Neuropsychology Society European Conference, Deauville, France. As cited in Marcel 1988.

McGinn, Colin. 1989. "Can We Solve the Mind-Body Problem?" *Mind* 98:349–366.

McGinn, Colin. 1991. *The Problem of Consciousness.* Oxford: Basil Blackwell.

Ratcliff, G., and F. Newcombe. 1982. "Object Recognition: Some Deductions from the Clinical Evidence." In *Normality and Pathology in Cognitive Functions,* ed. A. W. Ellis. New York: Academic Press.

Riddoch, M. J., and G. W. Humphreys. 1987. "A Case of Integrative Visual Agnosia." *Brain* 110:1431–1462.

Searle, John. 1983. *Intentionality.* Cambridge: Cambridge University Press.

Searle, John. 1992. *The Rediscovery of the Mind.* Cambridge: MIT Press.

Shallice, Tim. 1988. *From Neuropsychology to Mental Structure.* Cambridge: Cambridge University Press.

Stoerig, P., and A. Cowey. 1990. "Wavelength Sensitivity in Blindsight." *Nature* 342:916–918.

Van Gulick, Robert. 1990. "What Difference Does Consciousness Make?" *Philosophical Topics* 17:211–230.

Van Gulick, Robert. 1991. "Consciousness May Still Have a Processing Role to Play." *Behavioral and Brain Sciences* 14:699–700.

Van Gulick, Robert. 1992. "Time for More Alternatives." *Behavioral and Brain Sciences* 15:228–229.

Velmans, Max. 1991. "Is Human Information Processing Conscious?" *Behavioral and Brain Sciences* 14:651–669.

Von Eckardt Klein, Barbara. 1978. "Inferring Functional Localization from Neurological Evidence." In *Explorations in the Biology of Language,* ed. Edward Walker. Cambridge: MIT Press.

Weiskrantz, Lawrence, E. K. Warrington, M. D. Sanders, and J. Marshall. 1974. "Visual Capacity in the Hemianopic Field Following a Restricted Occipital Ablation." *Brain* 97:709–728.

Weiskrantz, Lawrence. 1986. *Blindsight: A Case Study and Implications.* Oxford: Clarendon Press.

Weiskrantz, Lawrence. 1988 "Some Contributions of Neurospychology of Vision and Memory to the Problem of Consciousness." In *Consciousness in Contemporary Science,* ed. A. J. Marcel and E. Bisiach. Oxford: Clarendon Press.

Emotional Disorder and Attention

Kent Bach

I don't know where I came from, I don't know where I'm going, and I don't know why I do the things I do.
Evel Knievel

Beginning to think is beginning to be undermined.
Albert Camus

Some would say that philosophy can contribute more to the occurrence of mental disorder than to the study of it. Thinking too much does have its risks, but so do willful ignorance and selective inattention. Well, what can philosophy contribute? It is not equipped to enumerate the symptoms and varieties of disorder or to identify their diverse causes, much less to offer cures (maybe it *can* do this—personal philosophical therapy is now available in the Netherlands). On the other hand, the scientific study of mental disorder has a long way to go. There is much disagreement and uncertainty about the nature, causes, and treatment of many specific disorders, as is evident from *DSM*'s (APA 1987) classification of them in predominantly symptomatic terms. And even if what is reflected in *DSM* were a consensus rather than a compromise, still this shifts periodically with each new edition. Moreover, it is a notorious fact that many patients who clearly have psychiatric abnormalities do not fit any of the recognized diagnostic categories.[1]

There are several obvious ways in which philosophy can contribute to the study of mental disorder. Questions raised in the philosophy of social science about methodology, explanation, and the fact/value distinction can be directed specifically at the theories, methods, and practices that treat of mental disorder. One noteworthy question in particular, raised not by a philosopher but by the psychiatrist Thomas Szasz (1974), concerns the legitimacy of the very idea of psychopathology and the suitability of the medical model for purely psychological conditions (no organic disease, trauma, or lesion and no anatomical, physiological, or neurochemical abnormality). Underlying this question are various fact/value issues, such as whether the label "disorder" is used to imply that something doesn't work properly or that it is undesirable in some respect.[2] Pertinent to these issues are various concepts that are grist for the mill of analytic philosophy, concepts such as *normality* and *disorder, health* and *disease, rationality, emotion, attention, agency, control, compulsion, freedom*, and *self.* Although I take up several of these concepts and their connections, I am primarily interested in the notion of an emotional disorder.

What makes a disorder an *emotional* one, as opposed to purely cognitive disorders like aphasias, agnosias, and attentional deficit disorder (ADD)? In most cases the disorder is specific to a particular emotion and concerns its character, cause, or consequences. In some instances the disorder is broader in scope and involves either enduring capacities for emotion or more transitory emotional tendencies and dispositions (moods). I will suggest that emotional disorders contain attentional and correlative motivational elements and that this is intelligible in light of the fact that emotions themselves are inherently attentional and motivational (consider such emotions as worry, fear, suspicion, resentment, guilt, shame, and confidence). Normally, the strength of an emotion is proportional to its attentional and motivational import, but in disorders there is a gross and chronic disparity between the amount of attention something deserves and the amount it receives; how one is motivated to act may be affected accordingly. Trivial matters can matter too much, and consequential ones too little, and there may seem to be no way to rectify the disparity. A sensitive subject matter may capture one's attention to an inordinate degree and, by its persistent and often ill-timed intrusion into one's experience, impose unreasonable demands and disrupt one's activities. This may lead to a vicious cycle of anxiety, distress, irrationality, and loss of control.[3] At the other extreme, a subject may be too touchy for focused consideration or even conscious awareness, and thereby chronically escape the attention it deserves. This may yield a blind spot in one's experience, which may in turn lead to constrictions or convolutions in how one confronts recurrent situations in one's life.

Defenses appear to play a role here. Defenses may be understood as unconscious devices or stratagems for managing one's attention. They can serve to keep something out of mind or, if it does come to mind, to get rid of it or at least put it in a favorable light. If, as seems plausible, some degree of defensiveness is necessary for mental health, too much or too little defensiveness can make for emotional disorder. Emotional disorders, as problems in attention management, may be regarded as emotionally based difficulties either in bringing things to mind when needed (overdefensiveness) or in keeping unwanted intruders out of mind (underdefensiveness). I will suggest that such problems in attention management are often due either to excessive or insufficent use of what I call *exclusionary categories*.

The conception of emotional disorder to be sketched here offers a descriptive framework for identifying and connecting several key elements of emotional disorder. To the extent that this conception goes beyond conceptual analysis, it may smack of armchair psychology, but at least it does not speculate heavily on underlying etiological questions.[4] Even so, I should note that whereas some emotional disorders may involve problems *caused* by emotions, others may only be problems *with* emotions, that is, emotional *effects* of cognitive, attentional, or perhaps ultimately neurophysiological causes.

1 Emotion and Attention

Philosophers often pretend that the only mental states recognized in folk psychology are beliefs and desires, and maybe intentions. In fact, most folks find a wide range of emotions in their own experience and cite emotions to account for the behavior of others. "Descriptions of character and temperament . . . are frequently couched in terms of people's dominant emotions" (George Graham, personal communication), such as "hostile," "melancholic," "timorous," and

"Pollyannaish" (Ekman 1992, 194). People recognize that they act out of anger, fear, gratitude, remorse, jubilation, jealousy, defiance, spite, etc. Yet philosophers, by ignoring emotions and by equating folk psychology with belief-desire psychology, implicitly assume that emotions are if not eliminable, at least reducible to beliefs and desires.[5] However, no one has ever tried to show that each type of emotion is reducible to some belief and desire complex or that the explanations ostensibly provided by emotions amount to mere belief and desire explanations. Fortunately, there are some philosophers who do not accept such an impoverished view of folk psychology and are not embarrassed to take emotion seriously. They may disagree in their accounts of emotion, but they agree that emotion is not mere feeling. Here I will not review these many accounts, which emphasize judgmental and motivational features.[6] I will instead focus on the attentional side of emotion.

Emotions, though sometimes still called "passions," need not be passive or irrational. Although some emotional episodes are uncontrolled reactions out of proportion to their objects, many such episodes, even if not calm and collected, are expressions of a person's considered attitude or outlook on something. Of course, people often do get overwhelmed by emotion (such as by grief, frustration, or guilt) and are motivated to take action appropriate to the emotion or are moved to express it physically. But even then the emotion normally runs its course: one gains perspective and adjusts to one's situation, and the various physiological changes associated with upsurges of the emotion eventually subside for good. Sometimes, however, emotions directed at particular persons, things, or events persist indefinitely and intensify out of proportion to their objects; they can even become detached from their objects. One can become, as we say, "consumed" by guilt, "paralyzed" by fear, "stricken" with grief, or otherwise overwhelmed by an emotion. Its persistence and unwelcome recurrence can make life unmanageable and unbearable.[7]

Emotion and attention are interrelated: attention on something (focusing on or just noticing it) can trigger emotion, and emotion can direct attention, either toward something or away from it. When an emotion focuses attention on something, it often makes certain features salient and puts the object of the emotion in a phenomenologically special light.[8] Although the onset of an emotion is typically characterized by its "unbidden occurrence" and an "automatic appraisal" of its object (Ekman 1992), its persistence may make one preoccupied with its object and oversensitive to the actual or possible presence (or absence) of its object. Sometimes there is a vicious cycle of emotion directing thought and thought triggering emotion.[9] Typical examples include negative emotions like embarrassment, alarm, worry, disgust, and envy, and positive ones like fascination, anticipation, pride, and awe. Such emotions are reasonable if they are commensurate with their objects, e.g., momentary fright at the sound of a loud but distant explosion or mild embarrassment at being seen in public with perspiration stains under one's arms. But if the frightening or embarrassing event becomes a preoccupation and the persistent state of fright or embarrassment leads one thereafter to avoid situations even remotely like the one in which the emotion originally occurred, surely it is irrational.[10] Similarly, anger or worry become irrational if they result in excessive alertness, respectively, to reasons for blaming the person one is angry with or to items to check and doublecheck. In these cases the emotion has "taken over," making something an issue of disproportionate importance at the expense of one's other concerns.[11]

Emotions can also have attentional effects, often lasting ones, that go beyond the direct object of the emotion. For example, disappointment at failure can lead one not only to relive the relevant events but also to become preoccupied with what one would have done if one "had it to do all over again." Anger at someone may lead to fantasies about ways to "get even" and to preoccupations with the person's undeserved successes and potential misfortunes. Gloom or grief may lead one into long trains of guilty thoughts, a "barrage [of] regrets and reproaches" (Beck 1976, 40), about what one could and should have done when one was young or when the deceased was still alive.

Take the case of a chronic fear, say of suffocating. You don't have lung disease, no one has ever tied a cord around your neck, you don't have plans to venture into a bank vault or a deep cave, and you don't live in Los Angeles, Mexico City, or Athens. In short, you have no reason to think that you will suffocate. Your fear is irrational not because suffocating isn't fearful—it is—but because it is so improbable. This fear, though unreasonable and chronic, could still be manageable. You might allay the fear by adopting the policy of keeping a window open wherever you are and otherwise avoiding places and situations where suffocation is even a remote possibility. This strategy might well suffice, and the fear would be under control. You would be like a person who manages his fear of flying or of snakes simply by avoiding airplanes and wriggly reptiles. On the other hand, circumstances might prevent you from successfully executing that strategy. Resorting to farfetched excuses, you might have to refuse important assignments and put your job at risk, or avoid normal social situations and put your personal relationships at risk. And even if external circumstances are cooperative, you might find yourself becoming subject to recurring bouts of idle but terrifying thoughts of suffocation. On such occasions you might worry that your air passages will constrict without warning, that your lungs will suddenly stop working, or that the carbon dioxide in the air will turn into carbon monoxide. At this point you are faced with a management problem: how to rid yourself of such morbid thoughts. You might remind yourself that the things that worry you at these moments aren't worth worrying about (air passages don't constrict without warning, lungs don't suddenly stop working, and carbon dioxide can't turn into carbon monoxide). However, even if dismissing such possibilities intellectually keeps you from taking them seriously, it might not get them out of your mind.

2 Control of Attention

It is tempting to equate control over a process with determining its every phase. In the case of skilled action, like doing gymnastics or playing a violin, control may indeed be a matter of determining each phase of the action (at least up to a certain degree of specificity and temporal resolution). Being skilled at something means knowing, at each moment, what to do next or at least how to figure out quickly what to do next.[12] However, if what is being controlled is not a course of action but merely an ongoing process, control involves merely regulating that process. Monitoring may be required (perhaps even vigilance), but action need be taken only to restore the controlled system to its range of normal or acceptable functioning (what counts as normal or acceptable is relative to standards, which may in turn be relative to circumstances). Intervention is needed if the process gets interrupted, goes off course, or is otherwise disrupted. Action must be taken against the cause of the disruption, which may be internal or external to the process being controlled.

In the case of attention, control is not a matter of determining its focus at every moment. Knowing what to think about next cannot require thinking what to think about next. Micromanaging attention is impossible, and you would go crazy trying obsessively to determine at every moment what comes to mind next. Exercising control over your attention just means regulating it so that, for example, whenever you are involved in an activity and irrelevant thoughts occur (memories, desires, fantasies), you are able to restore your attention to what you are doing. If you can't divert your attention even when you desperately want to, it is no longer under your control. On the other hand, having it under control also means that matters that might become worth considering are not foreclosed from consideration.

I am not suggesting here that every loss of attentional control constitutes an emotional disorder. In some cases the disorder is not really emotional but attentional or otherwise cognitive in nature (perhaps grounded in some anatomical defect or neurophysiological deficit). And, of course, temporary losses of control due to external circumstances or even to intense but transient emotional experiences should not be counted as disorders. After all, elation, grief, lust, embarrassment, and panic wouldn't be what they are if they could be "turned off" at will, but they are not disorders. Things would be different, of course, if such an emotion lasted indefinitely or flared up periodically without external prompting, as in manic depression or paranoia.

Unwanted thoughts aren't mere distractions or nuisances but can be seriously disruptive. By breaking one's concentration, they can interfere with what one is doing, and by becoming preoccupations, they can impede the pursuit of one's goals. Indeed, they can even enter into the definition of one's goals: the contents of persistently occurring thoughts, just by virtue of their persistence, can come to matter more and more. To appreciate how this situation might arise, consider that at any given time what matters to one, at least on the very short-term basis of that moment, is whatever one's attention is then directed at. In this narrow horizon, what matters is the matter of the moment. Moreover, the fact that this matters can, when one reflects on it, become the matter of the next moment. Then one faces the metaproblem of dealing with the fact that one's attention is being captured by something one deems unimportant or irrelevant. This metaproblem is the problem of regaining control of one's thought, feeling, and will; one needs to be able to attend to and act on what matters, and what matters is, in the longer term, generally not what one is attending to at the moment. Successful attention control, to the extent that it is possible, harmonizes one's short-term foci of attention with one's longer-term concerns.[13]

Whereas with emotional disorders there is a disparity between the amount of attention something receives and the amount it deserves, when one's attention is under control one is able to keep them commensurate.[14] But what does this ability involve? We must largely avoid considering what is not worth considering, and obviously we cannot spend time and effort on everything that might come to mind just to determine that it is not worth considering. Indeed, at every moment we implicitly judge things not worth considering by not considering them at all, or at least not for long. In this respect, the process of attention management is analogous to default reasoning. Just as effective reasoning, given our limited cognitive capacities and resources, requires the ability not to consider matters not worth considering while being sensitive to the presence of matters that are (Bach 1984), so it is with effective attention management. Since we have limited control over what attracts, maintains, or diverts our attention and over what reminds us of what, irrelevant thoughts will occur, but normally (see note 10) we can focus our attention on things that matter and disregard things that do not. Yet we must also be sensitive to the possible pertinence of things not currently considered or not currently considered pertinent. Effective attention management requires habits, skills, and strategies that enable one to get things done and to further one's aims without being blind to new considerations and possibilities. But, as we will see, these devices (so-called defenses) are not always effective, for they can be used to excess and keep worthy things from coming to mind, or they can be inadequate and fail to prevent distressing or disruptive matters from dominating one's attention.[15]

3   Attention and Defense

Although having your attention under control does not require determining its focus from one moment to the next, this does require being able to keep out of mind, or at least get out of mind, matters that you do not need or want to attend to. On occasion, however, an emotion that leads you to dwell on something can become so intense and involving as to be unmanageable.[16] For example, it could cause you to be haunted by fantasies or hallucinations that don't go away, no matter how hard you try to get rid of them. You might become preoccupied with humiliating episodes, terrifying situations, imagined misfortunes, unrequited-love objects, and lost loved ones. You might dwell on how horrible you are and on all the rotten things you've done. You might even fear that if you fall asleep, you won't wake up. Most of us most of the time are lucky enough not to be haunted by such thoughts and without conscious effort we generally avoid dwelling on them. This is fortunate, for if eternal vigilance were required, we'd go out of our minds trying to keep such thoughts from persisting or recurring.[17] Still, we can't always rely on touchy subjects to stay out of mind spontaneously. When they don't, we can often distract our attention from them by focusing on what we are doing or, if we are not doing anything, by immersing ourselves in a good book or movie, some exercise, a chore, or some other diversion. Sometimes, however, keeping such thoughts out of mind requires special devices, commonly (and aptly) called *defenses*.[18]

   There are various views of what psychic defenses are and of what they are defenses against. Freud thought they protect the ego from instinctual demands, and they have since been viewed as protections from such things as pain, stress, anxiety, insecurity, low self-esteem, and other people. Considered from the standpoint of attention management, a defense may be defined as any device for preventing the occurrence of an intolerable or unmanageable state, or at least for neutralizing or forestalling its effect. This conception is broad enough to include self-deception and selective inattention, as well as such classic defenses as rationalization, denial, repression, displacement, and projection. There are several sorts of evidence for the existence of defenses. For example, repressed traumatic experiences, such as of being abused as a child, can eventually reveal themselves, whether spontaneously or as the result of psychotherapy. If they are genuine memories (not fantasies or the product of therapeutic suggestion or manipulation) and are specific to the traumatic events, then their not having come to mind before was probably not due to a problem in memory. Also, people's resistance to a touchy subject can become evident if, whenever the subject is brought up, they resort to implausible rationalizations or engage in evasive tactics to get on to something else. An ever handy ploy is procrastination: one avoids not only doing something about an issue but even thinking about it, on the grounds that it can always be addressed later.

Philosophers sometimes wonder how processes like defenses can be purposeful yet unconscious. This is one facet of a broader question about unconscious motivation: how can a desire (or other motivational state, like a state of fear or jealousy) motivate one to act if one is not only unaware of being in that state but also unable to be aware of being in it? The answer to this question (unless the real philosophical worry here is how desires and other states can be unconscious at all) is straightforward. An unconscious state motivates in just the way that a conscious state does: by virtue of being in that state, one represents the desired outcome as to be achieved, one represents a way of achieving that outcome, and one acts in that way. Just as one can draw a conclusion from something one believes without being aware of believing it or thinking that one believes it (only a diehard Cartesian would insist that being conscious of a belief is necessary for making an inference from it), so one can act on a desire (or other motivational state) without being aware of it or representing oneself as having it. And action itself does not have to be conscious, much less intentional, and this includes the mental acts involved in defenses. One can be motivated to do something and act purposefully from that motive even if one is not acting consciously. Indeed, as Mark Johnston (1988) has suggested, "mental tropisms," or purpose-serving but subintentional mental mechanisms, are quite common.

The idea of unconscious defense, though not this way of describing it, is prominent in post-Freudian folk (some would call it "pop") psychology. It is widely accepted nowadays that people often engage in motivated, though unintentional, avoidance of painful or anxious thoughts. Popular discussions of such topics as death and terminal disease, rape and incest, POWs and torture, reflect the view that people sometimes "lie to themselves" and deny or perhaps even repress an extremely painful experience or fearful prospect because they cannot "deal with" it, cannot "face up to" it, cannot "bear the thought" of it. People even acknowledge this in themselves, at least retrospectively.

There seems to be a certain conception of mental health that underlies this view: one deals with something one cannot face up to by not facing up to it. Defenses are the means to that end. A defense is a routine for nullifying, neutralizing, or at least forestalling the damaging or debilitating effect of facing up to a certain subject matter or acting on a "dangerous" impulse. Different defenses offer different ways for one to respond to the problem posed by the dangerous or threatening subject. One can repress the thought of it, deny that there is a problem, put it off, immerse oneself in other things, or just trivialize it.[19] That is, different defenses serve, as the case may be, to get rid of the threatening thought (or dangerous impulse), to help one ignore the touchy subject for the time being, to enable one to work around it, or to make it seem innocuous.[20]

4   Exclusionary Categories

There is one particular kind of defense that, so far as I know, has not been explicitly identified. It is a form of rationalization that involves the use of what may be called exclusionary categories. An *exclusionary category* is a way of classifying an actual or potential target of attention in a way that ostensibly justifies not attending to it or, if one is already attending to it, not attending to it any further. These categories come in a variety of types, and whether or not they are applied for good epistemic reasons, they serve the practical purpose of keeping one's experience manageable. They fall into several broad,

Table 1
Examples of exclusionary categories

Class	Exclusionary category
Epistemic	absurd, baseless, hopeless, impossible, incoherent, insignificant, irrational, ridiculous, superstitious, unreal
Psychological	bigoted, crackpot, crazy, hateful, imaginary, inconceivable, misguided, unthinkable
Social	embarrassing, forbidden, offensive, outrageous, taboo, unspeakable
Evaluative	dangerous, filthy, hostile, incompetent, inferior, intolerable, obscene, perverted, selfish, shameful, stupid, unhealthy, unimportant, wicked, worthless
Ideological	blasphemous, communist, diabolical, extremist, fascist, irreligious, racist, sexist, sinful, subversive, un-American

overlapping classes, as illustrated by the heterogeneous list of examples in table 1 (they apply, depending on the case, to propositions, ideas, actions, or persons).

I am not suggesting that using an exclusionary category is inherently irrational or defensive. Many of these categories have perfectly legitimate applications quite apart from their role in attention management, although some are merely pejorative and cannot provide an objectively valid reason for excluding something from consideration.[21] But even the legitimate ones can be applied hastily, carelessly, indiscriminately, or zealously. On the other hand, even when a legitimate exclusionary category is applied for epistemically valid reasons, using it may also serve a collateral managerial purpose. This purpose can be cognitive, say to keep one's mind from getting too cluttered or changing too easily, or emotional, say to shield one from pain or anxiety.

Worth special mention is the use of exclusionary categories to sustain acceptance of what might be termed a *psychologically basic proposition*. It seems that most people have a fundamental need to believe such things as that one is competent, important, attractive, and well liked, that one's projects and goals are worthwhile, and that the world is safe and hospitable. The inability to sustain such "existential a priori" propositions (Needleman 1968) may lead to chronic and debilitating feelings of inadequacy, inferiority, insecurity, precarious-ness, rejection, or worthlessness. On the other hand, there are cer-tain propositions whose *acceptance* leads to such effects. Many people irrationally accept negative propositions about themselves, such as that they are helpless, worthless, repulsive, mad, or otherwise "differ-ent" and that others must inevitably despise, ignore, or mistreat them. They perpetuate such negative thoughts by perversely using exclusionary categories to keep from thinking anything positive about themselves.

Generally speaking, the use of exclusionary categories is continu-ous with the use of other categories for classifying and evaluating things (people, objects, events, possibilities, and courses of action) and plays key roles in the system that makes up one's overall theoreti-cal and practical view of the world. When an item does not fit into the system, either the item must be excluded or the system must be adjusted. Insofar as something in mind or threatening to come to mind fits the system, one knows what to think of it and what to do about it, or at least one knows how to go about figuring out what to think of it and what to do about it. One thereby knows what to do next with respect to that target of attention. Unfortunately, not ev-erything fits the system. Things that do not fit pose a paradoxical question: how is one to deal with what one can't deal with?

A person's basic repertoire of exclusionary categories provides a practical answer to that question. One deals with a recalcitrant item by classifying it as something that does not have to be dealt with. One can do this directly, by means of an exclusionary category like *absurd* or *impossible,* or indirectly, by means of a category whose application implies that the item does not deserve to be dealt with, like *blasphe-mous* or *obscene.* Applying an exclusionary category plays the role of getting something out of mind, in much the way that in the context of solving a problem one summarily rules a bad idea out of consider-ation. Indeed, prior application of an exclusionary category to an object or type of object may keep it (and things saliently like it or related to it) from coming to mind at all. Prior application may even produce an attentional aversion to the touchy subject, whereby one recognizes when the dangerous object even *threatens* to come to mind. The thought (or mention) of something distantly related to it may be enough to divert one's attention to something else.

There is no guarantee that a given exclusionary ploy will work. One may be unable to get or keep something out of mind even if one does subsume it under an exclusionary category. When this happens, either one bears the consequences or, to try further to exclude the recalcitrant item from consideration, one engages in a more elaborate scheme, which may invoke other exclusionary categories. The more elaborate scheme may have unpleasant or otherwise unfortunate side effects, producing irrational attitudes or behavior patterns like those delineated in the clinical literature. In particular, the use of exclusionary categories to avoid confronting a touchy subject may lead to excluding too much and disable one in some way. For example, categorizing sex as wicked might cause a person not only to avoid all thoughts about sex but to be frightened away from any social encounters.

Different types of ineffective or even self-defeating policies or strategies of attention management are epitomized by certain chronic attitudes towards problems that arise in everyday life (table 2). In each pair the first attitude is symptomatic of insufficent use of some exclusionary category(-ies), and the second involves excessive use.[22] So, for example, the chronic worrier (1 −) fails to exclude from consideration possibilities that are not worth taking seriously, whereas someone engaged in denial (1 +) always thinks of reasons (*impossible, ridiculous*) for not taking real possibilities seriously. Similarly, an impulsive person (2 −) is satisfied with the first solution that comes to mind and acts accordingly, failing think of why it might be *dangerous* or *stupid*, whereas a perfectionist (2 +) never fails to find reasons for not being satisfied with a solution.[23]

It is beyond the scope of this paper and its author to classify in detail the multitude of emotional disorders. However, it does seem to me that a great many involve ineffective use of exclusionary categories. In impulsive disorders they are not used enough,[24] but with phobias and in paranoia they are used to excess. Mood disorders seem to involve a generally excessive use of exclusionary categories, except with respect to the emotion specifically associated with the disorder (such as anxiety, despair, or excitement), where exclusion fails.[25] Obsessive-compulsive disorders involve not only the inability to get something (represented as needing to be done) out of one's mind but also the inability to neutralize the occurrence of the obses-

Table 2
Uses of exclusionary categories

	Insufficient use (−)		Excessive use (+)	
	Attitude	Trait	Attitude	Trait
1	There always is or may be a problem.	Chronic anxiety or worry	There is no problem.	Denial
2	The first candidate is the solution.	Impulsiveness	No solution is adequate.	Perfectionism
3	The problem must be solved now.	Obsessive-compulsiveness	The problem will be solved later or by someone else.	Evasiveness
4	I can always deal with it.	Overconfidence	I can't deal with this.	Panic, depression
5	It's always my fault.	Guilt	It's always someone else's fault.	Passive-aggressiveness

sive desire except by acting on it.[26] On the other hand, there are disorders that result from the repression of certain states (desires, memories, or emotions). They may involve the inability to address certain problems or to bring oneself to do certain things, and may even lead to a blind spot in one's experience, one that one can't even see as a blind spot. In inhibitions one shies away from doing a perfectly normal thing and maybe even from thinking about doing it. The extreme compartmentalization of experience in multiple personality disorder seems to be the result of massive repression, which perhaps involves the application of exclusionary categories to major chunks of one's personal history.

My original question was, What makes a disorder emotional? I raised it to focus on specific relations between emotions and disorders. Interestingly, there seems to be an intuitive sense of these relations in folk psychology, including an inchoate recognition of the role of attention. Partly by building on what is implicit in folk psychology, I have tried to make explicit certain attentional aspects of emotional disorder. From a descriptive point of view (I have not speculated on underlying etiological issues or on therapeutic methods[27]), they may be regarded as extreme versions of normal relations between emotion and attention. In the simplest cases they involve devoting either too much or too little attention to the object of emotion. In other cases an emotion or a mood (an impermanent emotional disposition) produces attentional and evidential biases by heightening one's attention to certain considerations and possibilities and diverting one's attention from others. It is normal, at least to some extent, to deal with things one cannot face up to by not facing up to them. Given our cognitive and emotional limitations, some degree of defensiveness is inevitable. This includes the use of exclusionary categories to avoid facing up to something, with at least some semblance of justification. I have suggested that different types of emotional disorder can be characterized in terms of loss of attention control through over- or underdefensiveness, and that this may involve excessive, insufficient, or otherwise ineffective use of exclusionary categories.

All in all, it appears that attention plays a key role in emotion and emotional disorder. Unfortunately, we will never fully understand how that role is played until we find out far more than we now know about why things come to mind when they do and what constrains transitions in mental state from one moment to the next. Equally unfortunately, these questions are, for the foreseeable future, hopelessly beyond reach. Fortunately, we can put them into the category of the unanswerable and thereby have good reason to turn our attention to something else.

Notes

1. "In most hospitals, about one-fifth," according to Goodwin and Guze (1989). They add, "The suitable label for these people is undiagnosed. One advantage of this term is that physicians who deal with the patient will not be biased by having a poorly grounded diagnosis in the chart. Another advantage is the sense of modesty it correctly implies" (1989, 299).

2. Jerome Wakefield (1992) argues, after disposing of six other theories, that a disorder is a "harmful dysfunction." Although I am concerned with what makes a disorder emotional rather than with the notion of disorder as such, my later suggestions—that in disorder emotion is not commensurate with one's values

and that disorder involves a problem in attention management—are consonant with the harmful-dysfunction view.

3. A classic example is Freud's Rat Man, whose "obsessions are recurrent persistent ideas (e.g., that something terrible will happen to his sweetheart), impulses (e.g., to cut his throat), and images (e.g., that a rat is boring into the anus of his father). He experiences them as alien and senseless (ego-dystonic) and evolves complicated formulas to ward them off. . . . As with the obsessions, he recognizes that the [compulsive] behavior is senseless and derives no pleasure from carrying it out, other than the release of tension" (APA 1981, 338).

4. Indeed, as Goodwin and Guze acknowledge, "For most psychiatric conditions there are no explanations. 'Etiology unknown' is the hallmark of psychiatry as well as its bane. Historically, once etiology is known, a disease stops being 'psychiatric'" (1989, xiii).

5. Psychologists do not suppose this (see, for example, Arnold 1960 and Ekman 1992).

6. Recent book-length accounts include Solomon 1976, Lyons 1980, and Gordon 1987.

7. This does not entail that the emotion is unreasonable. For example, chronic gloom can be justified by hopeless life circumstances (Graham 1990).

8. Solomon (1976) and de Sousa (1987), as well as one's own personal experience, provide numerous examples of this phenomenon.

9. Although I am emphasizing the relation between emotion and attention, I should note that emotions can be triggered by subliminal or what Aaron Beck calls "automatic thoughts" (1976, 29–37).

10. Beck describes the "spiraling of fear and anxiety" (1976, 149) , with its exaggeration of dire consequences and their probabilities, as indicative of an "overactive 'alarm system'" (p. 156) that is sensitive to idle as well as to realistic possibilities.

11. The topic of the rationality of emotions is far too complex to take up in any detail here (see de Sousa 1987 and Greenspan 1988). Nowadays philosophers of emotion reject the traditional view that emotions are inherently irrational and the Humean view that they are nonrational. Above I have indicated several ways in which they can be justified or unjustified, and undoubtedly there are many more. Also, emotions are sometimes said to be unjustified when they are based on unwarranted beliefs.

12. Knowing how to figure out or how to go about figuring out what to do next is itself, strictly speaking, knowing what to do next.

13. The notion of attention control is central to George Ainslie's (1992) intra-personal game-theoretic account of impulse management.

14. What counts as commensurate is a matter of opinion, and not necessarily the opinion of the person at the moment. Some people suffering from attentional problems like those described here will acknowledge the disparity between their opinion of the moment and their considered opinion. Some, on the other hand, may be so absorbed in an obsessive concern that they find their excessive attention on something to be perfectly reasonable. Still, they suffer from the consequences of this "opinion," which they eventually acknowledge should they ever seek therapy. What counts as one's "considered" opinion—and exactly why it should override one's opinion of the moment—is not as straightforward as it might seem.

15. After drafting this paper, I discovered the following apt passages in Beck 1976: "The patient has to grapple to retain voluntary control over concentration, attention, and focusing" (p. 78); the "disruption of voluntary control over focusing attention" is indicated either by the "mercurial nature of attention" or by a "involuntary fixation of attention" (p. 152), i.e., "attention-binding," in which the patient is "overly attentive to certain cues . . . and oblivious to others" (p. 79).

16. By "unmanageable" I mean more or less what J. K. Wing has in mind when describing "pathological" anxiety: "The main question is whether the condition has gone 'out of control,' producing symptoms that cannot be dealt with by consciously turning the attention to other matters, or withdrawing from the anxiety-provoking situation in good order, or simply exercising the will. The symptoms that result can be very severe: palpitations, muscular tremors, 'butterflies' in the stomach, giddiness, sickness, breathlessness, muscular tension, and faintness. In a total panic, there may even be loss of control over bowels or bladder" (1978, 60).

17. David Shapiro describes the "continuous state of volitional tension" (1965, 36) in the obsessive-compulsive, whose attention is "markedly limited in both mobility and range, . . . sharply focused and concentrated" (195, 27).

18. There are also teachable techniques, such as "thought stopping." As Rimm and Masters describe it, "The client is asked to concentrate on the anxiety-inducing thoughts, and, after a short period of time, the therapist suddenly and emphatically says 'stop' (a loud noise or even painful electric shock may also suffice), and the locus of control is shifted from the therapist to the client. Specifically, the client is taught to emit a subvocal 'stop' whenever he begins to engage in a self-defeating rumination" (1974, 430). This technique would seem to be particularly effective when what makes the thought unmanagable is not so much its content as its uncontrollable recurrence.

19. Immersion can be in attention-engaging activity or simply in fantasy. As John Neale remarks, "Frequent use of pleasant fantasies to distract oneself from unpleasant events or cognitions may make the fantasies more accessible and may heighten their reality" (1988, 146). Indeed, activity and fantasy can be combined, as in grandiose delusions. Neale suggests that "by distracting the person, guiding information processing, or occupying the limited processing capacity of conscious awareness, the grandiose delusion may function as an avoidance response, reinforced by the reduction of distress. . . . Grandiose delusions may have yet another function in that they produce the elated mood of the manic. Elated mood could make it less likely that the manic will access distressing cognitions from memory, an effect similar to the one discussed [in Bower 1981] for alcohol" (1988, 148).

20. Such ploys and stratagems are central to my account of self-deception (Bach 1981, 1992).

21. There are some positive categories—such as *attractive, friendly, pleasurable, productive,* and *sensible*—that some people perversely use for exclusionary purposes. Perhaps this use of such categories partly explains the self-defeating character of certain disorders.

22. In some cases, such as obsessive-compulsiveness (3−) and paranoia, an extreme version of 1−, "inclusionary" categories, like *urgent* or *menacing,* seem to be at work, categories that chronically provide reasons for considering certain sorts of things and whose persistent use repeatedly gets them and keeps them *in* mind.

23. Both insufficient and excessive use of exclusionary categories can aid and abet reliance on false assumptions, massive overgeneralizations, and rigid rules—three culprits identified by the cognitive therapist Aaron Beck—and can further help what Karen Horney called the "tyranny of the shoulds" (as cited by Beck [1976, 257]). David Shapiro describes how obsessive-compulsives experience these "shoulds" as "quasi-external . . . requirements of objective necessity" (1965, 39), whose observance leads to "overcontrol" and flatness of affect. Ainslie explains how compulsiveness can be "a side effect of personal rules" (1992, 205–227).

24. Shapiro, though aptly describing impulsive persons as "unmindful of consequences" (1965, 143), suggests that their "lack of planning is only one feature of a style of cognition and thinking in which active concentration, capacity for abstraction and generalization, and reflectiveness in general are all impaired" (p. 147). In Ainslie's intrapersonal game-theoretic account of impulse control, impulsive persons lack the techniques normally used to "precommit future behaviors" (1992, 130–144).

25. For example, "Thoughts of escape and avoidance are particularly prominent in the ideation of anxious and depressed patients" (Beck 1976, 39).

26. It is often supposed that what drives obsessive-compulsives is anxiety reduction. However, there may be, as Baer and Minichiello suggest, "two classes of obsessional behavior: one anxiety-increasing, and another anxiety-decreasing. Anxiety-increasing obsessions occur automatically in response to anxiety-provoking stimulation. Anxiety-reducing compulsions occur as a reaction to the anxiety, and their performance temporarily decreases anxiety" (1986, 53). It is easy to see how the second phase can involve the use, often desperate, of exclusionary categories.

27. George Graham, whom I wish to thank for his valuable comments and references, suggests that the method of treatment most consonant with my approach is cognitive therapy, with its emphasis on "control through reason and reasoning" (personal communication). However, I should note that control over thought and thought processes is also part of the cognitive approach, as Beck implies when he speaks of "breaking cognitive habits" (1976, 217) and "alleviat-[ing] psychological distress [by] correcting faulty conceptions and self-signals" (p. 214). It would take research on the effects of clinical practice to ascertain to what extent, and in which conditions and circumstances, improved reason and reasoning are enough to correct a psychological disorder. Insight might not be enough. Harrow, Rattenbury, and Stoll, in their discussion of schizophrenic delusions, distinguish three "important dimensions of patients' delusional ideation . . . : (1) patients' belief-conviction about the delusion, (2) their perspective on the delusion, and (3) their emotional commitment to the delusion" (1988, 185), and they suggest that these do not always correlate. In particular, then, one's "perspective on the delusion" may not help to get rid of it or its effects.

References

Ainslie, George. 1992. *Picoeconomics: The Strategic Interaction of Successive Motivational States within the Person.* Cambridge: Cambridge University Press.

American Psychiatric Association. 1981. *DSM-III Casebook.* Washington, D.C.: American Psychiatric Association.

American Psychiatric Association. 1987. *Diagnostic and Statistical Manual of Mental Disorders,* 3rd ed., rev. (*DSM*). Washington, D.C.: American Psychiatric Association.

Arnold, Magda B. 1960. *Emotion and Personality.* London: Cassel and Co.

Bach, Kent. 1981. "An Analysis of Self-Deception." *Philosophy and Phenomenological Research* 41:351–370.

Bach, Kent. 1984. "Default Reasoning: Jumping to Conclusions and Knowing When to Think Twice." *Pacific Philosophical Quarterly* 65:37–58.

Bach, Kent. 1992. Review of *Perspectives on Self-Deception*, ed. Brian P. McLaughlin and Amélie O. Rorty. *Noûs* 26:495–504.

Baer, Lee, and William E. Minichiello. 1986. "Behavior Therapy for Obsessive-Compulsive Disorder." In *Obsessive-Compulsive Disorders: Theory and Management*, ed. Michael A. Jenike, Lee Baer, and William E. Minichiello. Littleton, Mass.: PSG Publishing Co.

Beck, Aaron T. 1976. *Cognitive Therapy and the Emotional Disorders*. New York: International Universities Press.

Bower, G. H. 1981. "Mood and Memory." *American Psychologist* 36:129–148.

De Sousa, Ronald 1987. *The Rationality of Emotion*. Cambridge: MIT Press.

Ekman, Paul. 1992. "An Argument for Basic Emotions." *Cognition and Emotion* 6:169–200.

Goodwin, Donald W., and Samuel B. Guze. 1989. *Psychiatric Diagnosis*, 4th ed. Oxford: Oxford University Press.

Gordon, Robert M. 1987. *The Structure of Emotions*. Cambridge: Cambridge University Press.

Graham, George. 1990. "Melancholic Epistemology." *Synthese* 82:399–422.

Greenspan, Patricia S. 1988. *Reasons and Emotions*. New York: Routledge.

Harrow, Martin, Francine Rattenbury, and Frank Stoll. 1988. "Schizophrenic Delusions: An Analysis of Their Persistence, of Related Premorbid Ideas, and of Three Major Dimensions." In *Delusional Beliefs*, ed. Thomas F. Oltmanns and Brendan A. Maher. New York: John Wiley and Sons.

Johnston, Mark. 1988. "Self-Deception and the Nature of Mind." In *Perspectives on Self-Deception*, ed. Brian P. McLaughlin and Amélie O. Rorty. Berkeley: University of California Press.

Lyons, William. 1980. *Emotion*. Cambridge: Cambridge University Press.

Neale, John M. 1988. "Defensive Functions of Manic Episodes." In *Delusional Beliefs*, ed. Thomas F. Oltmanns and Brendan A. Maher. New York: John Wiley and Sons.

Needleman, Jacob. 1968. Translator's Introduction. *Being-in-the-World*, by Ludwig Binswanger. New York: Harper Torchbooks.

Rimm, David C., and John C. Masters. 1974. *Behavior Therapy: Techniques and Empirical Findings*. New York: Academic Press.

Shapiro, David. 1965. *Neurotic Styles*. New York: Basic Books.

Kent Bach

Solomon, Robert C. 1976. *The Passions: The Myth and Nature of Human Emotions.* New York: Doubleday.

Szasz, Thomas S. 1974. *The Myth of Mental Illness*, rev. ed. New York: Harper and Row.

Wakefield, Jerome C. 1992. "The Concept of Mental Disorder." *American Psychologist* 47:373–388.

Wing, J. K. 1978. *Reasoning about Madness.* Oxford: Oxford University Press.

The Problem of Despair

Richard Garrett

Despair comes in many sizes and shapes, but despair in its grandest form is philosophical, and it is despair of this sort that is the subject of this chapter. The central question I will explore is whether or not philosophical despair is rational. In what follows, I will consider the nature of philosophical despair, its central importance for philosophy, some of the major reasons given for it, solutions that have been proposed in response to the problem of despair, and some criteria relevant to the various solutions posed. Finally, I will consider what all of this has to do with the theory and treatment of depression, a phenomenon related to, but by no means identical with, despair.

1 The Problem of Philosophical Despair

We sometimes hear people say things like "I despaired over the dinner" or "John despaired of ever pursuing a career in music." The kind of despair referred to on such occasions is not philosophical. It is despair over some particular project or undertaking. But it is like philosophical despair insofar as it does entail a *belief* that something is not worth pursuing, a belief that something is hopeless, either because it lacks sufficient value or because it is not sufficiently possible. Such despair can be trivial (if the project given up is trivial) or earth-shaking (if the project given up is a marriage, career, someone's life, or something else of great importance). Nonetheless, trivial or important, such despair is not philosophical. So, to avert confusion, I simply refer to such despair as *project-specific despair*. We get closer to philosophical despair when we consider someone who despairs over the worth of their entire life, as when they say things like, "My life is meaningless" or "My life is useless." Such people are not simply giving up (or abandoning as futile) some career, relationship, or specific project or undertaking *within* their lives. Rather, they have come to believe that their entire life from beginning to end is a futile, meaningless gesture, an undertaking without any positive worth or good. Logically, it follows that they also believe that *all* particular undertakings and projects *within* their lives are also futile. For if a person's life as a whole is futile and worthless, then so are various, specific projects within that life. Hence such despair is greater in scope than project-specific despair, for it encompasses *all* of the specific projects within one's life and not merely one or two. But this is not yet philosophical despair. So, to avoid confusing it with project-specific despair on the one hand and philosophical despair on the other, let us call it *personal despair.*

When an individual comes to the grand conclusion that not simply their own life but everyone's life is, as a whole, futile, then we have genuine *philosophical despair.* It is despair of this sort that is of interest to philosophy, for it entails the proposition that no one's life is good or meaningful or even has the potential of being good or meaningful. To believe in such a proposition is to be a *pessimist*, in the philosophical sense of the word.

The central concern of this chapter will be to examine the question, Is philosophical despair or pessimism a rational possibility? Otherwise put, can a reasonable or rational case be made for subscribing to pessimism or for despairing philosophically?

It is often rational to despair of specific projects. If, for example, a woman's ninety-year-old mother has cancer of the liver and has only been given two weeks to live by several competent physicians, then it is certainly reasonable to despair of saving her life and focus on other issues, e.g., making her as comfortable as possible, saying goodbye, etc. Moreover, it is arguable that it is sometimes rational for *this or that person* to despair over their life as a whole. Suppose, for example, a child is born paralyzed from the neck down but is somehow kept alive. We might further imagine that this child was unhappy his entire life and that when the child came to be an adult, he chose to have the life support systems removed so that he could die and escape his tormented existence. People have argued that in even less extreme situations than this, the decision to despair over one's life is rational or reasonable. Whatever one's view of the matter, few would say it is *irrational or unreasonable* to despair under such extreme circumstances. So it may be that personal despair is sometimes rational or reasonable.

But when we come to philosophical despair, we are dealing with a despair of an entirely different order. For the pessimist is saying not simply that his or her own particular life is not worth living but that no one's life is worth living. And this is quite an extraordinary claim to make. But is it irrational or unreasonable? Or are things sufficiently ambiguous and uncertain that we must admit that it is a rational possibility, as rational as the alternative view, which is that life is, or can be, good or meaningful? It is this question that constitutes the problem of despair and with which I will primarily be concerned throughout this chapter.

2 The Good or Meaningful Life

As we will see below, people's conceptions of the good or meaningful life can vary enormously. Still, there are certain conditions that few would deny are ingredients of the good or meaningful life: the development of one's talents, self-governance or autonomy, and good interpersonal relationships are examples of such conditions that readily spring to mind. More important, there are two distinct perspectives from which we can view the value or worth of our lives. Each is compelling and each is inescapable for any rational, well-developed human being. For lack of better terms, I will call the first *the experiential perspective* and the second *the tribunal or judicial perspective*. Let us consider each of these.

No one relishes the thought of undergoing tremendous physical pain or deep mental or emotional suffering or anguish. Nor does anyone want to be bored or without interesting things to do. Indeed, we all find certain experiences pleasant, enjoyable, and in some cases even deeply pleasurable. Told two paths in the woods are entirely equal in all other ways, but will lead to entirely opposite experiences—one to terrible pain and suffering, the other to the most supreme joy and pleasure—we would naturally want to take the latter path. So we care about the quality of our consciously lived experience: whether it is painful (and the like) or pleasurable (and the like). Nor would we relish a life where we were alive biologically and behaviorally but consciously experience nothing whatever. In general, if we were to consider various possible lives, all else being equal, we would prefer and call better and more meaningful those lives that are most filled with pleasure, joy, and the like and least filled with pain and suffering and the like. This is what I mean by evaluating our lives from the *experiential perspective*.

As a rule, people prefer praise to condemnation. But praise is more meaningful, more apt to please, and condemnation more disturbing, more apt to sting, if it is delivered by someone whose judgment we respect or revere. For the more competent or wise the judge, the more likely their praise or condemnation is an indication of our truly being worthy of it. It is evident, therefore, that *being worthy of praise* (and not merely praise) and *not being worthy of condemnation* (and not merely not being condemned) are important to us humans. Moreover, of all the qualities we humans find praiseworthy, none is more universal or revered than moral character, especially moral courage (without which moral character is impossible). For heroes and heroines (the persons admired and revered in the world's literature) come in all sizes, shapes, and ages and vary in almost any quality you can name except for one: without exception they all have moral courage. And the more moral character and moral courage they have, the more they are loved and admired. In our heart of hearts, all of us would like to be worthy of praise and, above all, worthy of the highest praise, which is to say all of us would like to possess moral courage and high moral character. All else being equal, we would view a life that is worthy of praise to be superior to a life worthy of condemnation. When we evaluate our lives (or others') from this perspective, we are judging from *the tribunal or judicial perspective*.

However people may differ in other respects concerning the good or meaningful life, no one can dismiss these two perspectives as unimportant to one's estimate of the good or meaningful life. The supremely good life is experientially wonderful, while at the same time judicially admirable to the highest extent. When we consider the various reasons given for pessimism as well as the various solutions and their criteria, it will be important to keep these two perspectives in mind. Before discussing the various reasons given for despair, however, I want to consider the importance of the problem of despair for philosophy in general.

3 Philosophy's Central Problem

"Philosophy" meant love of wisdom to the ancient Greeks, and our present-day tendency in analytic philosophy to pursue everything but wisdom notwithstanding, the ancients were right to see the quest for wisdom as philosophy's central concern. For being ideally wise entails having a fundamental understanding of how we humans can live the very best life of which we are capable and I cannot conceive of any understanding of anything else being as important as this. If it is right to reason in this way, then there can be nothing more important for philosophy to pursue than wisdom.

This brings us to the good or meaningful life and the problem of despair. If the pessimist is mistaken and the good or meaningful life is possible, then to be wise is to understand this and also to understand the nature of the good or meaningful life. But if the pessimist is right and the good or meaningful life is not possible, then to be wise is quite a different thing. For in this case, being wise would amount to understanding that the good or meaningful life is not possible, understanding one's options, and also understanding which of these is best. Just so, the pursuit of wisdom, philosophy's central task, brings us face to face with the problem of despair: Is the good or meaningful life possible or not possible? Or is it as rational or perhaps more rational to believe, as the pessimists do, that the good or meaningful life is not possible?

4 Reasons Given for Philosophical Despair

Philosophical despair is as old as religion. Indeed, the world's great religions, without exception, all have their versions of the problem of despair, as well as their solutions to it. In this section I simply want to review some of the more important and more interesting kinds of meditations that have posed the problem. In all, there are four kinds of reasons or meditations I will discuss.

The first class of reasons arise from meditations about the worth of life from what I have called *the experiential perspective*, the perspective from which we evaluate our lives in terms of the quality of our consciously lived experience. When ordinary people speak of desiring to be happy, as a rule they are looking at their life from this perspective. For their concern in such cases is with living a life that is pleasurable and joyful and not full of pain and sorrow. People's conception of happiness varies in the sense that they sometimes have very different ideas about what would bring them pleasure and joy (and help them avoid pain and sorrow), but there can be little doubt that these are the things that ultimately concern them when they speak of living a happy life. One class of reasons given for saying that life is meaningless or that the good or meaningful life is not possible, therefore, derives from the assertion that happiness (in this ordinary sense) is not possible.

There are various meditations that lead people to conclude that human happiness is not possible. One very famous set of reasons was offered by Gautama Buddha.[1] According to Buddha, both the world and the self make their respective contributions to our unhappiness. The contribution of the world lies in the fact that everything (including the self) is conditional, and hence uncertain and impermanent. (Thus, unpredictable death, sickness, loss, etc. follow necessarily from the very structure of the world.) The contribution of the self lies in its self-centered and selfish clinging to things (which renders the self incapable of accepting things as they are). The result is universal unhappiness. Yet ultimately Buddha is an optimist, for he claims to have found a universal path for escaping this (initially) universal condition of suffering and unhappiness.

Arthur Schopenhauer, who was influenced by Buddha, offered a similar meditation in *The World as Will and Idea*. But Schopenhauer, unlike Buddha, saw the striving of an indestructible and inalterable will as the primary source of human suffering and so, seeing no escape from pain and sorrow, remained a pessimist.

The second set of reasons for pessimism have to do with what I referred to above as *the tribunal or judicial perspective*. From this perspective, it will be recalled, we evaluate our lives not in terms of our happiness but rather in terms of our praiseworthiness, which is to say our worthiness of being happy. In this case pessimism rests upon the claim that all humans are by nature morally corrupt, and so, unworthy of praise. Such a view is more or less implied by the Christian doctrine of original sin. Were it not for God's saving grace, according to this doctrine, we all would be hopelessly corrupt morally and spiritually, and in the tribunal or judicial perspective, this leads to pessimism. Since the doctrine holds that God's grace can save us all from sin, however, Christianity is ultimately optimistic rather than pessimistic. But a person need not be a Christian to feel that humans are hopelessly corrupt, and many embrace this view without seeing any means of redemption (such as God's saving grace), which easily leads to pessimism.[2]

The third set of reasons are derived from meditations that combine *both the experiential and the tribunal perspectives.* According to these meditations, there is no relationship between happiness and worthiness of being happy. Or worse, the relationship is the inversion of justice, so that while those who are morally good and innocent suffer, those who are morally corrupt are happy and prosperous. The book of Job in the Bible wrestles with this question. Job is represented as a righteous man (a man worthy of happiness) who is nonetheless afflicted with the worst pain, sorrows, and losses. The Holocaust is probably the most dramatic and most horrible example of such unjustified suffering in history, but it is by no means an isolated event. Kant's question "What can I hope for?" arises directly from Kant's perception of the immense injustice in the world. Kant argues, in effect, that we can avoid pessimism only if we assume both that there is a God and a life hereafter (Kant 1956).

The fourth set of reasons given for despair are based upon meditations *primarily involving the judicial or tribunal perspective.* But unlike the second set of reasons, they do not necessarily start from the assumption that human beings are hopelessly corrupt. Rather, it appears, they begin with the notion that the judicial or tribunal perspective has no objective grounds. What does this mean, and why should it matter?

An example of objectively grounding the judicial perspective is Platonic realism. According to the view Plato articulates in the

Republic, a person's life is morally good if it is an instance of an abstract form or universal, Goodness itself, where Goodness itself has an existence independently of all human contrivance or thinking. Another example is Western theism, where the worth of a human life is a function of the judgment of an absolutely perfect judge (God). In both cases the goodness of one's life is objective, in the sense that it transcends human contrivance or invention and even what humans think or value. Thus the meaning of our lives (in the sense of the merit or worth of our lives) is in no way arbitrary and indeed transcends all human judgment or striving. The distinction between being praised and being worthy of praise is thus quite real on such views. And the reason that this distinction matters to us is because, as noted above, we desire to be praiseworthy and not merely praised. For it is the thought that we are praiseworthy that makes praise so important to us, and so it is being praiseworthy and not merely being praised that makes our lives meaningful from the judicial perspective. To say that the judicial perspective has no objective validity, therefore, is to say that our lives have no meaning, objectively speaking. It is to say that objectively the entire worth of our lives is an illusion, a human projection.

Thus, some thinkers have been led to the conclusion that the judicial perspective is itself mere myth, a doctrine of human creation. So nothing (our lives included) has any meaning or worth. Albert Camus puts it thus: "And these two certainties—my appetite for the absolute and for unity and the impossibility of reducing this world to a rational and reasonable principle—I also know that I cannot reconcile them" (1955, 38). On the one hand, our "appetite for the absolute and for unity" is our need of a judicial perspective that is objectively grounded and therefore a perspective from which our lives are really, objectively worthy of being praised. On the other hand, "the impossibility of reducing this world to a rational and reasonable principle" is the impossibility of objectively grounding the judicial perspective. To say we cannot reconcile these two things is to say that we can't help desiring and needing such objective grounding and yet we can't expect to achieve it. And herein lies the absurdity, for it is really and profoundly to need what is nonetheless impossible.

5 Solutions to the Problem of Despair

By a "solution" to the problem of despair, I mean any view of the human situation that either averts despair or accepts despair but offers us a way of dealing with it. Let us consider examples of each type of solution.

Plato's view of the human situation averts despair. On Plato's view, none of the above reasons for despair holds up. In the *Republic* at least, Plato argues, in effect, that the judicial perspective can be objectively grounded via a knowledge of universals, and of the universal the Good in particular. So that takes care of the fourth reason given for despair. Plato argues, moreover, that moral corruption is a function of ignorance, which again can be removed through a study of the forms or universals. Plato further argues that all and only those who are moral are truly happy, and this takes care of the first three sets of reasons above. If we grant the view of the human situation that Plato defends in the *Republic*, then there is no reason to despair philosophically.

Theism similarly averts despair. For the theist, the judicial perspective is objectively grounded in God. Moreover, many theists believe that God ensures ultimate justice (the ultimate happiness of the righteous) and provides aid in overcoming moral corruption (for those who sincerely seek it), so all who choose to be can be both moral and happy. So, once again, there is no need to despair, granted the mainstream theistic conception of the human situation.

Karl Marx (1989) offers a historical-materialistic way of dealing with despair and B. F. Skinner (1948, 1971) a behavioristic solution to the problem. For Marx, unhappiness, immorality and injustice are all rooted in certain economic institutions (such as capitalism). But they will pass, Marx believes, and with them the problems they have caused us. Similarly, for Skinner, these problems are caused by failures in the culture, which can be removed or at least significantly reduced through the intelligent application of science, especially the application of the principles of reinforcement, by means of which human behavior can be modified and shaped as the culture requires. Although neither Marx nor Skinner address the fourth sort of reason for despair given above, one suspects that they would argue (mistakenly I believe) either that it is a pseudoproblem or that it can be dealt with in strictly psychological terms. So from their standpoints the problem of despair is a manageable problem, and we really have no reason to despair.

Examples of *positive solutions* that claim to avert or eliminate despair could be multiplied endlessly, for most major thinkers in the Western world have offered some vision or other of the human situation that makes it possible either to avert or to hope to eliminate any conditions that could give us serious cause for philosophical despair. There are, nonetheless, a significant minority of thinkers who have offered us what might be called *negative solutions* to the problem. In calling them negative solutions, I simply mean to imply that these solutions require us to accept philosophical despair in some form or other and instruct us on how to deal with the problem from that (negative) standpoint. That is, they entreat us not to try to overcome the meaninglessness of our lives but rather to learn to live with it as best we can. So they are all pessimists of one sort or another.

Probably the best known and least compromising pessimist in the Western world is Arthur Schopenhauer. According to Schopenhauer, unhappiness is an inescapable condition of human existence and it is by itself a sufficient condition for despairing, since, on Schopenhauer's view, happiness is everything. The only reason we should not commit suicide is because in doing so, we'd only be making a bad situation worse. For, according to Schopenhauer, the will (which is the ultimate source of our unhappiness) is indestructible, and the next life will only be worse than this one. So the reason to keep on living (the only reason) is not because this life is good but simply because the next one will be worse. The best thing we can do, therefore, is to cultivate the arts (which gives us a brief relief from our suffering) and, even better, to cultivate altruism, which (for Schopenhauer) essentially consists in having a feeling of sympathy for our fellow sufferers. But neither the arts nor altruism can transform our essentially bad situation into a good one. At best, they can only make what is a truly horrible situation a little less horrible.

Albert Camus, in *The Myth of Sisyphus* (1955), represents what must be called a qualified version of pessimism. Indeed, Camus did not think of himself as a pessimist at all, and he was genuinely shocked when, on one occasion, he was described as such. There is a sense in which Camus is right to deny that he is a pessimist. Let us consider first the sense in which he was a pessimist and then the sense in which he was not a pessimist. Camus was a pessimist insofar as he held that, from the objective point of view, life is meaningless, empty, futile, worthless. And the realization that this is so, said Camus, must forever be a profound loss. But Camus is also very far from being a pessimist in Schopenhauer's absolute sense, where life has no positive value whatever. For to the contrary, argues Camus, real living consists of the triumph of the spirit (of the subjective) over the world (over the objective). Camus holds human pride, in particular, above all else, particularly the pride of the man or woman who goes on living in the lucid awareness of the objective absurdity or meaninglessness of it all. It is this very pride that (subjectively) gives life its meaning (Camus 1955).

6 Evaluating Solutions to the Problem of Despair

Above, we have considered some possible solutions to the problem of despair. Without exception, such solutions presuppose rather comprehensive systems of beliefs about the human situation—both about human nature and about the nature of the world with which humans must deal. Because they are systems of *beliefs*, we can evaluate them by means of *standard epistemic* sorts of considerations: logical consistency, consistency with science and common sense, overall coherence with the rest of our beliefs, etc. If we evaluate purely in terms of such standard epistemic criteria, it is not possible to clearly reject the pessimist's arguments and so, clearly and decisively to say that philosophical despair is irrational. Fortunately, we can and must go beyond standard epistemic practices. For, in the first place, every lifestyle presupposes some sort of solution to the problem of despair, and in the second place, every solution to the problem of despair in turn entails assumptions that reach beyond our standard epistemic practices. Let us consider each of these points in turn.

First of all, no matter how people live their lives, the various things they do and the various choices they make necessarily reflect their values, and in particular the extent to which and manner in which they view life as good and meaningful or lacking in goodness and meaning. And normally these values in turn reflect their views of the human situation (in one way or another), and so their solution to the problem of despair. So all lifestyles presuppose some solution to the problem of despair. The way each of us lives reflects our solution to the problem. Hence there is no way to be neutral about the matter.

But a person's view of the human situation, however dim or ill thought out, or however carefully and systematically arrived at, necessarily entails beliefs that transcend what could even remotely be called knowledge, and so goes beyond our standard epistemic practices. This is obvious in the case of Plato and theism, for example, since Plato embraces the doctrine of forms or universals and theism embraces the belief in a personal God. It is also the case with Marx and Skinner, who assume versions of materialism and determinism. For both materialism and determinism are principles lying beyond the reach of human knowledge. And the same holds with Schopenhauer, who assumes the existence of a will that survives death and that is inalterable in any fundamental way. Nor is Camus any exception to this rule, for Camus assumes that it is best not to assume anything not known—surely an assumption of very far reaching consequences, both logically and practically speaking, and lying beyond the realm of human knowledge. So you may be metaphysical or anti-metaphysical if you wish, you are still going to have an impressive stock of assumptions that transcend our standard epistemic practices (i.e., that go beyond what is known). This fact itself is a very important fact about the human situation, for it means that all solutions to the problem of despair rest on some kind of *faith*.

But an assumption, just because it is not known and is a matter of faith, need not be irrational. To the contrary, if we appeal to extra-epistemic criteria, we can still distinguish between solutions to the problem of despair that are rational and those that are not on other grounds. On what other grounds?

Ideally, we would all like to live a life that is good and meaningful from both the experiential and the judicial perspectives, which is to say that we would all prefer to be both happy and worthy of being happy if somehow these were possible. We must, I think, keep this in mind when we evaluate the various solutions to the problem of despair. For all else being equal, a solution that holds more promise in making such a good or meaningful life possible must surely be preferable to one that rules out such a possibility from the very beginning. So if it can be empirically shown that certain solutions to the problem of despair more readily lend themselves to a life that (to all appearances) is happier and more moral then their competitors, then this is a very good reason to adopt such solutions. For such solutions are more rational than those that produce lives that are unhappy and/or immoral.

Viewing the matter this way, we can, I think, say that pessimistic solutions to the problem of despair are less rational than at least some of their positive alternatives. Indeed, it seems correct to say that they are irrational. For there is good evidence that pessimism is self-confirming, that it tends to produce the very unhappiness and immorality it predicts (Beck and Coleman 1981). So it is not rational to hold such a view. For to be pessimistic is to undermine the very thing we all want most, namely, the good life. If this is right, we can conclude that pessimism is indeed an irrational worldview, not (perhaps) judged simply by our standard epistemic practices but judged rather by these practices in conjunction with the additional criteria I am here proposing.

By means of these same criteria we can, moreover, evaluate the various competing positive solutions to the problem of despair. For among the positive solutions that are equally sound epistemically, some will likely go further in promoting happiness and moral character than others, and some may even promote unhappiness and/or immorality. So on such grounds we can distinguish which, among the competing positive solutions are more rational.

7 Rationality, Despair, and Depression

Despair is of interest to psychology as well as to philosophy. Some cognitive theories of depression (e.g., Beck and Coleman 1981) link despair very closely with depression, an illness of considerable importance to psychologists and to all of us, since it inflicts so many people. Perhaps as many as 75 percent of all psychiatric hospitalizations are cases of depression (Beck and Coleman 1981, 111). In particular, Beck and Cleman hold that the core of depressive illness is hopelessness (or despair) and negative expectancy. Speaking of their own theory, Beck and Coleman put the matter as follows:

> This cognitive model of depression states that the depressed person develops . . . a negative view of the self, the world, and the future that affects subsequent judgments about the person's interactions with the world. . . . This negative cognitive triad consists in a developing constellation of three categories of self conceptual ideas ranging from the general ("I am no good." "The world is unjust." "Things won't work out.") to increasingly more specific attitudes and beliefs about the self ("I can't speak coherently." "My memory is not what it used to be."). (1981, 112)

Despite significant experimental and clinical support for Beck and Coleman's model, it has been seriously challenged in the last decade or so by a phenomenon described in the literature as "depressive realism." Depressive realism seems indeed to challenge our commonsense notion that depressed people are less rational than nondepressed people, and in some cases it even suggests that they are more rational and more realistic than nondepressed people.

Very roughly, the notion of depressive realism has arisen from a variety of empirical studies in which depressed students and patients described themselves or their situation with greater accuracy and/or less bias than did nondepressed students and patients. In one series of experiments, for example, depressives accurately evaluated the amount of control they had in the experimental situation, while their nondepressed counterparts inaccurately exaggerated the amount of control they had (Alloy and Abramson 1979). Similarly, in other experiments the depressives were more accurate judges of the amount of success they could expect (Golin, Terrell, and Johnson 1977). Again, in a third set of experiments, nondepressives took more credit for positive outcomes than for negative outcomes, while depressives were more evenhanded, taking an equal amount of credit for both positive and negative outcomes (Bradley 1978).

Reviewing such experiments, one finds it hard to avoid the initial impression that laypersons and psychological theorists alike have had it all wrong: it is the depressed, not the nondepressed, that see the world (or at least themselves) more clearly. This certainly seems to fly in the face of theories, such as Beck and Coleman's (1981), that explicitly state that depression arises largely from irrational, illogical patterns of reasoning. There are nonetheless some very good reasons for resisting both of these conclusions. Let's consider them in turn.

First of all, depressive behavior is indeed maladaptive: depressed people are less effective and less happy then nondepressives. And, though I am not aware of empirical support for this contention, I strongly suspect that they are also less motivated to act or think in moral or socially useful ways. It is hard to see that their tendency to despair (personally and/or philosophically) does not play a significant role here. Nothing in the phenomenon of depressive realism is inconsistent with such conjectures. If all of this is so, it seems that we are after all justified in considering depressed persons less rational and (in a very important sense) less in touch with reality than nondepressives.

This last comment warrants more discussion. If, as a result of their despair-depression, depressives bring unhappiness upon themselves (and others) and are less capable of moral and socially useful action, then by their despair they destroy any hope of realizing a good or meaningful life, a life that everyone (including depressives) prefers to all others. Moreover, there are no good, clear empirical reasons for anyone to despair philosophically or, as a rule, personally. In fact, judged by our standard epistemic practices, there is no more support for despair than for hope. But this means that depressives hold as a matter of *faith* beliefs that make the pursuit of the good or meaningful life impossible, and I see no way of describing such beliefs as more rational or more realistic than beliefs that on the face of them make the good or meaningful life possible. Therefore, the greater accuracy of the depressives in certain kinds of self observation notwithstanding, we ought not leap to the conclusion that they are more rational or more in touch with reality than nondepressives.

Nor ought we to assume that Beck and Coleman's (1981) theory is beyond saving. In the first place, it is entirely possible that the experimental situations are quite unlike real-life situations to such an extent that the long-term cognitive strategies of the depressives that result in accurate descriptions in the laboratory distort things in the real world and vice versa for the nondepressives. Moreover, even if depressives are more accurate outside the laboratory (in daily life), they still may be less rational and less in touch with reality. Consider an analogy: It could turn out that the excessively jealous husband could give you a much more detailed and accurate description of his wife's comings and goings than his more trusting counterpart. It would scarcely follow that the excessively jealous husband is a better husband, more rational or for that matter more in touch with reality. And similar points could be made about people who are paranoid. Even if they could more accurately describe other people's behavior than nonparanoids, this would not make them more rational or more in touch with reality than normal, healthy, trusting people. People who trust the world, trust in themselves, trust their spouses, and in general trust others may get duped in many small ways. But people who trust little or not at all get duped in very big ways. They miss out on the good or meaningful life entirely. So even if (and this is a very questionable "if") they happen to see the individual trees better, they lose sight of the forest. And this leads them to do and say things that frustrate their deepest longings and best hopes.

The general point, then, is that even if it should turn out that depressives are more accurate than nondepressives in certain kinds of self-observation even in daily life, it by no means follows that they are more rational or more realistic than nondepressives. For to the contrary, what they miss is the larger picture, the larger truth that in general it is better to trust themselves, the world, and the future than not to. If this is right, then Beck and Coleman have no reason to abandon their claim that depressives are irrational and unrealistic. Nor need they abandon their thesis that depressives' distrust in themselves and the world lies at the core of their depression.

What about Beck and Coleman's recommendations concerning the treatment of depressives? If the reflections above are correct, eliminating despairing attitudes would seem to be the chief target such treatment procedures should have. Precisely how to go about such treatment must, of course, be an empirical matter. Nonetheless, if there is anything to the speculation above, one would expect the deepest and most lasting results would be achieved if patients could somehow be encouraged to construct for themselves positive solutions to the problem of despair that are both epistemically sound and prudentially and morally beneficial. In these reflections there are, moreover, some implications concerning the *prevention* of depression.

If depression is in part or primarily a function of despairing beliefs concerning the human situation and/or one's personal situation, it would seem wise for society in general and for parents and educators and others responsible for shaping young lives in particular to pay more careful attention to helping young people construct a view of life and the world that is positive and constructive in an enduring way.

Notes

1. This interpretation of the teachings of Buddha is defended by Walpola (1974).

2. See the letters of Saint Paul, especially his letters to the Corinthians.

References

Alloy, L. B., and L. Y. Abramson. 1979. "Judgment of Contingency in Depressed and Nondepressed Students." *Journal of Experimental Psychology: General* 108:441–485.

Beck, A. T., and R. E. Coleman. 1981. "Cognitive Therapy for Depression." In *Depression: Behavioral and Directive Intervention Strategies*, ed. J. F. Clarkin and H. I. Glazer. New York: Garland Press.

Bradley, G. W. 1978. "Self-Serving Biases in the Attribution Process." *Journal of Personality and Social Psychology* 36:56–71.

Camus, Albert. 1955. *The Myth of Sisyphus.* New York: Knopf.

Golin, S., F. Terrell, and B. Johnson. 1977. "Depression and the Illusion of Control." *Journal of Abnormal Psychology* 86:440–442.

Kant, I. 1956. *Critique of Practical Reason.* Trans. L. W. Beck. Indianapolis: Bobbs-Merrill.

Marx, K., with F. Engels. 1989. *Basic Writings on Politics and Philosophy.* Ed. L. W. Feuer. New York: Anchor.

Schopenhauer, A. 1964. *The World as Will and Idea.* Trans. R. B. Haldane and J. Kemp. London: Routledge and K. Paul.

Skinner, B. F. 1948. *Walden Two.* New York: Macmillan.

Skinner, B. F. 1971. *Beyond Freedom and Dignity.* New York: Knopf.

Walpola, R. 1974. *What the Buddha Taught,* 2nd ed. New York: Grove.

Mind and Mine

George Graham and G. Lynn Stephens

Is my mind my own possession? That purveyor of delusion, the delirious, the fatuous, and in frenzy or senility proved to be the very negation of mind.
Philo, On Cherubim

Being self-conscious with respect to my own mental life involves more than simply my being aware of the occurrence of various mental episodes. It also involves my being aware of them as *mine*: as my thoughts, my feelings. What must be added to my awareness of particular thoughts and feelings for me to be aware of them as my thoughts and my feelings? An obvious, if not deeply illuminating, answer is that I need to recognize the *subjectivity* of those events; that is, I need to grasp that they are episodes in my psychological history, that they occur within the boundary of my self rather than outside that boundary. However, certain cases reported in the literature on psychopathology suggest that recognizing the subjectivity of a given mental episode is not sufficient for recognizing that episode as my own. People sometimes experience a sort of introspective alienation. For example, they maintain that certain thoughts that they acknowledge to be occurring in their own minds are not their own thoughts but rather someone else's. In the chapter that follows we will consider how such cases of introspective alienation are possible and what their possibility shows us about the nature of human self-consciousness.

We divide the main body of the chapter into three parts. In section 1 we discuss various examples of introspective alienation drawn primarily from the clinical literature on psychopathology. This discussion will serve not only to make clear to the reader the sorts of cases about which we are talking but also to focus attention on introspective alienation as a general phenomenon of human self-experience. While instances of introspective alienation are frequently mentioned in the clinical literature, the discussion is distributed under a variety of separate headings, and connections among different instances of introspective alienation have gone unnoticed. For example, the clinical literature distinguishes delusions of thought insertion, where the subject believes that someone else's thoughts have been introduced into the subject's mind, from verbal hallucinations, in which the subject "hears" the voice of another person. Yet, as we will argue, many of the experiences classified as verbal hallucinations have much more in common with delusions of thought insertion than with typical instances of hallucinations.

In section 2 we turn to the task of making sense of experiences of introspective alienation. My report that a thought occurring in my mind is, nonetheless, *not* my thought but someone else's may seem not to express a coherent or intelligible belief on my part. Is it not true, as a matter of conceptual necessity, that any thought occurring in my mind is my thought? How, therefore, can I, without self-contradiction, acknowledge that a thought occurs in me but deny that it is mine?

We will argue that the key to making sense of such reports, the key to making them coherent, lies in recognizing a distinction between attributions of subjectivity and attributions of agency. When, in the throes of introspective alienation, I deny that a thought I find occurring in me is my thought, I am not denying that I am the subject in whose psychological history the thought occurs. Rather, I am denying that I am the agent or author of its occurrence. We will argue that it is not incoherent for me to suppose that I am the subject in whom a mental episode occurs but not the agent of that episode, nor is it incoherent to say that *another* person is the agent of an episode occurring in my psychological history.

We will devote the third section to examining the sense of mental agency invoked above and to explaining how I may come to believe that an episode in my psychological history is the expression of an agency other than my own. We will suggest that whether I take myself to be the agent of a mental episode depends upon whether I take the occurrence of this episode to be explicable in terms of my underlying intentional states. We will explain, in terms of this account, how I might come to believe that an episode occurring in my mind is attributable to another agent. Although such beliefs may be influenced by normative or evaluative considerations, we believe that they represent, for the most part, honest errors.

1 Introspective Alienation

Psychopathology often manifests itself in disturbances of the patient's self-consciousness or sense of self. Freud notes, for example,

Pathology has made us acquainted with a great number of states in which the boundary lines between the ego and the external world become uncertain or in which they are actually drawn incorrectly. There are cases in which part of a person's own body, even portions of his mental life—his perceptions, thoughts, and feelings —appear alien to him and as not belonging to his own ego. (Freud 1962, 13)

A type of delusion called "thought alienation" or "thought insertion" provides a particularly vivid example of the sort of case in which episodes in a person's mental life "appear alien to him." *Fish's Schizophrenia* (1984), a standard clinical handbook, characterizes the delusion as follows:

Thinking, like all conscious activities, is experienced as an activity which is being carried out by the subject. . . . There is a quality of "my-ness" connected with thought. In schizophrenia this sense of possession of one's own thoughts may be impaired and the patient may suffer from alienation of thought. [The patient] is certain that alien thoughts have been inserted into his mind. (1984, 48)

Mellor quotes a 29-year-old woman's report of such delusions:

I look out the window and I think that the garden looks nice and the grass looks cool, but the thoughts of Eamonn Andrews come into my mind. There are no other thoughts there, only his. . . . He treats my mind like a screen and flashes his thoughts onto it like you flash a picture. (1970, 17)

Mellor's patient makes two claims about her alien thoughts: (1) the thoughts occur in her own mind, and (2) they are not her thoughts but rather someone else's. The first claim is worth emphasizing because delusions of thought insertion are often said to involve inner/outer confusion or loss of ego boundaries (e.g., APA 1987, 188). Mellor's patient is not confused, however, about where the relevant thought occurs relative to the boundaries of her ego. She correctly locates it in her own mind rather than in the external world. Indeed, it is an essential feature of the delusion that the patient recognizes that alien thoughts occur in his own mind. He has the sense that, as Fish puts it, "others are participating in [his] thinking," "inserting" their thoughts into his stream of consciousness (1985, 43). He recognizes that the thought is something internal to him, and his distress arises precisely from his sense that another has invaded or penetrated his ego boundaries.

However, the patient's recognition that the thought occurs in her mind makes her insistence that it is alien—not her thought but someone else's thought—seem all the more bizarre. How can she regard it as someone else's thought if she acknowledges that it occurs in her mind? Nevertheless, clinical accounts of thought insertion emphasize that the patient does believe that the relevant thoughts are another's thoughts, not her own thoughts. In his account of thought insertion, for example, Wing insists, "The symptom is not that [the patient] has been caused to have unusual thoughts . . . but that the thoughts *themselves* are not his" (1988, 105). Likewise, Fulford distinguishes delusions of thought insertion from the experience of thought influence, or the belief that one's thoughts have been influenced by another:

The experience of one's own thoughts being influenced is like thought-insertion to the extent that it is, in a sense, something that is done or happens to one. But the similarity is only superficial. For in the normal case that which is being done is simply the *influencing* of one's thoughts: whereas in the case of thought-insertion it is (bizarrely) the thinking itself. (1989, 221)

According to the standard clinical story, then, these patients regard their thoughts as alien in some robustly literal sense, their recognition that these thoughts occur in their own minds notwithstanding.

We coined the term "introspective alienation" to mark off the sort of disturbance of self-consciousness found in thought insertion from disturbances that involve loss or confusion about ego boundaries. In the latter sort of case (the sort of case that Freud had in mind in the earlier quote of his) the subject takes a certain episode to be occurring in the external world when in fact it occurs in his own psychological history (or vice versa). A person mistakes his introspective awareness of something subjective for a perception of something objective. In contrast, the patient suffering from delusions of thought insertion recognizes that her access to the relevant episode is introspective rather than perceptual. Such recognition does not prevent her, however, from insisting that the episode represents somebody else's thinking rather than her own.

Verbal hallucinations or "voices" may seem to be an excellent example of the loss-of-ego-boundaries sort of disturbance of self-consciousness. Patients undergoing verbal hallucinations seem to themselves to "hear" the voice of another person. According to the dominant account of this phenomenon in the clinical literature, the voices that the patient "hears" are actually the patient's own verbal imaginings or inner speech (Hoffman 1986, Slade and Bentall 1988). But the patient supposes that his experience represents not introspective apprehension of his own inner speech but an auditory perception of another's speech. As Snyder puts it, "The voices are strictly the patient's own thoughts which he has chosen, presumably without conscious awareness, to project onto the outside world" (1974, 121).

The account above suggests an easy explanation of why the verbal hallucinator regards his voices as alien, as someone else's speech rather than his own. It seems to the subject that he is hearing someone speak. But his perceptual monitoring of his own body informs him that he is not speaking audibly. The speaker, he reasons, must be somebody else. On this explanation, the alien quality of verbal hallucinations is not attended by the sorts of conceptual puzzles that surround the alien character of inserted thoughts. Voices represent a disturbance of self-consciousness but not what we have called "introspective alienation."

Things are not so simple, however (as we show in more detail in Stephens and Graham 1994). From the earliest studies of verbal hallucination to the present, clinicians have consistently noted that many patients do not describe their voices as auditory or audition-like experiences. In 1846 Baillarger remarked that for many patients, the voice seems to come not from without but from "the interior of the soul," and he introduced the distinct terms "psychosensory" and "psychic hallucinations" to make this distinction (Flor-Henry 1986, 523). Blueler (1934, 51) notes that for many patients, "the voices are unlike spoken voices but are as of thoughts." Sedman's (1966) careful study of patient reports of voices provides several relevant examples. One patient says of her voice, "I felt it within me. It doesn't sound as though it's outside" (1966, 487). Other patients described the voice as "within my mind" or "in my head" and as appearing to be "a loud, strong thought" (1966, 487–488).

These clinical observations receive support from experimental studies by Junginger and Frame (1985) in which 41 percent of schizophrenic hallucinators rated their experience of their voices as more similar to introspective awareness of inner speech than to auditory perception of another's speech.

One might suppose that the tendency of some hallucinators to describe their experience of the voice as "soundless" or as similar to their typical awareness of their own inner speech reveals more about the cognitive penetrability of the experience than of its phenomenology. After all, many hallucinators, even schizophrenic hallucinators, know or at least strongly suspect that nobody is talking to them. Since they suppose that the voice is really only in their heads, they might be inclined to describe the voice as "thoughtlike," even if their experience of the voice was phenomenologically similar to their normal auditory experiences. This possibility was experimentally investigated by Junginger and Frame (1985). They found that patients' tendency to rate their voices as similar or dissimilar to auditory experiences varied independently of their reported convictions about whether the voice was real. That is, patients who acknowledge that the voice was probably only in their heads were no less likely to describe the voice as dissimilar to ordinary auditory experience than were patients who expressed the firm conviction that the voice was indeed that of another person. In his classic study of schizophrenia, Bleuler notes,

Many patients do differentiate between what they really hear and what is "imposed" on them. Nonetheless, even they are frequently inclined to attribute reality to the "voice." (1950, 110)

Allen, Halpern, and Friend report one patient's account of her experience:

The voices are not received as auditory events coming from without through the ears. . . . They feel distant and diffuse, "like thoughts," she adds ironically. "Ironically" because she cannot accept them as her own thoughts, but as messages sent to her by beings external to herself. (1985, 603).

Chapman and Chapman describe patients in their study as follows:

Many of our subjects described vivid *inner voices.* . . . Yet there was striking variation in beliefs about these voices. The most common interpretation . . . was that the voice represented their own conscience. . . . A few subjects, however, believed that the voices represented the intercession of other people. . . . A few subjects had *outer voices.* Again some subjects recognized these voices as the products of their own minds, while others developed delusional beliefs concerning their origins. (1988, 175; emphases added)

As the above evidence suggests, many cases of so-called verbal hallucinations actually are instances of introspective alienation. They are not hallucinations (or auditory hallucinations, at any rate); they are not cases of mistaking introspection of some inner event for perception of some event in the external world; they are not cases of ego-boundary confusion. Rather, they are cases in which the subject has the sense that the voice is alien, the voice of another, even though he realizes that the "voice" is in his own mind. Thus the problem of explaining the alien character of such inner voices is not categorically different from the problem of explaining why inserted thoughts seem alien to the subject. In the next section we turn to those problems.

2 The Intelligibility of Introspective Alienation

In this and the next section of our chapter we examine the question of how introspective alienation is possible. We divide this question into two. First, how are we to understand the experience of introspective alienation? That is, can we provide a coherent and plausible interpretation of the subject's assertion that an episode occurring in his mind is attributable to someone else rather than to himself? In this section we undertake to provide such an interpretation. Then in the next section we consider how introspective alienation is possible: what is it about the operation of human self-consciousness that makes us vulnerable to introspective alienation? It is possible, and we believe that what makes people prone to introspective alienation is some conscious evidence people may possess that the alien thinking is not their own activity.

We propose that the key to rendering introspective alienation intelligible lies in distinguishing the claim that a person is the subject in whom a given mental episode m occurs and the claim that a person is the agent or author of m. A person suffering from introspective alienation with respect to m acknowledges that he is the subject in whom m occurs, but he has the sense that somebody else is the agent of m. Mellor's patient (cited above) realizes that the relevant thoughts occur in her mind. However, she feels that it is not she but Mr. Andrews who *thinks* those thoughts.

Such is our proposed interpretation. We now need to develop and explain it. An analogy between attribution of mental activity and attribution of bodily action will be helpful.

It is a familiar point in action theory that I may acknowledge that my body moved in a certain way but deny that this movement is my action, something that I *did*. I may say, for example, that my arm went up but deny that I raised my arm. I have the sense that I am actively involved in some of the movements of my body but passive with respect to others. The former represents things that I do; the latter things that merely happen to or occur in me.

Just as I may experience myself as either agent or patient with respect to a particular bodily movement, I may experience myself as actively or merely passively involved in the "movements" of my mind, i.e., in particular occurrent episodes of mental activity. This sense of activity or passivity is especially marked in the case of episodes of thinking. Thinking a certain thought or thoughts is something that I often feel I do voluntarily, even deliberately. I may decide to recite silently the last line of Swinburne's "In the Garden of Proserpine"; I may cogitate with the intention of rehearsing Anselm's ontological proof for the existence of God. More commonly, I have a sense of deliberately directing my thinking toward a certain project or theme, such as crafting an apology, finding a solution to a problem, recollecting my trip to Berlin or Tenerife, without having some specific sequence of thoughts in mind at the outset. On the other hand, I may feel that certain thoughts occur in me through no doing of my own. The lyrics to an odious advertising jingle may run through my head unbidden and may continue despite my efforts to dismiss them. The name "Rosebud" may pop into my stream of consciousness without my being able to see how its occurrence is relevant to any cognitive project in which I am currently engaged. Regarding such episodes Harry Frankfurt observes,

Thoughts that beset us in these ways do not occur by our own active doing. It is tempting, indeed, to suggest that they are not thoughts that *we think* at all, but rather thoughts which we find occurring in us. This would express our sense that, although these thoughts are events in the histories of our minds, we do not actively participate in their occurrence. . . . It is not incoherent, despite the air of paradox, to say that a thought that occurs in my mind may or may not be something that *I think*. (1976, 241)

In our view, my admitting that thought, *m* occurs in my mind while denying that I think *m* is like my acknowledging that my arm went up but denying that I raised my arm. I accept that I am the subject in whom *m* occurred but deny that I am the agent responsible for *m*'s occurrence.

How does any of this help us understand instances in which a person claims that a thought occurring in her mind is somebody else's thought. Consider again an analogy with bodily movements. An event in the history of my body might be something that someone does, even if it isn't something that I do. Another person can raise my arm, for example, by grasping it and picking it up. In such a case the other person, and not I, would be the agent of the movement, although it happens in or to my body.

Interestingly, there is a class of delusions whose salient feature is the subject's belief that other persons are the agents of his bodily movements. Mellor quotes a patient's report: "When I reach for the comb it is my hand and arm which move . . . , but I don't control them. I sit watching them move and they are quite independent, what they do is nothing to do with me. . . . I am just a puppet manipulated by cosmic strings" (1970, 18). Bliss describes a patient suffering from multiple personality disorder who, "despondent and guilty on the anniversary of her mother's death, watched another personality put her arm in a fire. . . . The patient had no control over the movement and felt the pain as she watched the skin char" (1986, 140).

We propose that experiences of thought alienation involve an analogous impression or belief concerning one's thoughts. The subject has the sense that a thought occurring in her mind has been occasioned by and expresses the agency of another person. She attributes the "movement" of her mind to the other, saying that he is the person who has done or *thinks* it. She acknowledges her own involvement in this episode, but she sees herself not as the agent but only as the patient in whom the thought occurs. No doubt her belief is mistaken, but it is not incoherent or unintelligible. The sense in which she attributes the thought to herself is not the same as the sense in which she attributes it to the other and denies that it is hers. So her attributions may be taken literally, and they are mutually consistent. One attribution answers the question Who is the subject in whom m occurs? and the other answers the question Who is the agent who produces m (wherever m occurs)?

3 The Dynamics of Introspective Alienation

In the preceding section we offered an interpretation of what the patient experiencing introspective alienation believes. In this final section we attempt to explain how a person might come to entertain or hold such beliefs. We must mention the provisional and speculative nature of our project in this section of the paper. We try to sketch an account of how introspective alienation might work that is consistent with the clinical data and with otherwise plausible assumptions about human self-consciousness. We do not try to defeat alternative explanations or to arrive at a complete understanding. However, we do not see any means to arrive at an understanding of introspective alienation and its implications concerning the nature of self-consciousness except by trying to offer such a sketch.

If our interpretation of introspective alienation as a disturbance of the subject's sense of mental agency is on the right track, then to explain how we come to be vulnerable to such disturbances, we will need a general account of our sense of agency for mental events. For the subject, what distinguishes the episodes in her psychological history that she regards as her actions, things she does or *thinks*, from those that she regards as merely happening within her?

A line suggested by Dennett (1987, 1991) and Flanagan (1991, 1992) seems to us to provide a promising approach to this question. They hold that, in general, our sense of ourselves as persons and agents engaged in living a particular life depends on our proclivity for constructing self-referential narratives, or hypothetical explanations that organize disparate events into coherent projectible patterns. A favored narrative strategy consists of explaining behavioral episodes, for example, as expressions of underlying, relatively persistent intentional states. Such explanations serve to make sense of behavior retrospectively and also provide the subject with a framework of expectations regarding her future behavior. Collectively, such explanations amount to a sort of theory of the person's agency or intentional psychology. In Flanagan's words, they constitute "the story we tell to ourselves to understand ourselves for who we are" (1992, 196).

For example, consider Sam. Sam is walking in a certain direction because he wants to get some laudanum, believes the best way to obtain laudanum is to buy it at the corner pharmacy and believes that the store lies in the direction in which he is walking. He anticipates that upon entering the pharmacy, he will take out his wallet, because he believes that laudanum costs money and that his money is in his wallet, and he intends to purchase the laudanum with the money in his wallet. Sam's behavior seems sensible and predictable to him because he takes it to be an expression of his own underlying beliefs and desires. He therefore regards it as something he does, as his action, and sees himself as its agent.

Suppose that Sam finds that he is unable to account for his ambulatory behavior, given his beliefs about his intentional states. He does not take himself to have any beliefs or desires that would explain or "rationalize" his behavior or that such behavior would appropriately express. In such a case his behavior will not appear to him as something he does, as his action. It will not seem agentically his. At this point Sam has two options: (1) He may revise his theory of his intentional psychology, i.e., he may decide that he does have the relevant sorts of intentional states and that the behavior is his action after all. Or (2) he may decide that the walking is none of his doing and that he is involved in its occurrence only as patient and not as agent.

We suggest that the subject's sense of agency regarding her thoughts likewise depends on her belief that these mental episodes are expressions of her intentional states. That is, whether the subject regards an episode of thinking occurring in her psychological history as something she does, as her mental action, depends on whether she finds its occurrence explicable in terms of her theory or story of her own underlying intentional states. For thinking, as for overt behavior, having a sense that you are *doing* something involves a sense of *what* you are doing and *why* you are doing it. I find occurring in me the thought that a good dose of laudanum would really hit the spot right now. Do I regard this episode as my action, something that I think, or do I dismiss it as mere verbal imagery running willy-nilly through my head? The answer depends upon whether I take myself to have beliefs and desires of the sort that would rationalize its occurrence in me. If my theory of myself ascribes to me the relevant intentional states, I unproblematically regard this episode as my action. If not, then I must either revise my picture of my intentional states or refuse to acknowledge the episode as my doing.

We should stress here that we are not saying that subjects decide whether a thought counts as their action by somehow checking the thought against their independent observations of their beliefs and desires. We agree with critics of introspective access to beliefs and desires that apprehension of one's own beliefs and desires is composed of inferential components. We suppose that the subject experiences her intentional states only insofar as she takes them to be manifested in occurrent episodes, either thoughts or behavior. Intentional states such as beliefs and desires are theoretical entities postulated to explain the data provided by (introspective and perceptual) self-observation. In theorizing about ourselves, we proceed hypothetically or abductively (though we need not assume that our theorizing in this area conforms any more closely to the formal canons of abductive inference than does human theorizing in any other area). New observational data serves as a test of previously accepted hypotheses and may suggest the need for new hypotheses.

What we are suggesting is that the subject unproblematically accepts a thought as her action if, by her own lights, it accords with her intentional psychology—if roughly, it is the sort of thought she would expect herself to think given her picture of her self. If the thought is not what she expects, or more particularly if she expects not to think such a thought, she has the option of revising her self-theory, and hence finally accepting the thought as her doing, or of explaining its occurrence by appeal to factors independent of her intentional states.

Why might the subject fail to embrace an intentional explanation of the occurrence of a thought? Accounts of thought alienation and verbal hallucination in the clinical literature frequently suggest that a subject's failure to acknowledge her "alien" thoughts as her own is motivated by her negatively evaluative attitudes toward the thoughts in question. One variation of the account goes as follows: a conscious thought produces in a subject a conscious feeling of aversion or fear, and the negative feeling influences or motivates the subject to dissociate. Snyder, for example, writes,

All these features of the voices heard by schizophrenics go along nicely with the notion that the voices are strictly the patients own thoughts, which he has chosen . . . to project onto the outside world. . . . A simple way of thinking about it is to suppose that by dint of his hallucinations the schizophrenic needs no longer take responsibility for his own unbearable mental processes. (1974, 121)

Our account of attribution of mental agency can readily accommodate this proposal. We need only suppose that the subject's tendency to entertain or accept hypotheses concerning her intentional states may be biased by her evaluative attitudes toward the sorts of states in question. Should a blasphemous thought occur in her, for example, her preference for maintaining an image of herself as a pious person might make her unwilling, or even unable, to accept the hypothesis that she harbors the sorts of beliefs and desires that would find their natural expression in blasphemous thoughts. She would feel that this thought could not be her doing.

However, our account does not *require* that the subject's failure to acknowledge responsibility for a thought be regarded as motivated self-deception, as motivated by negative evaluation. Even if she is mistaken in denying that the thought involves her agency, it could be an honest mistake, rather than a self-serving evasion. And indeed, the clinical literature does not support the notion that the subject's failure to acknowledge her alien thoughts as her own is necessarily motivated by her disapproval of the intentional states they seem to express. Studies of verbal hallucination in schizophrenia note that while comments made by "voices" often are persecutory or demeaning, they sometimes encourage or console the subject (Bleuler 1950, 96; Snyder 1974). Modell (1960) emphasizes that voices are often innocuous, offering neutral comments or advice. Chapman and Chapman (1986, 175) report the case of a young woman who persistently heard the voices of her deceased father and her paternal grandmother advising her on various decisions that she faced, such as whether to buy a car. She experienced their intervention as well intentioned and actually helpful to her. There seems to be no obvious reason why this patient's self-esteem would be soiled by her admission that she is the sort of person who would think about the advantages or disadvantages of purchasing an automobile.

On our account, what is critical is that the subject find her thoughts inexplicable in terms of beliefs about her intentional states. We are not committed to any particular tale about why she finds them intentionally inexplicable. Indeed, there is no reason to rule out the possibility that she fails to find an intentional explanation because there really isn't one. Thoughts may occur in her that are not expressions of (or appropriate expressions of) any of her underlying intentional states. Hoffman (1986), for example, proposes an explanation of verbal hallucinations according to which hallucinators suffer a breakdown in the processes that normally guide the production of inner speech (what he calls "discourse planning"). As a result, they produce inner speech that is discordant with their expectations and that is not explicable by reference to their intentional states. Whether or not Hoffman's specific proposals are correct, we can see no reason to assume that all the thoughts that occur in a person's mind are expressions of her underlying intentional states. Insofar as those who experience their own thoughts as alien deny merely that they are the agents of those thoughts, what they say may be perfectly plausible.

Of course a subject experiencing delusions of thought insertion does more than deny that she is the agent of her alien thoughts: she maintains that somebody else is the agent. She does not deny that there is an intentional explanation for the occurrence of the relevant thoughts in her; rather, she explains their occurrence by reference to someone else's intentional states. Why should she experience her thoughts as *alien*, as expressions of another's agency, rather than as mere mental happenings?

A possible explanation for such an extraordinary hypothesis would be that, despite her conviction that an episode of thinking does not express her own intentional states, the episode might seem to her quite intentional. It may be topically relevant—for instance, speaking to concerns that she acknowledges in herself. Unlike nonvoluntary verbal imaginings, such as snatches of doggerel running unbidden through her head (which are notable for their lack of connection with, and tendency to distract one from, one's current concerns), the contents of alienated thoughts tend to be personally salient for the subject (Bleuler 1950, 97; Mott, Small, and Anderson 1965). They mean something to the person; they tend not to be isolated from a person's interests or concerns. Likewise, in the case of voices at any rate, alien thoughts typically exhibit the sorts of grammatical forms appropriate for conversational or communicative speech. They are frequently in the second person, for example (Linn 1977). Often they are in the imperative mood (Bleuler 1950). Their content is appropriate to communicative acts like giving advice or criticism, issuing threats and orders, offering condolence or encouragement.

For example, a young mother, concerned with her child's welfare and her own maternal responsibilities, might find the thought "Bad mother" or "You're hurting your child" or "Joan Crawford" occurring in her consciousness. She does not acknowledge in herself the sorts of intentional states that would naturally find expression in such utterances. She represents herself to herself as a caring, competent mother, utterly and unequivocally devoted to her child. So these are not the sorts of comments she would make or wish to make to herself. Nonetheless, it is hard for her to dismiss her thoughts as random verbal imagery. They seem to betray an agency, an intelligence, that accounts for their coherence, salience, and directedness.

Thus she may have the strong impression that someone is communicating with her here, that her deceased mother, her ex-husband, or God is addressing her.

Whether her impression becomes a delusional conviction doubtless depends upon a variety of factors—cultural, psychosocial, neurological—that go beyond the mere phenomenology of her experience. Our hypothesis is just that the apparently conversational, communicative character of her thoughts may provide an experiential basis for her attributing her thoughts to other agents. The person experiences the thoughts as agentic but not of her doing.

Another example involving overt behavior may be helpful here. Suppose I find myself taking up a pen and rapidly inscribing marks on a piece of paper. To my surprise, I discover that these marks form English words and sentences: words and sentences that would naturally be used to express undying love for someone named Beatrice. My movements with the pen seem to be producing a letter. Such literary production suggests authorial direction. But I am not aware of providing such direction. I recollect no one named Beatrice; I do not seem to myself to have any beliefs and desires that such a letter would appropriately express; I have no idea which sentence will appear next on the page or when the letter will end. Still, it hardly seems possible to me that there is no intelligent agent behind my performance.

If I remain convinced that composing the letter is an intelligent performance, an action or activity, I have two options. One is to suppose that the writing is after all something that I am doing. In this case I revise my account of myself so as to accommodate in my psychology the sorts of intentional states that I take to be required for such a performance: "I do, after all know, a Beatrice." "I do, after all, want to express my love to her." "I am, after all, the agent of this letter." Perhaps I will supplement this revision with some explanation of why I was previously unaware of these intentional states: "Beatrice is my neighbor's wife." "I dread the thought that I covet my neighbor's wife."

The other option is to suppose that someone else is using me to write a love letter to Beatrice, writing the letter through me or through my body. I conclude that I am possessed, that my movements are directed by the intentional states of another and express his or her beliefs and desires.

Now imagine by analogy that instead of finding myself taking up a pen and writing to Beatrice, I find myself thinking of such a person and entertaining love of her. Similarly, the movements of my mind, my thoughts or inner speech, may seem to me to be intelligent but not to express my own intelligence. Instead, they seem to be expressions of another. Doubtless attribution to another would be an extraordinary hypothesis in the case of writing to Beatrice, and an extra-extraordinary hypothesis regarding the provenance of these thoughts about Beatrice. However, the highly atypical character of my current thoughts or perhaps my imperative emotional needs or some bizarre breakdown of my cognitive economy may lead me to embrace it.

4 Conclusion

The defining feature of our whole approach to thought alienation is that we think it wise to distinguish two aspects of self-consciousness or two senses in which a person may be self-conscious. One is being conscious of one's subjectivity or ego boundary, where thoughts are taken to occur within one's own stream of consciousness or psychological history. The other is being conscious of one's own actions, where thoughts are taken to express one's own underlying intentionality or agency.

Admittedly, the grain of our distinction is rather coarse. To detail the character of our approach requires expanding our account of agentic self-attribution as well as our description of mental agency. It also requires answering questions about susceptibility to thought alienation and divisions between thought alienation and types of closely related phenomena (such as thought influence). These are topics we hope to address on other occasions. When trying to achieve more detail, we must be cautious that psychopathological data of the sort cited in this paper make interpreting peoples' behavior and introspective reports a complex matter. But our idea is that no matter the complexities, there is a central distinction in self-consciousness between realizing that something occurs in my mind and experiencing it as agentically mine.

References

Allen, J. F., J. Halpern, and R. Friend. 1985. "Removal and Diversion Tactics and the Control of Auditory Hallucinations." *Behaviour Research and Therapy* 23:601–605.

American Psychiatric Association. 1987. *Diagnostic and Statistical Manual of Mental Disorders*, 3rd ed., rev. Washington, D.C.: American Psychiatric Association.

Bleuler, E. 1934. *Textbook of Psychiatry.* Trans. A. A. Brill. New York: Macmillan.

Bleuler, E. 1950. *Dementia Praecox or the Group of Schizophrenias.* Trans. J. Zinkin. International Universities Press. First published in 1911.

Bliss, E. 1986. *Multiple Personality, Allied Disorders, and Hypnosis.* Oxford: Oxford University Press.

Chapman, L. J., and J. P. Chapman. 1988. "The Genesis of Delusions." In *Delusional Belief,* ed. T. F. Oltmanns and B. Mahrer. New York: Wiley.

Dennett, D. C. 1987. *The Intentional Stance.* Cambridge: MIT Press.

Dennett, D. C. 1991. *Consciousness Explained.* Boston: Little, Brown, and Co.

Fish, F. J. 1984. *Fish's Schizophrenia,* 3rd ed. Ed. M. A. Hamilton. Bristol: Wright. 1st ed., 1962.

Fish, F. J. 1985. *Clinical Psychopathology.* Ed. M. A. Hamilton. Bristol: Wright.

Flanagan, O. 1991. *Varieties of Moral Personality: Ethics and Psychological Realism.* Cambridge: Harvard University Press.

Flanagan, O. 1992. *Consciousness Reconsidered.* Cambridge: MIT Press.

Flor-Henry, P. 1986. "Auditory Hallucinations, Inner Speech, and the Dominant Hemisphere." *Behavioral and Brain Sciences* 9:523–524.

Frankfurt, H. 1976. "Identification and Externality." In *The Identities of Persons,* ed. A. O. Rorty. Berkeley: University of California Press.

Freud, S. 1962. *Civilization and Its Discontents.* Trans. J. Strachey. Boston: Norton.

Fulford, K. W. M. 1989. *Moral Theory and Medical Practice.* Cambridge: Cambridge University Press.

Hoffman, R. 1986. "Verbal Hallucinations and Language Production Processes in Schizophrenia." *Behavioral and Brain Sciences* 9:503–517.

Junginger, J., and C. Frame. 1985. "Self-Report of Frequency and Phenomenology of Verbal Hallucinations." *Journal of Nervous and Mental Disease* 173:149–155.

Linn, E. L. 1977. "Verbal Auditory Hallucinations: Mind, Self, and Society." *Journal of Nervous and Mental Disease* 164:8–17.

Mellor, C. S. 1970. "First Rank Symptoms of Schizophrenia." *British Journal of Psychiatry* 117:15–23.

Modell, A. 1960. "An Approach to the Nature of Auditory Hallucinations in Schizophrenia." *Archives of General Psychiatry* 12:595–601.

Mott, R. H., J. F. Small, and J. M. Anderson. 1965. "Comparative Study of Hallucinations." *Archives of General Psychiatry* 12:595–601.

Sedman, G. 1966. " 'Inner Voices': Phenomenological and Clinical Aspects." *British Journal of Psychiatry* 112:485–490.

Slade, P. D., and R. P. Bentall. 1988. *Sensory Deception: A Scientific Analysis of Hallucination.* Baltimore: Johns Hopkins University Press.

Snyder, S. 1974. *Madness and the Brain.* New York: McGraw Hill.

Stephens, G. L., and G. Graham. 1994. "Voices and Selves." In *Philosophic Perspectives on Psychiatric Diagnostic Classification*, ed. J. Sadler, O. Wiggins, and M. Schwartz. Baltimore: Johns Hopkins University Press.

Wing, J. K. 1988. *Reasoning about Madness.* Oxford: Oxford University Press.

Going to Pieces

John Heil

Many forms of human irrationality stem from our capacity to exploit mental machinery that otherwise serves us well. The very mechanisms that enable me to ignore irrelevant evidence, for instance, make it possible for me to ignore relevant evidence and thereby to form beliefs on the basis of wishful thinking. The selective focusing of attention is a technique useful in the exercise of self-control, but this same technique can be deployed in support of self-defeating ends.

This, at any rate, is what I shall argue here. My target is Donald Davidson's partitioning model of irrationality. That model, I contend, invokes a needlessly complex depiction of wayward, though nonpathological agents. Of course, even if I am right in supposing that everyday sorts of irrationality are best understood in terms of the operation of unremarkable, mostly adaptive mechanisms, severe pathological cases might well be importantly different. We might discover, for instance, that it is impossible to regard such cases as extremes on a continuum that, at one end, includes simple indiscretion, slides into wishful thinking and self-deception, and then, at the far end, shades into paranoia, amnesia, and multiple personality.[1] Ultimately, something like Davidson's partitioning model might be required to make sense of pathological phenomena.

I intend to dwell on topics that inform explanations of behavior but often go unremarked. The most important of these, perhaps, is the notion of charity as applied to ascriptions of states of mind. It is easy to dismiss charity as a relic of a discredited, aprioristic conception of mind. This would be a mistake. Charity, I shall argue, plays an interpretive role analogous to parsimony. Moreover, considerations of charity are at bottom what motivate appeals to mental partitions or multiple selves.

I shall begin with a discussion of assorted background issues, move to an account of Davidson's conception of mental partitioning, and conclude with some remarks on my own view of the landscape. Along the way I hope to illuminate matters that are too easily lost sight of in discussions between philosophers and nonphilosophers.

1 The Pull of Coherence

The concept of a divided mind has an ancient and honorable history, going back at least to Plato's account of the tripartite soul in the *Republic*. In our own century, the phenomenon of multiple personality has attracted considerable attention and found its way into into popular consciousness.[2] Our well-documented capacity for self-deception, for "compartmentalizing," for losing track of painful or inconvenient information, all suggest a picture of the mind as an array of "loosely organized systems composed of relatively autonomous subsystems . . . , [a] medieval city of relatively autonomous neighborhoods" (Rorty 1988, 213–214).

The image is a powerful one. Appeals to mental divisions enable us to make sense of actions that might seem baffling otherwise. Some aspects of my behavior might strongly intimate that I hold a certain belief or embrace a particular value, while other aspects suggest the opposite. Under the circumstances, you may be inclined to suppose that one part of me harbors the belief or value in question, while another part remains detached from this commitment. It is important to see that, in reasoning thus, we are driven by a unifying ideal: agents, qua agents, are coherent; they exhibit unity and consistency. When this is lacking, we find it natural to postulate multiple agents, each of whom exhibits what all, taken together, lack. It is not, or not just, that we regard unity and consistency as a good thing. It is rather that we have no choice. If you have evidence that I hold p, for instance, and evidence that I hold not p, you do not thereby have evidence that I hold both p and not p.[3] Evidence for the one undermines evidence for the other.

A coherence requirement is constitutive of the scheme we employ in understanding ourselves and others as acting on reasons. To the extent that a creature's behavior fails to be interpretable in light of this scheme, the creature's behavior resists explanation by reference to the vocabulary of reasons: beliefs, desires, motives, intentions. In attempting to understand one another and ourselves, we react to the pull of coherence. In dividing the mind, we compromise intelligibility, but we do so, it seems, for the sake of improved overall intelligibility. I shall argue presently that the interests of coherence are often better served by means of less dramatic devices. Before venturing into deeper waters, however, it might be useful to look briefly at the dynamics of rational choice.

2   Rationality and Coordination

Common wisdom has it that we cannot compare apples and oranges. Yet we are obliged to make such comparisons more or less continuously. I want apples and oranges, but I have enough room in my shopping basket for one or the other, not both. I am compelled to choose. Even if I am indifferent, my indifference expresses a straight-forward comparison between apples and oranges, and this comparison is eventually reflected in my choice. Many real-life cases require choices over far more disparate kinds of object. I must choose between flying to Barcelona for a conference, attending the wedding of a cousin in Detroit, or remaining at home and completing a project required for promotion. I am pulled in different directions. In settling on a course of action, I thereby exclude endless others.

Sometimes we are confronted with choices along a single, well-defined continuum. I am torn between a napoleon and an éclair. On further consideration I conclude that the éclair offers a larger culinary payoff, and so select it. If my evaluations are evenly balanced, or if the éclair proves disappointing, I may experience regret. Still, other things equal, I am making a choice from within a homogeneous range of possibilities. The trouble is, it is rare that other things *are* equal. I may regard the éclair as superior to the napoleon in certain respects (it is larger and sweeter), the napoleon as preferable in others (it is less expensive yet connotes sophistication). Occasionally we are led in this way to awkward violations of transitivity: I prefer a fresh éclair to a less-expensive napoleon, and the napoleon to a 25¢ oatmeal cookie. The inexpensive cookie, however, may strike me as preferable to the costly éclair (see Heil 1986).

We find ourselves, in this way, inclined in many directions at once. Life poses coordination problems of arbitrary complexity. I must weigh interests in one domain against those in other domains and assess my prospects. Sometimes the choices we make line up with our better judgments, sometimes they do not. I judge it best to forego a pastry at lunch, yet succumb to my desire for an éclair. In so doing, I may revise my better judgment, but I may not. If I do not, and if my desire is not irresistible, I act *acratically*. Acratic action—weakness of will—is possible in part because our desires exhibit a degree of motivational clout that can fail to conform to their overall evaluative standing (see Mele 1987). I am faced with a choice between incompatible actions a and b. I consider my circumstances and these options and, on this basis, judge a preferable to b. Nevertheless, if b outweighs a motivationally, I may deliberately do b, and I may do so without revising my better judgment. In so acting, I act on my strongest desire, perhaps, but not in a way I consider best.

Although acratic choices are certainly plentiful, there are powerful internal pressures to conform to the principle of continence:

Principle of continence   Act in accord with one's better judgment (Davidson 1986, 81).

The principle is partly constitutive of our overall motivational structure; it is an essential component of the machinery of coordination. Faced with recalcitrant desires, we may engage in efforts at self-control. I judge it best to forego the éclair while recognizing that I am apt to succumb to temptation. I may endeavor to diminish the éclair's attractiveness by calling to mind both unattractive consequences of my eating it and various benefits I might expect from abstention. If I am successful, I have excercised a degree of self-control and tempered my desire for the éclair; if not, if my desire gains the upper hand, I may exhibit weakness of will and act acratically.

Behind all this lies a dynamic evaluative structure. Human beings exhibit and continually evolve values or norms subsuming a variety of domains of interest. Some of these may be finely articulated, others less so. Each of us possesses culinary, economic, sartorial, aesthetic, moral, epistemic, and social standards. Coordination problems arise when domains overlap, as they inevitably must. You ask my opinion of your haircut. My aesthetic norms are offended, etiquette demands that I find it attractive, and morality that I say what I think. My response expresses my solution, whatever it is, to an unremarkable coordination problem.

Where does rationality fit into this picture? Do we possess a special set of rational norms alongside, or perhaps above, the rest? Might rational norms be overridable? And might their being overridden be reasonable on occasion?

Such questions betray a confusion about the character and role of normative systems. Imagine that I have strong evidence that p and no evidence, or only insignificant evidence, against p. Is it reasonable for me to believe that p? If I fail to believe that p, perhaps because I find the prospect distasteful or depressing, am I thereby guilty of irrationality? Prima facie, my embracing p could be epistemically reasonable without thereby being reasonable all things considered. How are cases of this sort different from those in which I overrule aesthetic norms, for instance, in order to satisfy some competing economic end? I forego a Ferrari for a Plymouth because, although the former surpasses the latter aesthetically, it would prove financially ruinous. Here the reasonableness of my choice is tied to something approximating an overall all-things-considered assessment. Suppose, now, that my forming the epistemically laudable belief that p would result in unacceptable nonepistemic consequences. My having the belief would make life no longer worth living, perhaps, or lead me to actions that could result in disaster. Were that so, my forming the belief might well fail to be reasonable in some broader, all-inclusive sense. More particularly, although my forming the belief would be epistemically reasonable for me, it could fail to be reasonable for me tout court.

An account of this sort need not be taken to imply that forming beliefs is something we do voluntarily. I can, of course, elect to take steps that will result, predictably, in the formation or inhibition of particular beliefs. Pascal's wager is merely the most famous instance of this sort. Pascal argues that we have strong, indeed overriding, prudential grounds for bringing ourselves to form the belief that God exists. Were Pascal right, then, depending on my normative makeup, this belief might be reasonable for me even if its evidential credentials were, by my own lights, patently inadequate.

Although we evidently lack control over most of the beliefs we form, we are adept at enhancing or inhibiting the influence wielded by a particular belief. In this respect, beliefs resemble desires. Suppose I find myself unable to shake the belief that a colleague is dishonest despite a deeper conviction that this belief is unjust. I may, reasonably perhaps, employ various techniques—self-deception being only the most extreme example—calculated to mitigate the belief's effects on my cognitive economy. These techniques are essential equipment for anyone hoping to negotiate a less than perfectly cooperative world. We are taught at an early age, explicitly and by example, to avoid thinking about matters that needlessly disturb us. Once in place, strategies useful in maintaining self-control extend smoothly to the epistemic domain. I may diminish the desire for an éclair by making vivid particular consequences of succumbing to the desire. Similarly, I may temper the effects of (and, if I am lucky, eventually cancel) a belief in the dishonesty of a colleague by focusing on evidence to the contrary, dwelling on the obligations of friendship, and the like.

It is natural to think of irrationality as involving an internal conflict of some sort. The presence of conflict, however, is by itself insufficient grounds for describing an agent as irrational. I may harbor inconsistent beliefs without realizing that I do so, and desires can be straightforwardly at odds. In neither case am I necessarily irrational. Irrationality arises when I act in ways recognizably inconsistent with standards to which I am committed. Consider my failing to form the belief that p when that belief is mandated by evidence in my possession. I am culpable only to the extent that I myself am committed to the evidential principles in question and that I in some sense appreciate the bearing of my evidence on p.

This cannot be the whole story, however. I have noted already that agents are constantly faced with choices that subsume incommensurable normative domains. In such cases an agent's acting in accord with one set of norms may necessitate flouting, often in full awareness, other norms to which the agent is committed. I choose McDonald's over Les Trois Faisans, a Plymouth over a Ferrari, knowing that in so choosing, I am apt to satisfy certain economic ends while frustrating important culinary and aesthetic values.

An understanding of ordinary irrationality requires an understanding of the dynamics of choice. I have suggested already that there is ample reason to regard intelligent agents as harboring commitments to evolving collections of norms. Norms afford guidance within specific domains. Culinary norms enable me to rank possible states of the world along culinary dimensions. Economic norms, or norms governing etiquette, or morals, or evidence, dictate rankings along different dimensions. A single option, my dining at McDonald's, may rank high in one domain, low in another. Norms provide us with a basis of choice, but they do not exhaust the mechanism of choice. Given the (often disparate) evaluative standing of options open to me, I must settle somehow what is best, all things considered. It is tempting, but misleading, to imagine that this must be a matter of bringing to bear an additional, higher-order set of norms. It is rather a matter of my ascertaining what is the best option, given my values (those norms to which I am committed) and my beliefs about the circumstances.

My decision reflects my values. It is normatively based in the sense that it is made in light of norms to which I am committed. It need not, however, manifest commitment to some further, global standard. Decision is the province of practical reason. Norms provide guidance concerning what I ought to do to satisfy ends of particular sorts. Practical reason provides guidance concerning what I ought to do. This will seem strange only to theorists who have lost sight of the fact that normative guidance must come to an end somewhere, principles must be applied. I can cultivate, in myself and in others, moral or aesthetic or economic values, but I cannot, in the same way, cultivate distinctively practical norms.[4] Attempts to formulate such norms inevitably fall short. One might try: do what one most wants to do. But what is that? I have a culinary interest in Les Trois Faisans, an economic interest in McDonald's. How are these interests to be weighed? This is not to say that we cannot compare interests across domains; it is to say only that, in the end, such comparisons do not involve the application of further standards. Nor is it that practical reason is unprincipled. On the contrary, the normative structures it invokes provide it with all the principles and bases of comparison that it could possibly need.

The most prominent function of practical reason is that of settling on courses of action. I have suggested that doing so need not be a matter of appeal to a distinctive collection of practical principles. This is not to say that practical decision is chaotic or unprincipled. It is merely to state the obvious: something must take us from norm to action. Imagine, for a moment, that practical reason operated with a set of distinctively practical norms. I might then have strong practical reasons to do *a*, though perhaps reasons of other sorts to do *b*. What ought I to do, then, all things considered?

My suspicion is that there is a tendency to confuse practical reason with the exercise of prudence. But prudence is merely one value among others. There is no special puzzle about cases in which one opts for an imprudent, though perhaps moral or heroic, course of action. Moral theorists would like to think that moral norms trump the rest: what is reasonable must be morally permitted. Although there are undoubtedly individuals for whom this is so, it is scarcely guaranteed by the character of practical reason.

If I am on the right track here, it may be possible to obtain a clearer view of the phenomena for which it seems most plausible to posit mental divisions or agencies. It is to these that I shall now turn.

3 Multiplication and Division

Theorists appeal to multiple selves not only in accounts of self-deception, weakness of will, and self-control but in discussions of conflicts among desires and between long- and short-term interests as well.[5] It is common to imagine that these selves exhibit one-sided or unbalanced traits of character. When I waiver between doing the right thing and doing what is expedient, I am being pulled in one direction by my moral (or "social") self and in the opposite direction by my expedient ("economic") self. The latter may or may not incorporate my earthy, primordial self, the self that clamors for attention whenever I am obliged to choose between courses of action that promise to satisfy, respectively, desires for long- and short-term ends. On such a view, a rational agent is one in whom these various selves operate in harmony, each asserting itself, as Plato puts it, "without internal division, each element . . . rightly performing its own function" (*Republic* 586e).

Such conceptions of the human psyche afford one way of describing and making sense of ranges of behavior that otherwise appear unintelligible. What is rather less clear is whether we might not be able to offer simpler, more straightforward accounts of the same phenomena, accounts not obliging us to appeal to multiple agents or mental domains. This, at any rate, is the question I intend to pursue in this section and the next. I shall focus not on clinical lore but on a latter-day philosophical treatment of irrationality. This seems to me a useful exercise in a volume devoted largely to discussions of clinical literature. My aim is to make salient matters that nonphilosophers sometimes take for granted, and so ignore. I shall begin with some general comments on the character of distinctively psychological explanation in hopes of providing a better sense of considerations that might be taken to motivate conceptions of the divided mind.

Earlier I advanced considerations tending toward the conclusion that, to the extent that we are describable as having propositionally characterizable states of mind, we are rational animals. But here looms a paradox. We rely on a principle of charity in the ascription of states of mind, and charity mandates rationality.[6] If anything is obvious, however, it is that rationality is an ideal seldom fully realized: each of us fails to be rational some of the time, and some of us fail more often than we care to admit. What remains to be determined is whether charity, while proscribing sweeping irrationality, might fall short of demanding, unreasonably, perfect rationality.

The matter is a subtle one. Our taking agents to harbor beliefs, desires, intentions, hopes, fears (the so-called propositional attitudes) necessitates substantive constraints on our ascriptions. As we have seen, however, this need not be taken to imply that we could never have grounds for attributing wayward states of mind to agents. These might reasonably be postulated when so doing would somehow optimize the coherence of the system as a whole. Regarded in this light, charity may be likened to parsimony. The ascription of nonstandard beliefs, desires, or intentions to an agent in one way complicates our conception of that agent. And complications are warranted only when there is some independent reason for them, something the complicating factor explains that would be mysterious otherwise. It is useful, then, to regard charity as parsimony applied in the mental realm.

Against this background, Donald Davidson has suggested that familiar sorts of irrationality might be accommodated by imagining that irrational agents comprise subsystems or partitions.[7] The notion that minds are divided into units, each in some respects self-contained yet at various times in collusion or competition with its neighbors, is a familiar clinical and psychoanalytic theme. We can now see that by partitioning agents in this way, we are in effect extending charity in ways that make sense of a range of performances that would otherwise resist interpretation. We preserve overall intelligibility by postulating subsystems that are themselves perfectly rational but operate at cross-purposes. Part of me wants to know the truth, and part of me wants to be happy. Ordinarily, these aims are independently satisfiable. At times, however, they compete. When this happens, there is an opening for irrationality.

Despite obvious similarities, there are a number of respects in which Davidson's notion of partitioning differs from traditional conceptions of the divided self. On Davidson's view, subsystems are not to be regarded as agents, even attenuated subagents.[8] There is but one self, one source of deliberative agency. Partitioning merely restricts or diverts access to the usual array of deliberative resources. I believe, against the evidence, that my child is innocent of some offense. The evidence or perhaps my recognition of its import or perhaps both (the cases are importantly different) is in some manner screened off or partitioned. My irrational belief is supported by favorable evidence left behind. In the same way, I may act acratically, act against my considered better judgment, when that better judgment is partitioned, kept apart from the motivational basis of the intention I form to act as I do.

These examples point to a second important respect in which Davidson's conception differs from more familiar clinical or psychoanalytical conceptions. Partitions, unlike Freudian psychic divisions, are not to be thought of as permanent mental fixtures. Partitioning is intended as a metaphor, a way of describing agents whose deeds might otherwise be indescribable, hence (psychologically) incomprehensible. Conflicting mental states and episodes are assigned to

distinct psychic regions. By so doing, we uphold the practice of ascribing these states and episodes to an agent while at the same time
accounting for their misfiring in that agent's global psychological
economy. The idea is not to advance an account of the machinery of
irrationality but merely to provide a framework within which irrational states of mind can be sensibly assigned (see, e.g., Davidson 1982,
300–301).

This brings us to a third respect in which Davidson's partitioning
differs from the traditional image. Partitions are functionally circumscribed. Material that fails to engage an agent as it should, for instance, is relegated to a distinct partition, a mental region cut off
from the mainland. Such material, it should be noted, need not be
banished to the unconscious, only isolated functionally from the rest.
Arguably, it is this sort of functional separation that is most important for our notion of the unconscious. Materials kept from consciousness might fail to figure in an agent's ongoing deliberative
activities, for instance, hence manifest none of their usual efficacy.
What is important in such cases is not that the agent is unaware of
particular wishes or thoughts but that the effects of those wishes or
thoughts in the agent's psychological economy are not rationally mediated. The idea, it should be clear, is not to deny the existence of
nonconscious mental events but merely to introduce a functional
criterion that cuts across the familiar conscious/unconscious divide.

We need, in any case, some such criterion. It enables us to account
for cases in which apparently *conscious* (or consciously accessible)
items fail to engage as they should, and to make sense of the evident
fact that beliefs, desires, and wishes may assert themselves in perfectly normal ways in our psyche even when we do not explicitly acknowledge their presence. Irrationality, or at any rate an important
species of it, occurs when these are, by whatever means, prevented
from interacting appropriately with our practical and theoretical deliberations, or when the results of our deliberations fail to take hold.
The mechanisms involved doubtless include those that inhibit our
bringing certain items into awareness. But they include, as well, those
that block our putting two and two together (as in cases of "compartmentalization" or "framing"), and those that prevent what may be
consciously appreciated from *sinking in*, suitably engaging the machinery. In all such instances there is at least a functional separation

John Heil

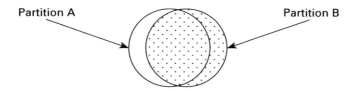

Figure 1
The partitioning model.

(see Tversky and Kahneman 1981, Kahneman and Tversky 1983, Heil 1984).

Davidson's picture, then, incorporates functionally distinguishable mental regions. Regions can overlap; indeed, we are to imagine that they *mostly* overlap. They are best depicted with Venn diagrams, rather than flowcharts (see figure 1). On Davidson's holistic view of the mind, the character of a belief is fixed in part by relations it bears to other beliefs. If that is so, we must suppose that partitions overlap considerably. Only in that way is it possible to make sense of cases in which partitioned beliefs are held in common. My incontinent belief about my child's innocence is a belief about the very same child concerning whom I possess unhappy evidence. The partition to which my incontinent belief belongs, then, must share countless be-liefs, including beliefs about my child, with the partition to which belong those features of my psychological economy in light of which that belief is incontinent.

It is worth pausing briefly to consider the relations that we might suppose mental partitions—whether these are regarded as fully-fledged agents, personalities, or agent-aspects or merely as divisions within agents—bear to one another. In a classic study of multiple personality, Morton Prince (1905) describes the personalities of Miss Beauchamp as standing in asymmetrical relations to one another. The relationship is discussed by Hilgard (1986, 31), who, following Prince, provides a diagram resembling figure 2. The arrows are in-tended to illustrate Prince's contention that while personality *C* en-joys access to the states of mind of both *A* and *B*, *A* has access only to *B*, and *B* persists in apparent ignorance of either *A* or *C* (see also Ludwig et al. 1972; Hilgard 1986, 33).

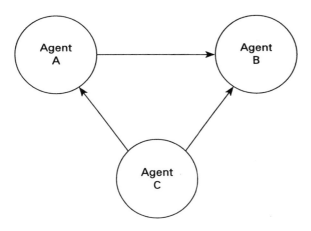

Figure 2
Multiple agents.

One difficulty with this way of representing mental divisions is that it ignores the fact that even in severe cases of dissociation, personalities or subagents may share states of mind. In the case of Miss Beauchamp, for instance, *C* seems not to be a mere spectator of the experiences of *A* and *B*, but to undergo those very experiences as well. More important, as suggested above, *A*, *B*, and *C* must have countless beliefs in common. *A*, *B*, and *C* share beliefs about and desires concerning particular people, landmarks, pets, and the weather. This, at least if we accept a modest holism, requires a shared background of belief, a framework to which individual beliefs owe their character. For this reason, among others, it would seem preferable to represent partitioned agents and some instances of multiple personality not as distinct nodes but as concentric spheres of influence (see figure 3). This is required, I think, if our accounts are to be intelligible.

4 Partitioning and Parsimony

Let us return now to Davidson's own deployment of mental partitioning. We have seen that the conception is in many ways an

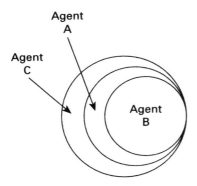

Figure 3
Multiple agents: concentric configuration.

attractive one. At the very least, it portends a striking solution to a notorious puzzle. What could entitle me to ascribe to you irrational states of mind? It would appear that evidence that you hold p and evidence that you hold not p could not add up to evidence that you hold both beliefs. Evidence for the one neutralizes evidence for the other and is itself simultaneously neutralized. How, then, could I ever be warranted in taking you to harbor inconsistent beliefs? Similarly, whatever entitled me to imagine that your behavior is uncoerced and deliberate would thereby be evidence that you have acted in accord with an all-things-considered better judgment. What, then, could lead me to describe you as acting acratically, acting without compulsion and against your considered better judgment?

Partitioning respects the demands of charity and at the same time preserves the possibility of genuinely irrational thought and action. The point may be appreciated by considering a two-person analogue. Imagine that I withhold evidence from you because I have an interest in your forming a belief that I recognize is defeated by my evidence. Should you then form the belief, you may do so perfectly reasonably. The belief is unwarranted relative to evidence that you and I together possess, but not in light of your evidence alone. In partitioning, this explanatory strategy is applied *intra*personally. Embarrassing evidence resides in a partition functionally isolated from that containing the awkward belief. As in the two-person case, the partitions are individually unremarkable but jointly at odds. Parti-

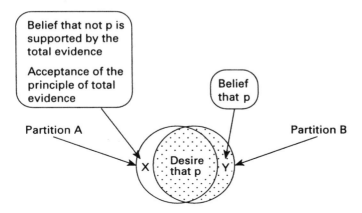

Figure 4
Irrational belief.

tioning thus provides us with a technique for describing agents in whom "a mental event [causes] another mental event without being a reason for it."[9]

Difficulties arise, however, when we attempt to move beyond the metaphor. As Davidson suggests in the passage just quoted, partitioning is to be invoked in instances in which some mental occurrence (my wanting my child to be innocent, for instance) is the cause of another mental occurrence (my believing that my child is innocent) for which it is not a reason. Thus, according to Davidson, because my wanting it to be the case that p is not evidence for p, it cannot be a reason for me to believe p. My believing p on the basis of such a want and in the absence of appropriate evidence, then, is apparently irrational.[10]

A model for one sort of irrational belief is set out in figure 4. In the diagram, Y represents my believing that p, and X includes my recognition that I ought, epistemically, not to believe that p, together with my acceptance of a principle authorizing belief only on the basis of sufficient evidence. X and Y fail to interact, and so reside in distinct partitions, A and B. This seems clear enough. It is less clear, however, what Davidson could have in mind in insisting that an irrational belief must be caused by a mental element that is not a reason for it. In our example, for instance, what element is supposed to

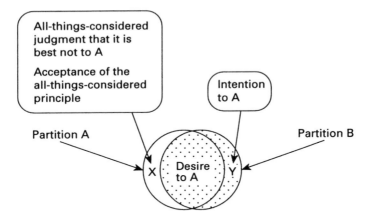

Figure 5
Irrational intention.

function as a cause that is not a reason? The desire that *p* seems an obvious candidate. Such a solution, however, fails to extend smoothly to other cases, and it appears likely that the answer is more complicated than the example suggests.

Consider a case of irrational *intention* (depicted in figure 5). I have a strong desire to insult Wayne, a student whom I have detected yawning surreptitiously as I lecture on Aristotle's theory of self-control. I judge that, all things considered, it would be better not to insult Wayne. Nevertheless, I succumb to my urge and heap abuse upon him. My acting as I do—intentionally but against my better judgment—is classically acratic.[11] Here, presumably, my desire to insult Wayne leads me to form the intention to insult him, and does so in a way that is unaffected by the force of my contrary all-things-considered better judgment.[12] How are we to invoke partitioning in this case? We need to locate a mental cause and a corresponding mental effect for which the cause is not a reason and use these somehow to plot a boundary.

The case differs importantly from one in which a belief is formed or held on the basis of wishful thinking. Thus, the relevant cause and effect pair cannot be my desire to insult Wayne and my forming an intention to carry out the insult. The desire is straightforwardly a reason for me to form the intention. Nor can the cause be my judging that, all things considered, I ought not to insult Wayne and the effect my intending to do so. It is my desire to insult Wayne, surely, not my all-things-considered judgment, that leads me to form the intention and act as I do. What is required is something rather more convoluted, I think. The cause of the irrational item, here an intention, cannot be a reason for it. A desire to A remains a reason to form the intention to A even when one judges it best not to A. Hence the desire to A cannot be the irrational cause. What is irrational, however, is my forming the intention to A on the basis of a desire to A *together with* my judging that, all things considered, I ought not to A, *and* my acceptance of the principle of continence: act always in accord with one's all-things-considered better judgment. The cause of my forming the intention to A, then, is my being in the complex state comprising all (or most) of what is included in partition A (X and the desire to A in figure 5).

If these observations are on the right track, it is now possible to make better sense of the case of incontinent belief modeled in figure 4. There the cause-that-is-not-a-reason for an irrational belief that p is the complex state encompassed by partition A. The belief that p is irrational, then, not solely in virtue of its being caused by a desire that p. The belief is caused by that desire together with the agent's acceptance of something like a principle of total evidence and his appreciation that, given his evidence, the principle does not permit the belief that p.

We have come a long way from the simple notion of partitioning with which we began. This, it might be thought, ought to raise suspicions. For all its apparent naturalness, Davidson's conception of partitioning, when pushed, may seem needlessly complicated. In any case, simpler, less cumbersome characterizations of the phenomena are available, characterizations that leave room for irrational thoughts and deeds within a framework broadly constrained by charity.

Consider again my epistemically ill-advised belief about the innocence of my child. The case was one in which I formed a certain belief in the teeth of the evidence and on the basis of a strong nonepistemic, prudential motive. Davidson considers an instance of this sort as one in which a mental cause (a cause that includes my wanting to believe in the innocence of my child) issues in a mental effect (my forming that belief) for which it is not a reason. This suggests that only evidential beliefs could count as reasons for holding other beliefs. But why should anyone think that?[13] There is a perfectly unexceptional sense in which my longing for the truth of a given proposition can give me a reason—a nonepistemic, prudential reason—for believing that proposition (see Heil 1983, 1992). I have argued already that it is the function of practical reason to sift through reasons for and against courses of action, a function that involves crediting reasons across normative boundaries. This is not to say that believing is, often anyway, the result of a decision; it is only to say that our psychological economy is such that considerations from disparate normative domains are bound to figure, even if only indirectly, in the determination of whatever we believe or do.

A view of this sort should not be taken as an endorsement of wishful thinking. We need only concede what is obvious anyway: epistemic norms can, on occasion, be reasonably usurped. Charity enjoins us to optimize rationality in ascribing states of mind to agents. But this need not mean that when it comes to the ascription of belief, we are to optimize only epistemic rationality. Self-serving attitudes make sense precisely because we can understand nonepistemic motives as providing agents with powerful reasons for holding particular beliefs, reasons that may finally out-muscle epistemic competitors.

Something like this can lead, on occasion perhaps, to a kind of mental bifurcation, as when we compartmentalize or frame doxastic territories (see Tversky and Kahneman 1981, Kahneman and Tversky 1983). Glenda, a molecular biologist, holds religious views on the basis of evidence that she would, in the context of her laboratory, regard as entirely specious. If these religious beliefs afford great comfort, Glenda could do so, it seems, reasonably. The possibility is intelligible, in part perhaps, because we conceive of Glenda's religious and scientific beliefs as occupying separate evidential spheres. Glenda fails to put these together, and of course she has strong prudential grounds for maintaining them apart just as she does. Imagine that Glenda holds a certain belief and does so partly on the basis of evidence that counts in favor of that belief. The belief affords nonepistemic, prudential advantage, perhaps by freeing her to pursue interests she would be unable to pursue otherwise. Moreover, Glenda finds it painful to scrutinize or evaluate evidence for the belief, and so does not. Here the causes of Glenda's believing what she does may be taken to be reasons for the belief, though not exclusively epistemic reasons. We render her intelligible without appeal to partitions.[14]

Everyday varieties of irrational action too seem not to require an appeal to mental partitions. Recall the acratic act previously discussed, my deliberately insulting Wayne, a mildly impertinent student, against my better judgment. In such cases it may simply be that a certain desire, here the desire to insult Wayne, enjoys motivational clout disproportionate to my evaluative assessment of it.[15] In judging what I have most reason to do, I assign the desire a relatively low evaluative ranking. Unfortunately, the desire manifests affective strength out of line with its evaluative standing, and as a result, I acquire an intention to insult Wayne and subsequently act on that intention. My action is irrational not because I fail to act on what is, in one obvious sense, my *strongest* desire but because I act against my considered better judgment, a better judgment that assigns a diminished ranking to that desire.

By distinguishing in this way between the motivational strength possessed by desires and their evaluative standing, we can account for a broad range of irrational actions without resorting to mental divisions. We can see how a recalcitrant desire could defeat a better judgment and induce action by means of the very mechanisms that ordinarily operate to make desires line up with better judgments. Similarly, forms of local dissociation in which evidence fails to take hold may be due to its failing to incorporate its epistemically prescribed weight. Were that so, the situation would be analogous to one in which I act against my better judgment, but on my strongest desire: items in my cognitive economy possess influence disproportional to their evaluative standing.

5   Concluding Remarks

Where does this leave us with respect to partitioning? First, we certainly must concede the conceptual importance of the notion of mental regions functionally circumscribed. The point of dividing the mind to explain particular sorts of irrationality and psychic malfunction is largely to maintain a measure of functional separation. This may be achieved by assigning elements to an unconscious realm. However, what is crucial for these elements is not that they persist outside of our awareness but that they fail to engage the rest of the system as they should. Functional detachment, then, is an important notion, one bound to have application in our understanding of psychodynamics.

Second, however, there is no reason to suppose that drawing mental boundaries is inevitably required to account for many familiar sorts of apparent irrationality. Acratic action and wishful thinking, for instance, are more straightforwardly explicable. Further, it seems likely that with a suitable account of the relation between practical and epistemic rationality, the need for appeals to distinct psychic regions would be further diminished. I have likened charity to parsimony. Both discourage the widespread application of the picture favored by Davidson. We need not, of course, abandon the idea that incontinent action, wishful thinking, and the like are to be seen as stemming from the operation of complex mental causes that fail, in one way or another, to warrant the beliefs, intentions, or actions they induce. Were this *all* there were to partitioning, we should find it untroubling. It is, however, worth bearing in mind Davidson's appeal to the two-person case as a metaphor for what he has in mind. We may (indeed, I have argued, we *ought* to) jettison the metaphor and the picture it encourages.

This is not to deny that we might be driven to something like partitioning in making sense of severely disordered agents, in some cases of multiple personality, for instance. In so doing, however, we are employing a rather more robust form of mental division, one that envisages a person as harboring separate and partially autonomous agencies—the original partitioning metaphor taken more or less literally. In other, less extreme nonpathological cases, however, partitioning seems merely to muddy the water.

Notes

This paper develops ideas originally discussed in Heil 1989 and 1992. I am indebted to my colleague Alfred Mele for much helpful discussion and to Stephen Braude and the editors of this volume for comments on earlier drafts.

1. I am not suggesting that irrationality of whatever sort might not come in degrees, or that there could not be borderline cases, only that an adequate understanding of all the phenomena may require that we employ different, even incompatible, models.

2. Popular fascination with the possibility of multiple personality may stem largely from *The Three Faces of Eve* (Thigpen and Cleckley 1957) and from the movie inspired by that book. Interest in the topic, however, antedates the twentieth century (see, e.g., Hogg 1969). The philosophical dimensions of multiple personality are discussed usefully and at length in Braude 1991.

3. It is important to distinguish different cases: (1) an agent s holds p and s holds not p; (2) s holds p and not p; (3) s holds p and s does not hold p. Case (3) is logically impossible (though see Rorty 1972, 393–394), and case 2 is not obviously possible. That leaves case 1, that in which an agent apparently holds inconsistent beliefs, as the interesting case.

4. Practical norms are in this sense to be distinguished from deliberative principles ("consider available options," "examine alternatives carefully," and the like).

5. For a useful catalog, see the introduction to Elster 1986.

6. On charity, see Quine 1960, 59; Davidson 1980, 221. A fascinating real-world application of charity can be found in Chadwick 1958.

7. See Davidson 1982, 1986; see also Pears 1984, chap. 5. A penetrating critique of Davidson's and Pears's conception, one to which this chapter owes much, can be found in Mele 1987, chaps. 6 and 10.

8. David Pears is less inhibited (see Pears 1984, 87).

9. Davidson 1982, 300. I should note that partitioning is intended to account both for cases in which what ought to cause some mental effect does not do so and for cases in which what ought not to cause some mental effect does.

10. Or at least it is irrational given that I hold the principle that I ought to believe only what best fits my evidence, a principle that comes close to being constitutive of doxastic agenthood. See Davidson 1982, 298, and 1986, 84, 91.

11. See "How Is Weakness of the Will Possible?" in Davidson 1980, and also see Mele 1987, chaps. 2 and 3.

12. The intention I form may be unaffected by my considered better judgment or merely moderated by it. Thus, while not preventing me from issuing the insult, my better judgment might at least result in my issuing a milder insult than I would otherwise have done. I owe this observation to Alfred Mele.

13. Davidson at one time endorsed such a conception: "The wish to have a belief is not evidence for the truth of the belief, *nor does it give it rational support in any other way*" (1982, 298; emphasis mine). More recently, however, he has distinguished "between having a reason to be a believer in a certain proposition, and having evidence in the light of which it is reasonable to think the proposition true" (1986, 85).

14. Edward McClennen has argued that we have powerful incentives to occupy certain "perspectives" in the evaluation of prospects. McClennen rejects "separability," the idea, roughly, that reasonable choices necessarily reflect the agent's perspective at the time of the choice (see, e.g., McClennen 1992). If this is right, then deliberative mechanisms that adjust the relative salience of options might prove adaptive. Once in place, of course, such mechanisms can be exploited in a variety of ways, and lead to a variety of suboptimal ends.

15. The account of acratic action and belief alluded to here is defended in detail in Mele 1987. See also Heil 1984.

References

Braude, S. 1991. *First Person Plural: Multiple Personality and the Philosophy of Mind.* London: Routledge.

Chadwick, J. 1958. *The Decipherment of Linear B.* Cambridge: Cambridge University Press.

Davidson, D. 1980. *Essays on Actions and Events.* Oxford: Clarendon Press.

Davidson, D. 1982. "Paradoxes of Irrationality." In Wollheim and Hopkins 1982, 289–305.

Davidson, D. 1986. "Deception and Division." In Elster 1986, 79–92.

Elster, J., ed. 1986. *The Multiple Self.* Cambridge: Cambridge University Press.

Heil, J. 1983. "Believing What One Ought." *Journal of Philosophy* 80:752–765.

Heil, J. 1984. "Doxastic Incontinence." *Mind* 93:56–70.

Heil, J. 1986. "Does Psychology Presuppose Rationality?" *Journal for the Theory of Social Behaviour* 16:77–87.

Heil, J. 1989. "Minds Divided." *Mind* 98:571–583.

Heil, J. 1992. "Believing Reasonably." *Noûs* 26:47–62.

Hilgard, E. 1986. *Divided Consciousness: Multiple Controls in Human Thought and Action,* expanded ed. New York: John Wiley and Sons.

Hogg, J. 1969. *The Private Memoirs and Confessions of a Justified Sinner.* Oxford: Oxford University Press. First published in 1824.

Kahneman, D., and A. Tversky. 1983. "Choices, Values, and Frames." *American Psychologist* 39:341–350.

Ludwig, A., J. Brandsma, C. Wilber, F. Bendfeldt, and D. Jameson. 1972. "The Objective Study of a Multiple Personality, or Are Four Heads Better Than One?" *Archives of General Psychiatry* 26:298–310.

McClennen, E. 1992. "The Theory of Rationality for Ideal Games." *Philosophical Studies* 65:193–215.

Mele, A. 1987. *Irrationality.* New York: Oxford University Press.

Pears, D. 1984. *Motivated Irrationality.* Oxford: Clarendon Press.

Prince, M. 1905. *The Dissociation of a Personality.* New York: Longmans, Green, and Co.

Quine, W. 1960. *Word and Object.* Cambridge: MIT Press.

Rorty, A. 1972. "Belief and Self-Deception." *Inquiry* 15:387–410.

Rorty, A. 1988. "The Deceptive Self: Liars, Layers, and Lairs." In *Mind in Action: Essays in the Philosophy of Mind,* pp. 212–228. Boston: Beacon Press.

Thigpen, C., and H. Cleckley. 1957. *The Three Faces of Eve.* New York: McGraw-Hill.

Tversky, A., and D. Kahneman. 1981. "The Framing of Decisions and the Psychology of Choice." *Science* 211:453–458.

Wollheim, R., and J. Hopkins, eds. 1982. *Philosophical Essays on Freud.* Cambridge: Cambridge University Press.

Multiple Identity, Character Transformation, and Self-Reclamation

Owen Flanagan

1   Multiple Identity and Multiplex Identity

Consider the following propositions:

Proposition 1   We abide by a "one self to a customer" rule (Dennett 1989). Normally, each body houses one person, one self. Having one and only one self is normative for us.

Proposition 2   But identity is scalar. It admits of degrees. Our conception of personal sameness allows for change and transformation. Indeed, our norms of personal and moral development require that the self changes.

Propositions 1 and 2 might seem to conflict. We want each individual to have one and only one self. But we want this self to be malleable enough to undergo even radical changes. We want the self to maintain its identity over the course of a life, and yet we want and expect the self to become complex and multifaceted, and to change, modify, and adjust itself, sometimes radically, over this course.

The prima facie conflict or tension between these two propositions can be reduced by accepting a third proposition:

Proposition 3   The conditions governing personal sameness require not strict identity or absolute sameness but rather that certain relations of psychological continuity and connectedness obtain. We require that there be *narrative connectedness* from the first-person point of view, that I be able to tell some sort of coherent story about my life.

In addition, we expect the following to hold:

Proposition 4 The narrative connectedness that obtains is caused in part by active *authorial work* on the agent's part: by working at integration[1] and working at making one's plans and projects materialize.[2]

The overall idea is to think of personal identity as a scalar relation of psychological continuity and connectedness caused in part by the agent's own activity in light of his plans and visions for his own development. Thinking about identity in terms of agency makes sense of future concern, and thus of self-adjustment, reclamation, transformation, and the like. It allows the possibility that I may participate authorially in the creation of a changed person to whom I am nonetheless narratively connected at each point in the reclamation or transformation project.[3]

Augustine's *Confessions* is an autobiography. It is the story of single self. This is established in part because Augustine is able to produce an account that narratively links up the multifarious episodes of his life from the first-person point of view. What events he remembers are *all* events in *his* life, and the changes he undergoes from philanderer to Bishop of Hippo are changes that involve, at each point, deployment of his own developing sense of the kind of person he wants to be. Augustine is often thought to be atypical because his transformation was so radical. And indeed it was. But Augustine is typical because his character is complex and his plans, projects, and desires are multifarious—and they are, to a certain extent, in tension with one another both synchronically and diachronically.

I will refer to a single self that is like this as a *multiplex self*. Normal selves are multiplex. When a single individual experiences herself or expresses her being with different narrators who cannot grasp the connection between or among the narratives or narrative segments, the individual is a *multiple*.

Individuals with multiple personality disorder (MPD) present multiple narrators, multiple selves. These different selves sometimes display different allergies and immunological reactions and have different visual acuity! True believers in MPD think the multiple narrators reflect multiple, functionally and qualitatively distinct selves inside a single body. Skeptics about MPD see suggestible individuals who are capable of mimicking various socially available personas. It seems to me that in either case—whether the individual really experiences what it is like to be each self she displays or is merely adept at simulating or feigning multiplicity—there is a problem there. I'm not going to try to resolve the thorny question of exactly in what sense multiplicity exists. I assume only that there are cases in which persons actually become different selves in the sense that there is something it is like for them to be the different selves they display, *or* that there are cases in which individuals feign or mimic alternative selves while under some sort of delusion or misapprehension that they are, in some sense, the self they mimic. Perhaps both kinds of multiplicity exist. It is interesting that the titles of the two newsletters written by MPD patients, "Speaking for Ourselves" and its successor "Many Voices," display, one might say, a certain ambivalence over whether to tie speaking in different tongues to bona fide different selves or merely to represent the phenomenon as involving speaking in different tongues.

I focus on MPD cases because of their special vivacity. But I want it to be clear at the start that I think that MPD cases represent only one of the ways in which the process of identity formation, development, and maintenance can go awry. My aim is to see how the idea of the self as a narrative construct can shed light on multiplicity and the process of transformation from a multiple to a multiplex self, and conversely, to use the phenomena of multiplicity to help us think more clearly about ordinary multiplex selfhood and identity. It might be thought to be a bad idea to try to analyze and refine two obscure notions in tandem. But for better or worse, that is my strategy. Whether illumination results is for the reader to judge.

2 Narrative Self-Representation

Many thinkers have converged on the insight that a narrative conception of self is the "essential genre" of self-representation (Bruner 1983, 1986; Dennett 1988, 1989; Kermode 1967; MacIntyre 1981). One useful way of conceiving of the self is just a kind of structured life, structured in part by its temporal components—its beginning, middle, and ending—and by the relations among the various characters who figure in our lives.[4]

Although personal identity proper can be grounded in the thinnest thread of biological or psychological continuity, the sort of connectedness that constitutes a normatively acceptable self or life is the sort that makes for a contentful story that involves an unfolding rationale for the shape it takes.

Why is narrative structure natural? Several reasons come to mind. First, human life in fact has the property of being lived in time. Second, our memories are powerful. We possess the capacity to appropriate our distant past and draw it into the present. Life and consciousness can be as streamlike as you want, but if memory is weak, if the present thought is not powerfully "appropriative" of what has gone before, then no narrative can be constructed. There is simply the here and now. Third, as beings in time, we are navigators. We care how our lives go. Successful concern requires attentiveness to the long term. We look toward the future, attentively both planning insignificant things and making monumental life plans, and we do so with a grasp of our present beliefs and desires and a grasp of who we are, given our past (Bratman 1987). Fourth, we are social beings. We live in society and in predictable and unpredictable interaction with other people. Characters abound to fill out the complex story of our lives. Fifth, because the story of any individual life is constituted by and embedded in some larger meaning-giving structure and because it is only in terms of this larger structure that a life gains whatever rationale it has for unfolding in the way it does, a life is illuminated, both for the person who lives it and for others, by seeing it against the background of this larger structure.

Although numerous characters appear in our life stories, each of us has but one character that constitutes his self. With narrative selves the basic principle is, as I have said, "one to a customer." Multiple chapters, novel twists and turns, even radical self-transformations are allowed. But these have to be part of the life of a single self. A self can change, but the changes, we prefer, should make sense. I need to understand your conversion from a hedonist to an ascetic Buddhist in a way that locates *you* both before and after the conversion. In those rare cases where this is not possible, we say that some individual is no longer the same person. From the insider's and outsider's point of view, different judgments may be rendered about narrative flow and personal sameness. Despite my judgment that you are no longer *you*, you may well judge otherwise and see your radical transformation as part of the perfectly coherent narrative of your life.

Oneness reigns when it comes to selves. It makes sense to have one and only one inner persona, given the complexities of rationally guiding action in a complex and ever-changing social world (Dennett 1989, 171). Severe amnesiacs have less than one full self, whereas persons suffering from multiple personality disorder (MPD) have too many selves. Normally, persons suffering from MPD can represent the self that is in the driver's seat. Since they are wholly or partly amnesic of other personalities they house, they cannot represent these selves until they, so to speak, become them.[5] The sort of self that severe amnesiacs have too little of and MPD patients have too many of is the self that is "the center of narrative gravity" (Dennett 1988).

We narratively represent our selves in part in order to answer certain questions of identity. It is useful to distinguish two different aims of self-representation that in the end are deeply intertwined. First, there is self-representation for the sake of self-understanding. This is the story we tell ourselves to understand ourselves for who we are. The ideal here is convergence between self-representation and an acceptable version of the story of our actual identity. Second, there is self-representing for public dissemination, whose aim is underwriting successful social interaction. The two are closely connected. Indeed, the strategic requirements of the sort of self-representation needed for social interaction, together with our tendencies to seek congruence, explain how self-representation intended in the first instance for "my eyes only," and thus, one might think, more likely to remain true, could start to conform to a false projected social image of the self, to a deeply fictional and farfetched account of the self.

Self-represented identity, when it gets things right, has actual identity (or some aspect of it) as its cognitive object. Because representing the self is an activity internal to a complex but single system, it does not leave things unchanged. The activity of self-representation is partly constitutive of actual identity. This is true in two senses. First, even considered as a purely cognitive activity, self-representation involves the activation of certain mental representations and cognitive structures. Once self-representation becomes an ongoing activity, it realigns and recasts the representations and structures already in place. Second, the self as represented has motivational bearing and behavioral effects. Often this motivational bearing is congruent with motivational tendencies that the entire system already has. In such cases, placing one's conception of the self into the motivational circuits enables certain gains in ongoing conscious control and in the fine-tuning of action. Sometimes, especially in cases of severe self-deception, the self projected for both public and first-person consumption may be strangely and transparently out of kilter with what the agent is like. In such cases, the self as represented is linked with the activity of self-representation but with little else in the person's psychological and behavioral economy. Nonetheless, such misguided self-representation helps constitute, for reasons I have suggested, the misguided person's actual full identity.

One further point is worth emphasizing. Although self-represented identity is identity from the subjective point of view, it invariably draws on available theoretical models about the nature of the self in framing its reflexive self-portrait. We represent ourselves by way of various publicly available hermeneutic strategies. Psychoanalytically inspired self-description is most familiar in our culture. But genetic and neurobiological models are increasingly visible in the self-understandings of ordinary people. When multiples (MPD patients) present alters, they invariably present themselves as characters from the historical and contemporary stock of characters known about by persons in their culture.

3 The Center of Narrative Gravity: Emergence and Development

The self that is "the center of narrative gravity" (Dennett 1988)—the self that answers questions about who a person is, what he aims at, and what he cares about—is a complex construct. It is both expressed and created in the process of self-representation. The self in this sense, what I call "self-represented identity," is a causally efficacious part of the whole system, and it affects both the cognitive content and the qualitative character of new experiences. The causal efficacy of a representation of the self is fairly obvious when a person is actively engaged in self-representing. It is also plausible to think that once a complex model of the self has been constructed and is in place, it exists as a complex dispositional structure in the brain and is often involved in structuring experience, albeit unconsciously. That is, the causal efficacy of the self model is compatible with its making only infrequent and partial appearances in consciousness and with its having differential effects in different situations from behind the phenomenological scenes.

The construction of a self begins in earliest childhood as parents try to shape the emerging character of the charges they love. Since we abide the "one self per customer" rule, we try to assist the child in building an integrated self that comprehends basic social norms and is equipped with a system of beliefs, desires, and values that will help it to live successfully and well. The "one self to a customer" principle is not just an arbitrary social construction. Productive relations with a single body favor minimal cognitive dissonance and maximal integration at the level of conscious thought and action guidance (although harmony at the top may well belie all sorts of disagreement and competition among lower-level processors).[6]

In both normal and abnormal cases, the process of constructing the self starts in interaction with elders, and it begins well before the child uses language. There is some evidence that the child, if given social interaction, may be innately disposed to develop a theory of mind, a theory of its own mind and those of others, a theory primed by evolution to frame the self and other selves as single integrated intentional systems (Wellman 1990). The parents provide models for constructing the self in what they do and say and in how they express their own formed beings. Increasingly, as time proceeds and especially with the development of speech, the child engages her parents with her own emerging self as *agent* and modifies their attempts to shape her. With language, time, maturity, and elaborate and multifarious interactions with others, there emerges the self, a relatively autonomous and integrated self.

The construction and maintenance of the self involves many players. Whether I know it or not, "others made me, and in various ways continue to make me the person I am" (Sandel 1982, 143). Our selves are multiply authored. Lest this sound too deflationary, it is important to emphasize that normally we are one of the main authors of our identity. Once our character is well formed and we have a good grasp of it, our powers of self-authorship increase dramatically. We gain the power to guide our life more self-consciously in terms of our model of who we are and who we want to become. We modify and adjust our self-conception unconsciously and effortlessly in response to social feedback, as well as consciously, with effort, and with mixed success in response to our judgment of fit between who we are and who we aspire to be.

Coming eventually to consciously grasp one's self does not require—at least in the early stages—that there already is a full-blown self in place. There is wide agreement among psychologists and philosophers who have thought carefully about identity formation that it proceeds largely unconsciously and that many aspects of identity never come into view for the agent who has that identity (Erikson 1968; Kagan 1984, 1989; Sandel 1982; Stern 1985; Taylor 1989).[7]

The main point is that selves are just like most other things. They are complex effects that do not in any way precede their causes. They don't need to. They emerge naturally in complex interactions with the world and other persons. And they acquire autonomy and increased causal efficacy as they develop, mature, and come to constitute character and personality.

Self-represented identity is emblematic. Multiplex selves in complex environments display different parts of their narrative to different audiences. Different selves—my philosopher self, my baseball-coach self, my religious self, my parental self—are played for different audiences. Different audiences see who we are differently. Different selves surface in different interpersonal ecological niches. Displaying a self and getting my audience (or myself) to posit one or the other as my center of narrative gravity is, in a sense, to produce a sort of illusion, since to me, in the first personal, my different selves are part of an integrated and unified narrative that contains, as proper parts, the different selves that I sometimes display in isolation. What distinguishes a multiplex self from a multiple self is, first and foremost, the fact that a multiplex self is not amnesic with respect to these selves, they permeate each other in ways the selves of multiples typically do not. Furthermore, I draw my selves together, through the force of narrative gravity, and I comprehend my self in terms of a single, centered narrative in which they all fit together (but not without tension, various confusions, and much second-guessing). Taken together and consciously interwoven, they give my life what I take to be its unique qualitative character.[8]

The self is an extremely complex construct. Indeed, it is multiplex. Different portions or aspects of the self are played in different environments. Nonetheless, there are pressures to coordinate and bring into reflective equilibrium the different ways of conceiving the self. I will speak, therefore, of the *self model* to refer to the highest-order model of the self that contains the various components of the self as proper parts or aspects. We can think of the self model as a construct that draws functional distinctions among various roles, characteristics, and personas, but recognizes these as part of one self and experiences the self as a qualitative whole. Thinking of the self model as involving recognition of functionally distinct aspects of a qualitatively integrated self allows us to think of the self model as a complex construct without advancing the dubious idea of true proliferation of the self. The effects of different *aspects* of the self can explain everything that several different selves can explain without undermining the phenomenological sense of coherence of the self that most people experience. Most people, but not people with MPD perhaps, experience qualitative wholeness of being across time.

The person for whom my narrative self plays is I, a whole conna-tively rich information-processing system from which the narrative self emerges and for which it plays a crucial role. Often I express and grasp snatches of my narrative self and utilize these representations in monitoring and guiding my life. This way of thinking about our reflexive powers makes matters fairly unmysterious. I am a system constituted in part by a certain narrative conception of self. Sometimes I hold that conception in view as I think about things. I, being more than my narrative self, can comprehend it, utilize it, and, in concert with outside forces, adjust it. What am I? This organism. This thinking thing.

4   The Fictional and Nonfictional Self

I have suggested that the self is constructed. Dennett is committed to the stronger thesis that the self that is the center of narrative gravity is a fiction, a useful fiction, but a fiction nonetheless. "Centres of gravity" are "fictional objects . . . [that] have only the properties that the theory that constitutes them endowed them with" (1988, 1016). The idea that the self is a fiction is, in part, a way of expressing the fact that it is, for the reasons given, a construction. Mother Nature does not give us a robust self. She starts us off caring about homeostasis, and she equips us with the equipment to distinguish "me" from "not me." But she hardly wires in a personality or an identity. Identity is the joint production of many sources, including one's own evolving self.

To conceive of the self as a fiction seems right for four reasons: it is an open-ended construction; it is filled with vast indeterminate spaces, and a host of tentative hypotheses about what I am like, that can be filled out and revised post facto; it is pinned on culturally relative narrative hooks; and it expresses ideals of what one wishes to be but is not yet.

But there are two important respects in which the analogy of the self with a piece of fiction is misleading. First, there is the issue of constraints. The author of a true piece of fiction has many more degrees of freedom in creating her characters than we have in spinning the tale of our selves. Despite the indeterminacies operative in construction of the self and despite the fact that different narrative emphases will be reinforced in different communities, there are more firm and visible epistemic constraints in construction of the self than in ordinary construction of fiction. There are, after all, the things we have done, what we have been through as embodied beings, and the characteristic dispositions we reveal in social life. Third parties will catch us if we take our story too far afield. We may also catch ourselves. There are selection pressures to keep the story that one reveals to oneself and to others in some sort of harmony with the way one is living one's life.

Second, some people, of course, are massively self-deceived. Self-deception only makes sense if selves are not totally fictive, that is, only if there are some facts constraining what is permitted in our self narrative. So real selves are fictional to a point. But they are less fictional than fictional selves because they are more answerable to the facts. The self can be a construct or model, a "center of narrative gravity," a way of self-representation, without being a fiction in the problematic sense. Biographies and autobiographies are constructs. But if they are good biographies or autobiographies, they are non-fictional or only semifictional. For Dennett (1989), there are, it seems, only normal fictive selves and invasive fictive selves, such as those suggested by abusive caretakers who posit imaginary selves for the abused child. One father gave his daughter biblical names, displaying at once his anti-Semitism and his need to sanctify his great sinfulness. Not surprisingly, this sort of abuse is sometimes causally effective in giving multiplicity a foothold. That said, there is considerable and increasing controversy, as yet empirically unresolved, over the degree to which MPD depends on actual abuse (see Ganaway 1989).

The distinction between fictive and nonfictive selves is important, but its application in the case of multiples is exceedingly tricky. On one plausible interpretation, multiples qualitatively feel, and therefore first-personally are, the self they narratively posit, for the time of the posit. Whether the posited self is real or fictive depends, among other things, on whether the narratively posited self has the features and has done the deeds that the narrator claims, and on whether third parties recognize the posited self as having historical standing from the objective point of view. Alters on equal qualitative footing from the first-person point of view will not have equal status from the third-person point of view. Not surprisingly, the differences between first- and third-person judgments about the realism and the historical validity of various alters will determine the direction of therapy.

5 Unmaking Multiplicity

We are in a better position now to address directly the issue of how modification of the self might work, even in extreme cases where there are several or many selves in one individual. One thing we have seen so far is that we needn't frame the task as one of how a multiple can regain unity, since in a certain sense no one is a unity. Selves, even very normal selves, are multiplex. The project is to move from multiplicity to mutiplexity. Multiplex selves live lives that are continuous, connected, functionally coherent, and qualitatively more or less homogeneous. Multiplex selves are integrated.[9] Or to put it another way, even if a multiplex person is perceived as unintegrated by some third-party norms, he is integrated if he is in control of his own mode of organization or disorganization. Individuals with MPD are unintegrated, despite there being a certain amount of integration within each alter: "Alters who claim (and appear) to be aware of another alter's mental states and actions, typically refer to them as 'his' or 'hers,' not as 'mine'" (Braude 1991, 71). Furthermore, there is no center of control.

How might a multiple become whole again? There are two senses of wholeness that seem relevant. The first is the multiple becomes whole in the sense of reexperiencing himself or herself as a single qualitatively integrated self, as a single qualitatively integrated center of narrative gravity. The second is that the multiple becomes whole in the sense of having something like a complete personality. The notion of a complete personality is a normative concept, and it can be satisfied in multitudinous ways.

The overall idea is that the individual experience himself or herself as whole in the first sense and, in addition, that his or her personality display the kind of fullness or completeness that we deem necessary for attributing a full *character* in the second, normative sense.

The question of how a multiple might become whole *again* makes sense for the first sense of wholeness, for multiples presumably once experienced themselves as single centers of self-consciousness and were once single centers. Indeed, even as multiples, they often experience wholeness of being in this sense. The trouble is that they experience themselves as qualitatively distinct centers of self-consciousness at different times. The aim, then, is to have the multiple regain the sense of a single center of self that is the same center over time. Third parties definitely prefer that persons they deal with be whole in this first sense. Multiples, once multiplex, prefer it as well.[10]

The question of how a multiple might become whole *again* makes less sense for the second sense of wholeness, character wholeness or personality wholeness. This is because multiples often begin to dissociate at a very early age. They were never whole or complete in the normative sense of having achieved a stable, mature, full character.

This last point suggests that if a multiple becomes whole *again*, it cannot usually involve becoming who he or she "really" is or was beneath or behind the multiplicity of selves he or she displays. This is because there is no self he or she "really" is or was before multiplicity took hold. This suggests that thinking of self-reclamation in any literal sense may be misleading, since it suggests getting back again what one once was or had.

To explain this point and extend reflection on the transformation from multiplicity to multiplexity, it will be useful to say a little more about the etiology and progression of multiplicity. According to the philosopher Stephen E. Braude,

Multiple personality has two main causal determinants. The first is the capacity for profound dissociation; in fact MPD patients tend to be highly hypnotizable. The second is a history of (usually severe and chronic) childhood trauma—typically, a combination of emotional, physical, and sexual abuse. The significance of high hypnotizability (in this case, really, *self*-hypnotizability) is that MPD patients have a coping mechanism at their disposal not available to victims of abuse or trauma who do not become multiples. To put it roughly, through dissociation the subject is able to avoid experiencing or dealing with an intolerable episode by turning it over to an alternate personality (or *alter*) who undergoes those experiences in his place. (1991, 39) [11]

Modern multiples average between six and sixteen personalities. One author reported a patient with 4,500 alters. Not surprisingly, the proliferation of alters appears to give them a certain ghostly shape. So Braude writes that many alters "are perhaps better described as personality *fragments*, since their functions tend to be highly circumscribed, and because they do not exhibit the more extensive range of traits and dispositions found in more personality-like alters" (1991, 41). But clinicians agree that even the more "personality-like alters" are "two-dimensional compared to normal persons, even a very young child" (Braude 1991, 59).

It is not at all surprising that a person with powers to do so might create an alter to fend off the pain of abuse and the recognition that someone he or she loves is an abuser. But it is obscure why there is so often proliferation beyond one alter. One hypothesis is that proliferation is a complex effect of therapeutic suggestion, involving the therapist's belief in multiplicity and his conveying to the patient the possibility of fitting the description (indeed, a savvy patient may well know that multiplicity is a genuine and increasingly popular way to be damaged or express damage). This is why one leading worker in the field thinks that MPD is "grossly overdiagnosed [especially among females] . . . and is heavily dependent upon cultural influences for both its emergence and its diagnosis" (Aldridge-Morris 1989, 4). Aldridge-Morris recommends that one "should only diagnose multiple personality when there is corroborative evidence that complex and integrated alter egos, with amnesiac barriers, existed prior to therapy and emerge without hypnotic intervention by clinicians" (1989, 109). Braude is less skeptical about the existence of MPD, but he is skeptical about determining the exact nature and character of the predissociative self and of there being some determinate number and types of personalities a given MPD patient has even if they have not, so to speak, shown themselves yet. "It is far more reasonable to maintain that a multiple's array of alters *at any time* represents merely one of many possible dissociative solutions to contingent problems in living" (1991, 127). The philosopher Ian Hacking thinks that "many, or most, but not all, of the panoply of alters, up to 100 in number, are a product of a therapy" (1991, 860). Hacking rejects the idea that the "entire array of alters is a real part of the patient's structure of personalities." And he thinks that there is no answer to the question of how many alters a multiple has before he or she displays them. Multiplicity is potentiality. How many and what type of multiplicity develops depends on the nature of the therapy, the cultural availability of alter types, the patient's knowledge of these types, individual capacities to dissociate, and so on. Just as it is neither true nor false that there is a good lacrosse player inside me now (I've never played), even if, after trying lacrosse, I become good at it, so too it is neither true nor false that some multiple has at time t_1 the alters that he or she displays for the first time at t_2.

In any case, there is considerable and increasing controversy, as yet empirically unresolved, over the degree to which MPD depends on actual abuse (Ganaway 1989), on therapeutic suggestion, or on an individual's knowledge of the possibility of adopting this form of sickness or defense and their powerful abilities to self-hypnotize (Aldridge-Morris 1989, Braude 1991). Commitment to both the reality of MPD and the assessment of it as a pathological solution to problems of living are compatible with a certain agnosticism about its exact causes. What seems fairly clear is that some cases of MPD are caused by actual abuse.

The question arises, When a person who has had his or her identity mutilated during personality formation, who has been so deflected in the normal project of finding or maintaining a unified personality, tries to gain unity or tries to transform herself, *toward which self, old or new, is he or she trying to transform himself or herself?* And if he or she is a multiple, which self, if any, orchestrates the change? To answer this question, we need to clarify the nature of what, in the literature, is called the *host* personality or the *primary* personality, since one obvious thought is that the host orchestrates the change.

Indeed, until very recently it was thought that the project of therapy with multiples involved reintegrating the alters with the host. One trouble with conceptualizing things in this way is that the host is usually a very emotionally flat self, and many of the alters have characteristics that one should not much want. The integration of a host with all its alters gets you a radically transformed but more or less unified personality. However, it also gets you a limited self, normatively speaking. Remember, the host is at best a very damaged root system, and the alters are all creations to maintain damage control in a radically unhealthy environment. Furthermore, even if such a reintegrated self has resources to go on, that is, even if the victim, once reintegrated, possesses the agentic capacities to try to make a better life for herself, these resources are, for the same reasons, likely to be very poorly developed and malformed. To be sure, such persons can be helped. But we would be less than honest if we denied that in many such cases the damage is both real and irremedial.

Another trouble Braude puts as follows:

One striking feature of the recent literature on MPD is that one sees almost no references to *primary* personalities. By contrast, around the turn of the century it was commonplace to refer to alters as either primary or secondary. There seem to be two main reasons for the current reluctance to designate an alter as primary. First, within the personality system discovered by the clinician, there may be no personality whose *role* within the system is primary in any deep way. . . . One might think that the *presenting* personality should be considered primary. But that alter often turns out to be relatively recent and fairly peripheral in the multiple's total system of alters. Similarly, there might be an alter who acts as *host* for the others, or who initially shows his or her face to the world before yielding to alters awaiting their appropriate times to emerge. And there might be alters who—for a time, at least—dominate the multiple's life. But host personalities might serve no vital function other than serving as 'masters of ceremonies' (so to speak), and both they and dominant personalities generally may be replaced by others who dominate for a while or act as host. (Braude 1991, 56)

Traditionally, the term "primary personality" referred to the personality that had historical primacy, the one that was there before multiplicity took over. The trouble with this way of conceptualizing things is that although there was normally some single center of self-consciousness prior to multiplicity, there is no basis, for the reasons just given, to think that there was anything like a complete personality in place prior to multiplicity. If all splitting took place in late adolescence or adulthood, then it would be possible that there was. But because dissociation typically begins in childhood, there is no reason to think that there is usually a bona fide personality in place that was historically primary and might be regained or, what is different, is worth regaining.

Indeed, there is little justification for regarding any active personality as the historically primary one, even if we presume that there was a complete personality in place prior to becoming a multiple. This is because, even when there was some single, historically memorable character in place prior to multiplicity, "rarely (if ever) does an alter seem to be *that* personality, or any clear evolution or descendant of that personality" (Braude 1991, 57).

The principle reason for this has to do with the functional specificity of alternate personalities and a pair of related phenomena called *attribute distribution* and *attribute depletion*. In general, clinicians believe that as alters are created to deal with quite specific traumas, the traits and abilities manifested by or latent in the predissociative personality begin to get distributed throughout the members of the personality system. Moreover, as alters proliferate, they apparently become increasingly specialized, and one is less likely to find any personality having the complexity or range of functions that might have been (but usually were not) possessed by the subject prior to the onset of splitting or that have the shape of a whole self.

How might a person overcome the damage to her identity after suffering from physical or sexual abuse as a child and developing an identity scarred by this abuse and taking the defensive route of multiplicity? One image is this: The abused person consciously accepts that these awful things have happened to her, have ruined her self-esteem, have made her identify with certain unworthy values and characteristics of her abusers, and have, in engendering multiplicity, created massive identity confusion in her. Armed with this recognition, she simply decides—by executive fiat, as it were—to move on, to reclaim her "real self" or make a "new" self, and to allow the scarred and mutilated self or selves to pass into oblivion.

But this view is much too Panglossian. First, there is the problem of finding a self with the power to set out and execute such orders. Second, there is the problem mentioned earlier with the idea of reclaiming a "real self." Besides the problem of attribute depletion and distribution and problems with the ideas of a host or primary personality that is most "real," there is also the problem that if one accepts that a self is a center of narrative gravity, then a multiple has to engage in the project of *self dissolution*. Since self dissolution is a bad and dangerous project in normal cases, it is hard to see why it wouldn't constitute yet another form of damage to a multiple to have to undermine and dissociate from selves she has come to identify with to various degrees.

Perhaps this is why the standard way of thinking about curing multiplicity is framed as involving *integration* or *reintegration*, although for reasons we have seen, the picture cannot be one of drawing all the dissociated selves back into the single narrative center of some host self (except in a sense to be explained shortly) or into some historically primary self. Furthermore, since alter selves often possess conflicting traits, desires, and values, hate each other, and so on, they cannot simply be reunited—at least not without undergoing constitutional changes, allowing various successions, and reaching certain peace treaties.

There is another reason that the aim of therapy or integration or reclamation of self cannot involve bringing into a single unified center of narrative gravity the "lives" lived by each alter. This is because some, indeed many, of these lives are utter confabulations, involving confabulated persons with confabulated lives. For example, many multiples typically become good at telling what they have been up too since their last appearance as a narrative center. But to lay claim to frequent visits to Disneyland and to consorting with Madonna, because that is what one of my alters says he has been doing while not making appearances, is to allow my unified narrative to be guided too much by the shape of other narratives that are perhaps, in some sense notionally lived but are, in large measure, fictive.

We want the eventual integrated center of narrative gravity of a multiple to seek convergence with his or her actual full identity. This will require recognition of what it felt like to be the various alters and of what the alters did and thought they did. But it will not, indeed it should not, involve appropriating the memories of all the alters as true memories. Among other things, there will be chaos and too many overlapping, incompatible events if this is allowed. Nor can the move from multiple to multiplex personhood involve retaining the autonomous feel of each alter if there really is to be a return to a single narrative center. This, I admit, is a thorny issue. I am not saying that a multiple should remember *all* that he or she thinks he or she was and did as each alter and disclaim what he or she did not do. It is probably best if a lot is forgotten. What I am claiming is that insofar as the individual remembers being certain ways, having certain traits, and having done certain things, that individual will need to mark off certain acts and traits as *alien* and *undesirable* and certain memories as false. Living out a narrative makes certain things true, but not everything. Normal multiplex selves face the problem of making their narrative self cohere with their actual identity and shedding undesirable characteristics. Multiple selves face this problem in spades. They not only need to see certain contentful acts as misattributed; they must also come to see some of the selves who allegedly did the things that never really happened as *alien*, fictive, unwanted, and undesirable in some strong sense. It will not be a mistake to think that they once felt or thought in certain ways or even believed that they did certain things. It will just be that they will want to disengage from certain alters and deny that some of the things the alter thought it did were done. In cases where the alters did in fact do things that are not consonant with the projected ideal, these will need to be accepted as done, but by one of the individual's now conceptually *alien* selves.

The proposal to which this is leading is this: Something like integration is part of what it takes to move from being multiple to multiplex. But not all aspects of all alters can or should be integrated. The therapeutic process will involve some disidentification, some dissolution of self. This is a bad thing because it is alienating. But it is not unconditionally bad. It is usually worse being a multiple or living lies. Furthermore, the alienation involved in shearing alters is mitigated somewhat when a multiple comes to see the ways in which certain of his or her alters are understandable as defensive maneuvers but are not the sort of selves one should want to be.

What I have said so far leaves open the question of which self orchestrates the process of change. Since I have expressed skepticism about the idea of a host or primary personality or a single "real self" beneath the manifold clutter, it becomes hard to say which self orchestrates the difficult transformation required. My view is that no particular self is necessary as orchestrator, so long as some self seizes executive control and projects a model, even an inchoate one, of a healed multiplex self. This self model held in view and encouraged in therapy, as it certainly is socially by the "one self to a customer" principle, can lead, especially in highly suggestible (hypnotizable) persons, to the breakdown of amnesic barriers and can engender the various compromises, dissolutions, and integrations required for personal wholeness in the two senses discussed earlier.

The idea that active consciousness of self and modeling an improved self can be causally efficacious is not mysterious (Calvin 1990; Craik 1943; Dennett 1988; Flanagan 1991a, 1991b, 1992; Johnson-Laird 1983, 1988; Stephens and Graham 1994). We needn't even think of some single self as in charge of working over a family of alters. Let every self be an alter. It makes no difference, so long as some alter comes forward with the strong desire for the system to become whole, and so long as the circumstances of that individual's life afford him or her the therapeutic environment to do the work required.

It is not even necessary to think that once the process of becoming multiplex begins, the alter who puts forward or embraces the plan to become whole again stays in place as orchestrator. The picture of one self at the head of a council table talking over matters with various ghostly selves, each in turn abandoning their seat at the table and entering the self at the table's head, is misleading in a variety of ways. Among other things, it stays too close to the picture of an alter with primacy, as if host's shape and character set down the basic parameters or guidelines for the operation of making the person whole again. Indeed, some alters are easier to work with than others (both first-personally and third-personally), and there may be certain traits of the alter who announces the plan to become whole that are maintained throughout. But there is no self, especially once multiplicity is deemed undesirable from the first-person point of view, who isn't in certain respects ghostly or at least a candidate for being booted out of the club. The project is to have some alter announce an action plan based on the normative ideal of multiplex wholeness and then to have the cognitive system, in conjunction with a therapist, work out a way of conforming both the narrative center and the actual life to the envisioned ideal. Since the multiplex self at the end of therapy did not exist at the beginning of the effort to become whole, there is a sense in which it is new. But because becoming that self involves an active, agentic working over of possibilities, ideals, and narrative structures available in the multiple, there is, in a certain sense, continuity and authorial connectedness. Multiplicity ends when a single multiplex narrative center is achieved. The multiple has recovered in the sense that he or she has gotten better. But the multiple has not recovered any self that he or she once was or that was lying beneath the surface wholly integrated and waiting to emerge. The whole process is a complex one involving at once some recovery and reclamation, some evolution, some transformation, and some creation. While a multiple is a multiple, it is fair to say that she is not the same person she was before she became a multiple. This is because when a multiple is a multiple, she is a cluster of narrative fissions many of which, indeed too many of which, are the closest continuer of whatever antecedent self there was before fissioning took place. Paradoxically, however, when a multiple becomes multiplex again, we *can* think of the individual as the same person throughout her life. This is because in regaining a single center of narrative gravity, the individual will regain memory connections to her premultiple life, as well as memories about her alters during her life as a multiple. Furthermore, and as important as the memory connections, the individual will achieve multiplex wholeness through efforts involving active consciousness of self and projection of who she wants to become—recognizing, incompletely at first, what she is like now.[12]

6 Authorship of Self, Therapeutic Rage, and Moral Luck

One way such passing from multiplicity to multiplexity in therapy of multiples involves anger, rage, and fury at the abuse. This rage may pass; perhaps it is even best that it eventually pass. But experiencing it and directing it at the perpetrator of one's abuse is typically a necessary condition for moving on. If this is right, then what P. S. Strawson called the reactive attitudes are backward-looking but at the same time are essential components of moving forward, of identity reclamation, transformation, and so on. Certain authorial transformations may *require* blame, fury, anger, and rage at the victimizer. When the blame, anger, and rage are vivid, consciously recognized, and actively orchestrated by the victim, the work of overcoming is most likely to succeed. In such cases and where the agent engages her own reactive attitudes and uses them to excise damage, it is also safe to say that we have the same person on the other side of the transformation. When the process works more unconsciously and with little agentic involvement, it is less clear what to say about sameness of identity.

So far I have been thinking of cases where moving forward requires shearing aspects of self-identity that are unworthy, unwanted, and imposed without the agent's own involvement. What is shorn is guided in some important respect by some image of the self the agent intends to reclaim or become. In cases of multiple personality disorder, unlike some other identity disorders, venting all one's anger at the external source of one's malformation is straightforwardly justified. Parental abuse is a paradigm case in which the parent or caretaker has grossly violated moral norms and has caused the malformation. Any complicity that the child or her grown-up self may feel is inappropriate.[13] The trouble is that philosophical or legal clarity about where fault lies is of little help to a damaged person who feels as if she has been party to her own ruination. Indeed, it is partly constitutive of her ruination that she feel this way. There is some reason to believe that such cases are made more difficult for victims because the culture at large has problematic views about complicity, and thereby makes it harder for victims to overcome these feelings. We know this is true in the case of rape. This suggests that more refined views widely shared by philosophers, legalists, therapists, and the public at large could change the climate of assumptions about complicity and thereby help victims not to be so tempted to blame themselves for what they in no way deserve. But this is easier said than done.

One final concern is this. I've been focussing on MPD as a problem of individuals to be solved in concert with professionals. But it is important to keep in mind that MPD reflects and raises problems that transcend individuals: problems of communal responsibility and of social practices with deep historical roots that lead to the malformation of many persons. In almost every case of abuse, there is a point to rage at the abuser. Such rage is a necessary part of moving forward, of identity repair and reclamation. The problem, however, is that any close look at almost any abuser will suggest an explanation in that abuser's life history that will explain why they themselves are so awful and why they did what they did.[14]

This point seems to me to raise some especially difficult problems. Victims of oppression and abuse need to feel and express rage at the perpetrators of that abuse, and they need to blame these individuals for the harm these individuals have caused them. One might think that it is the rage that is important and not what it is directed at, and thus that it could just as well be directed at the larger context of what caused one's abuser to be the way he is rather than at the abuser himself. I have trouble thinking this is true. The overall view does seem, as Gary Watson puts it, to simultaneously demand and preclude that we regard perpetrators of evil as victims. If we allow the considerations that preclude directing rage and blame at some individual to win out, we are in danger of losing focus on the very capacities of agency that give the victimized the power, courage, and confidence to try to go on. But if we give in to the considerations that direct *all* the blame at the perpetrator, then we are in a sense simply blaming another victim. So we seem to need to keep both points of view in mind at once, despite the tension between them.

This is a familiar plight once philosophical reflection reaches a certain depth. But it is nonetheless troubling. One way of making it less troubling is to think of what could happen that would require less use of this cognitively dissonant solution of both blaming particular agents for the harm they cause and seeing the harm they cause as something they are caused to do. One thing that would reduce the need for the cognitively dissonant solution is there being less evil, less harm, less personality malformation, less abuse and exploitation. How could there be less of these things? I admit that I have little in the way of a detailed plan about how to reduce of these things. But I do know that it requires collective work to change the forms of life in which evil flourishes. At this point work on identity, agency, and ethics must yield to the work of politics, to the work of political action designed to change poisonous social structures. This, it seems to me, is where the solution lies, but it involves the hardest work of all.[15]

Notes

1. I want to emphasize from the start that when I speak of integration, I do not posit some particular model of a "well-integrated person." The crucial thing really is that whatever form integration takes, there is a first-person qualitative unity of the experience of the self and this integration (which can come in very disorganized forms) is in some large measure under one individual's control capacities. I thank Todd May for pressing me on this point.

2. Christine Korsgaard writes, "Authorial psychological connectedness is consistent with drastic changes, provided these changes are the result of actions by the person herself or reactions for which she is responsible" (1989).

3. Throughout this paper I am using terms like "self" or "person," even "I," to mean that which grounds or constitutes personality, rather that whatever is denoted by "I" in its strict indexical use. Issues such as MPD as treated within philosophy of psychology have important implications for questions of personal identity, including metaphysical questions of numerical identity over time. But it is best if we leave the issue of the meaning and reference of the essential indexical "I," in its strict metaphysical sense, to one side here.

4. Spence (1982, 22) thinks that continuity, coherence, and comprehensiveness are the ideals of narrative explanation. I favor more emphasis on correspondence truth in thinking about narrative selves, and I think that our expectations about comprehensiveness are moderate.

5. This is true of "unreclaimed" multiples but not of "reclaiming" multiples, who can, indeed must, represent the different selves they house. Furthermore, even "unreclaimed" and "unreclaiming" multiples sometimes speak of or write about alters, but they do so from the third-person point of view and often without the knowledge that the alters are their alters.

6. Dennett writes, "There is in every country on earth a Head of State. . . . That is not to say that a nation lacking such a figurehead, would cease to function day-to-day. But it is to say that in the longer term it may function much better if it does have one. . . . The drift of the analogy is obvious. In short, a human being too may need an inner figurehead—especially given the complexities of human social life" (1989, 171).

7. Erikson writes that the process of identity formation is "a process taking place on all levels of mental functioning. . . . This process is, luckily, and necessarily, for the most part unconscious except where inner conditions and outer circumstances combine to aggravate a painful, or elated, 'identity-consciousness.'" (1968, 22–23). Furthermore, our innate temperamental traits (Kagan 1989), our differential natural intelligences (Gardner 1983), are productive forces in identity formation from the start. These aspects of our self may never be seen very clearly in the first-personal, in self-representation, but they are indispensable pieces of the puzzle of who we are. They are causally efficacious aspects of our actual full identity.

8. This is why we should be wary of William James's claim, "*A man has as many social selves as there are individuals who recognize him* and carry an image of him in their mind. To wound any one of these images is to wound him. . . . We may practically say that he has as many different social selves as there are distinct *groups* of persons about whose opinion he cares" (1961, 46).

9. "Although non-multiples may dissociate in any number of ways, and even experience amnesia, they tend nevertheless to retain only one center of self-consciousness. No matter how differently a non-multiple might act, think, or feel about himself on separate occasions, those changes generally 'refer' or apply to the same center of self-awareness, even from the person's subjective point of view. That is, not only would an outsider say that the changes were changes *in* the same individual, but that person generally experiences the changes in that way and would refer to successive states as 'mine'" (Braude 1991, 70).

10. Stephen Braude writes, "In all the cases I know of where a multiple has been integrated extensively enough to feel what it is like to be a person with different

and often conflicting desires, preferences, and interests, the integrated state has been preferred. Granted, the internal group of friends may have disappeared, but the integrated multiple recognizes that their distinctive quality tends to remain. In fact, the integrated multiple will tend to experience those qualities in a somewhat enhanced and enriched way, as they blend for the first time with and become augmented by other attributes previously limited to specific alters" (Braude 1991, 46). Some of the reading I have done, as well as conversation with Jennifer Radden, have convinced me that this claim that multiples always prefer integration (once they have achieved it) is controversial.

11. One of the first widely discussed case of multiplicity was that of Mary Reynolds (1793–1854). Miss Reynolds case was described by S. Weir Mitchell, and William James quotes his report at length in volume one of his *Principles* (1976). Miss Reynolds has two distinct personalities, each of which displayed the classical amnesic symptom with respect to the other. Miss Reynolds regularly remained a distinct self for a month or more, while alternating selves over the course of 15 years.

12. Virgil Aldrich pointed out to me that although we are inclined to speak of "multiple personalities" in the same body, we are not inclined to speak of "multiple persons" in the same body. This is right, and one reason for it, I think, is that bodily continuity is important to us in ascribing personhood. So Jane is one person with many personalities because "Jane" names this continuous organism. She is not a multiple person; she is an individual with many different personalities. The importance of bodily continuity in thinking about the identity of persons helps to explain why, when multiplicity yields to multiplexity, we are willing to think that we have the same person we had before multiplicity took hold, even though we do not think this when the person is in the full grip of MPD. During multiplicity, standards of psychological continuity and connectedness are rightly most weighty and undermine the ascription of personal identity.

13. One MPD patient who was repeatedly raped by her father was confused by the fact that she had played along with certain of what her father called "daddy games." This father, perhaps to reduce his own cognitive dissonance, suggested a new name for his daughter when they played "daddy games." I have come across another case in which the abusive father actually laid the ground for alters to take in his daughter hold by providing names for them (Humphrey and Dennett 1989).

14. Gary Watson provides a vivid example. Watson first describes the case of Robert Harris, a reckless and unfeeling murderer capable of enjoying his lunch immediately after pumping two innocents full of bullets. He needed their car to commit a bank robbery after lunch. Harris, according to his sister, "cared about nothing." He was born to a mother sent into labor from the hemorrhaging caused by a beating she, 6½ months pregnant, suffered at the hands of her

alcoholic husband. Harris's father was convicted several times of sexually abusing his daughters, and his mother also eventually became an alcoholic and was arrested several times, once for bank robbery.

Watson writes, "The fact that Harris's cruelty is an intelligible response to his circumstances gives a foothold not only for sympathy, but for the thought that if *I* had been subjected to such circumstances, I might well have become as vile. What is unsettling is the thought that one's moral self is such a fragile thing. . . . The awareness of moral luck, however, taints one's own view of one's moral self as an achievement, and infuses one's reactive attitudes with a sense of irony" (1987, 276–277).

Watson goes on to write, "Harris both satisfies and violates the criteria of victimhood. His childhood abuse was a misfortune inflicted upon him against his will. But at the same time (and this is part of his very misfortune) he unambivalently endorses suffering, death, and destruction, and that is what (one form of) evil is. With this in focus, we see him as a victimizer and respond to him accordingly. *This ambivalence results from the fact that an overall view simultaneously demands and precludes regarding him as a victim*" (1987, 275, my emphasis).

15. I first started thinking about some of the issues discussed in this paper when I was invited to comment on Claudia Card's paper "Responsibility and Moral Luck" at the Eastern Division meetings of the American Philosophical Association in Baltimore in December 1989. I am grateful to George Graham and Lynn Stephens for their immensely perceptive and helpful comments on several earlier versions of this paper. Jennifer Radden and Ruth Anna Putnam also provided especially close critical readings. My colleagues at Wellesley helped when they read the paper for our departmental seminar, as did audiences at Oberlin college, Wake Forest University, University of Utah, Clemson University, and Syracuse University. Virgil Aldrich, Michael Lynch, Todd May, Philip Peterson, and Peter Van Inwagen made especially helpful points. Steven Braude neatly identified the main difference between us as involving the need to posit some sort of "transcendental ego" in order for self construction to get going. Braude thinks we need such an ego. I think not.

References

Aldridge-Morris, R. 1989. *Multiple Personality: An Exercise in Deception*. Hillsdale: Lawrence Erlbaum Associates.

Bratman, M. 1987. *Intentions, Plans, and Practical Reason*. Cambridge: Harvard University Press.

Braude, 1991. *First Person Plural: Multiple Personality and the Philosophy of Mind*. New York: Routledge.

Bruner, J. S. 1983. *In Search of Mind: Essays in Autobiography*. New York: Harper and Row.

Bruner, J. S. 1986. *Actual Minds, Possible Worlds.* Cambridge: Harvard University Press.

Bruner, J. S. 1991. "The Narrative Construction of Reality." *Critical Inquiry* 18:1–21.

Calvin, W. H. 1990. *The Cerebral Symphony: Seashore Reflections on the Structure of Consciousness.* New York: Bantam.

Craik, K. 1943. *The Nature of Explanation.* Cambridge: Cambridge University Press.

Dennett, D. C. 1988. "Why Everyone Is a Novelist." *Times Literary Supplement,* September 16–22, p. 459.

Dennett, D. C. 1989. "The Origins of Selves." *Cogito* 2:163–173.

Erickson, E. H. 1968. *Identity: Youth and Crisis.* New York: W. W. Norton.

Eysenck, H. J., and M. W. Eysenck. 1985. *Personality and Individual Differences.* New York: Plenum.

Flanagan, O. 1991a. *Varieties of Moral Personality: Ethics and Psychological Realism.* Cambridge: Harvard University Press.

Flanagan, O. 1991b. *The Science of the Mind,* 2nd ed. Cambridge: MIT Press.

Flanagan, O. 1992. *Consciousness Reconsidered.* Cambridge: MIT Press.

Ganaway, G. K. 1989. "Historical versus Narrative Truth: Clarifying the Role of Exogenous Trauma in the Etiology of MPD and Its Variants." *Dissociation* 2, no. 4: 205–220.

Gardner, H. 1983. *Frames of Mind: The Idea of Multiple Intelligences.* New York: Basic Books.

Hacking, I. 1991. "Two Souls in One Body." *Critical Inquiry* 17, no. 4.

Humphrey, N., and D. Dennett. 1989. "Speaking for Ourselves." *Raritan* 9:69–98.

James, W. 1961. *Psychology: The Briefer Course.* New York: Harper and Row. First published in 1892.

James, W. 1976. *The Principles of Psychology,* 3 vols. Cambridge: Harvard University Press. First published in 1890.

Johnson-Laird, P. N. 1983. *Mental Models.* Cambridge: Harvard University Press.

Johnson-Laird, P. N. 1983. *The Computer and the Mind.* Cambridge: Harvard University Press.

Kagan, J. 1984. *The Nature of the Child*. New York: Basic Books.

Kagan, J. 1989. *Unstable Ideas: Temperment, Cognition, and Self*. Cambridge: Harvard University Press.

Kermode, F. 1967. *The Sense of an Ending: Studies in the Theory of Fiction*. New York: Oxford University Press.

Korsgaard, C. 1989. "Personal Identity and the Unity of Agency: A Kantian Response to Parfit." *Philosophy and Public Affairs* 18:101–132.

Luria, A. R. 1987. *The Man with the Shattered World*. Cambridge: Harvard University Press. First published in 1972.

MacIntyre, A. 1981. *After Virtue*, 2nd ed. Notre Dame: Notre Dame University Press. With postscript, 1984.

Sacks, O. 1985. *The Man Who Mistook His Wife for a Hat and Other Clinical Tales*. New York: Summit.

Sandel, M. 1982. *Liberalism and the Limits of Justice*. New York: Cambridge University Press.

Spence, D. 1982. *Narrative Truth and Historical Truth: Meaning and Interpretation in Psychoanalysis*. New York: W. W. Norton.

Stephens, G. L., and G. Graham. 1994. "Voices and Selves." In *Philosophical Perspectives on Psychiatric Diagnostic Classification*, ed. J. Sadler et al. Baltimore: Johns Hopkins University Press.

Stern, D. 1985. *The Interpersonal World of the Infant*. New York: Basic Books.

Taylor, C. 1989. *Sources of the Self: The Making of Modern Identity*. Cambridge: Harvard University Press.

Watson, G. 1987. "Responsibility and the Limits of Evil." In *Responsibility, Character, and the Emotions: New Essays in Moral Psychology*, ed. F. Schoeman. Cambridge: Cambridge University Press.

Wellman, H. M. 1990. *The Child's Theory of Mind*. Cambridge: MIT Press.

Autism and the "Theory of Mind" Debate

Robert M. Gordon and John A. Barker

Recent research has established that by the age of 4 most developmentally normal children understand that people sometimes respond to the world not as it actually is but merely as they believe it to be. With this understanding, children are better able to anticipate the behavior of others and to attune their own behavior accordingly. In mentally retarded children with Down's syndrome, attaining such competence is delayed, but it is generally acquired by the time they reach the *mental* age of 4, as measured by tests of nonverbal intelligence. Thus from a developmental perspective, attainment of the mental age of 4 appears to be significant for acquisition of what we call *psychological competence:* possession of the skills and resources people routinely call on in the anticipation, explanation, and social coordination of behavior.[1]

There is one notable exception, however. Most *autistic* children lack much of this competence even at significantly higher mental ages, according to a number of recent experimental studies. Most do not seem to understand that people's actions and emotions depend on their beliefs. Rather than treating other people as subjects with "points of view," they frequently give the impression of "treating people and objects alike" (Kanner 1943). Asked what the brain does, autistic children speak of it as making people move or run, whereas most children first mention thinking or feeling. Philosophers have sometimes found it useful to invent imaginary people who treat their fellows as, literally, mindless beings.[2] The exotic creatures of philosophical fiction appear congenial and well adjusted, however, in comparison to those real people who are severely handicapped by autism. People with autism, even many of the most intelligent among them, apparently never succeed in developing a normal understanding of many of the psychological dimensions of human existence, and as a result, they fail to achieve normal interactions with other human beings.

Many autistic people are also abnormal in respects other than psychological competence. The majority are mentally retarded. But their striking failure in many psychological tasks does not appear to be accountable in terms of any broad deficit in intellect. It has therefore been argued by a group of leading researchers that autism is characterized by a specific deficit in psychological competence, a deficit in what they call possession and use of a "theory of mind" (Baron-Cohen, Leslie, and Frith 1985; Leslie 1987; Frith 1989; Baron-Cohen 1990).

1 Some Pivotal Experimental Results

According to many accounts, the major watershed in the development of psychological competence is the capacity to deploy the notion of belief, and in particular the capacity to attribute beliefs that are false or contrary to fact. A classic experimental study, Wimmer and Perner 1983, focuses on false belief and establishes that in normal children this capacity becomes apparent at approximately the age of 4. In the original experiment, children are presented a story, illustrated with puppets, in which the protagonist places an object in one location and subsequently, while he is out of the room and without his knowledge, someone else relocates the object. Where does Maxi go to retrieve his candy when he returns to the room? *We*, of course, would predict that he will look for it in the wrong place, and so do most children of age 4 or older. Children under about the age of 4, however, point to or otherwise indicate the actual present location of the candy. Evidently, they are unable to adjust for the fact that the protagonist was not in a position to know that the object was relocated. They treat all the facts presented to them in a story as accessible to the protagonist, as if nothing were beyond his ken. It doesn't matter whether something happens in plain sight of the protagonist or whether he is epistemically handicapped. The experiment has been replicated a number of times, and it has held up very well and been supported by other research.

Even more striking than the results of the original experiment were those reported in Baron-Cohen, Leslie, and Frith 1985. In this study, a test similar to the one used in Wimmer and Perner 1983 was applied to a group of clinically normal 4-year-old and 5-year-old children, a group of mentally retarded children with Down's syndrome (mean chronological age = 10, mean nonverbal mental age = 5), and a group of highly functional children with autism (mean chronological age = 11, mean nonverbal mental age = 9). It was found, on the one hand, that the mentally retarded Down's syndrome subjects gave the right response about as frequently as the normal children did. On the other hand, most of the highly functional autistic subjects gave the wrong response. Even those who had attained the mental age of 9 typically performed at the 3-year-old level on false-belief tasks. Despite being smarter than the other subjects, the autistic children appeared to suffer from a specific deficit in at least this aspect of psychological competence.

Results for the most part consistent with those reported in Baron-Cohen, Leslie, and Frith 1985 have been obtained in a variety of subsequent studies.[3] In addition, a later study by Baron-Cohen, Leslie, and Frith (1986) employed a largely nonverbal test in which children were asked to put the frames of a picture story into the proper sequence. Where the sequence was one of mechanistic causality, children with autism performed at least as well as normal children and those with Down's syndrome. But where the right sequence (recognized immediately by normal adults) depicts a story involving false belief, the performance of autistic children was no better than chance and far worse than those of normal and Down's syndrome subjects.

2 Is Psychological Competence Based on a Theory?

We assume in this chapter that the available evidence largely favors the hypothesis of a specific deficit in psychological competence. Whether we should characterize it as a "theory of mind" deficit, following Baron-Cohen, Leslie, and Frith (1985, 1986), depends on whether we wish to accept the implicit assumption that psychological

Robert M. Gordon and John A. Barker

competence consists in the possession and use of a *theory*. This is indeed a popular assumption. For the past quarter century a dominant view in philosophy and the cognitive sciences has been that the resources that underlie commonsense explanations and predictions of behavior chiefly consist of a tacit body of propositional knowledge roughly comparable to a scientific theory. The alleged theory posits unobservable mental states such as beliefs, desires, intentions, and feelings, linked to each other and to observable behaviors by "lawlike" principles. These principles are applied to observable situations by way of logical inferences that generate predictions and explanations of behavior. The theory is supposedly called on by people of all cultures and virtually all levels of intelligence to explain and predict the behavior of others. To apply the theory, it is said, one neither needs nor typically possesses any conscious awareness of the principles one is applying. Careful reflection, however, can often bring them to light. And once they are provided with verbal garb, the principles typically seem obvious, commonplace, and platitudinous—which is taken to be good evidence that they constitute unquestioned presuppositions of a tacit folk theory.

The view that commonsense explanations and predictions of behavior are theory-based is called the "theory theory." Despite general acknowledgement that this view has serious deficiencies, until recently it was widely conceded that it had no plausible alternative: it was, as Jerry Fodor put it, "the only game in town." Indeed, it has been presupposed in most debates in the philosophy of mind, particularly the debate between those, such as Fodor, who think our tacit commonsense theory likely to be vindicated in large part by future science and those (the "eliminativists") who believe future science will show it to be radically mistaken and misconceived.

According to some developmental psychologists who accept the theory theory, children acquire psychological competence by a process of theory construction and theory change, replacing inadequate laws or principles with better ones, progressing toward mature conceptions of mental states such as belief and desire. Consider how, on this view, one might explain the difference between the way in which a 3-year-old and a 4-year-old answers the question, "Where will Maxi go to get his candy?" A 3-year-old might reason (consciously or unconsciously) as follows:

To get *x*, people will go to wherever *x* is.

Maxi's candy is in location *b*.

Therefore, to get his candy, Maxi will go to location *b*.

(The same conclusion could also be reached using an immature notion of belief shaped by the principle "If it is the case that *p*, then people believe that *p*.")

In contrast, a typical 4-year-old can deploy the notion of a belief that may or may not correspond to fact. The child might reason, consciously or unconsciously, along the following lines:

Principle: People who put an object in location *l* will typically believe just afterward that it is currently in location *l*.

So just after Maxi put his candy in location *a*, he believed that his candy was currently in location *a*.

Principle: People who believe that something is currently in location *l* will typically continue to believe that it is in location *l* unless they come to believe it (was) moved.

Principle: Typically people come to believe that *x* (was) moved only if they saw *x* move (being moved) or are told that *x* (was) moved.

But Maxi neither saw his candy being moved nor was told that it was moved.

So when Maxi returned, he believed that his candy was currently in location *a*.

Principle: To get *x*, people will go to wherever they *believe x* is.

Therefore, to get his candy, Maxi will go to location *a*.

The assumption that psychological competence consists in the possession and use of a theory is shared by many recent investigators of the development of psychological competence. The field of investigation has even come to be called "the child's theory of mind." Developmental psychologists inherited the term "theory of mind" from an article that asked whether the chimpanzee has a theory of mind (Premack and Woodruff 1978). The authors of that paper used the term very loosely, however. They gloss the term as follows: "In saying that an individual has a theory of mind, we mean that the individual imputes mental states to himself and others" (1978, 515).

This suggests that Premack and Woodruff were introducing the term "theory of mind" merely as an abbreviation of "capacity to attribute mental states." If that were their sole intent, then, of course, they would be leaving open the question "What is the *basis* of the capacity to attribute mental states?" But their choice of the term *theory* suggests that they were not leaving this question open but rather were taking for granted a certain answer to the question. They were accepting the conjecture that it is possession and use of a theory that gives individuals (human beings and possibly chimpanzees) the capacity to attribute mental states. Indeed, they did attempt to justify their use of the term *theory* on the grounds that mental states are not observable and that people are able to make predictions on the basis of these attributions. And at the time they were writing, there seemed to be no plausible *alternative* way of explaining how people might make predictions on the basis of attributions of states that lie "behind" behavior.

Some of the developmental psychologists who borrowed the term "theory of mind" from Premack and Woodruff also slide too easily from "capacity to attribute mental states" to "theory of mind" (as noted in de Gelder 1993). They vacillate between the innocuous assertion that by age 4 children are able to attribute mental states and the extravagant speculation that by age 4 children have a relatively mature *theory* on the basis of which they are able to attribute mental states. Considerable care should be given, therefore, to interpreting Baron-Cohen's claim that people with autism have a "theory of mind" deficit. If he is taken as saying only that normal children and those with Down's syndrome have a capacity to make a type of attribution that autistic children do not make, then he is putting forward a very interesting claim that does appear to be warranted by the experimental results he cites. But if he is taken as saying that normal children and those with Down's syndrome possess and use a *theory* (or part of a theory) that autistic children alone do not possess and use, then he is making a claim that appears to be called into question by some of the experimental results he cites in its support.[4] For children afflicted with Down's syndrome, who evidently have the psychological competence characteristic of their mental age, are notably deficient in theoretical abilities, whereas children afflicted with autism, who appear to be psychologically incompetent, are *not* generally deficient in theoretical abilities for their mental age. Why would autistic children who in some cases do even better than the average normal child in mastering theories of other sorts, fare so badly in this particular domain? And even more counterintuitive, how can it be that Down's children with IQs as low as 50 are able to master this "theory" about as well as normals do (albeit a few years later), when they master no other theory? In short, one drawback of the theory theory is that it is not easily squared with the findings regarding the psychological competence of children with Down's syndrome and the psychological incompetence of relatively intelligent children with autism.

We think the evidence suggests that the psychological competence that normal children develop but autistic children do not develop is based not on a *theory* but rather on a *skill* that does not essentially require the aptitudes tested in typical "IQ" tests. This is why retarded children with Down's syndrome, even those who in large degree lack these further aptitudes, prove to be psychologically competent. (Of course, one may reasonably expect the relevant skill to be refined and enhanced by these further IQ aptitudes. Hence it is not a consequence of our view that low-IQ Down's syndrome children are as likely as normal children to become successful novelists, playwrights, or psychologists.)

Although clearly not deficient in theoretical powers relative to their mental age, autistic children are in other respects very markedly different from other children of the same mental age, including those with Down's syndrome. Some of these differences can reasonably be attributed in large part to their impaired psychological competence. For example, autistic people are notoriously odd and limited in their capacity to communicate with others, both verbally and nonverbally. They also have a severely diminished capacity to enter into normal social relationships, especially with peers. Although these handicaps no doubt set them further behind the pack in psychological competence, the more important causal relationship seems to be the converse: without a level of psychological competence beyond that attained by most autistic people, normal communication and normal social relationships are altogether impossible (Baron-Cohen 1988, also Frith 1989). Thus whatever proves to be the key to the psychological incompetence of autistic individuals will probably also be the key to their social and communicative impairments.

3 Pretending and Simulating

There are, however, other autistic abnormalities that cannot be attributed chiefly to psychological incompetence. Among these is the often-remarked failure of autistic children to engage in spontaneous pretend play, whether in conjunction with others or alone. Normal children and Down's syndrome children spontaneously initiate pretend play and develop the ability to participate in complex, interactive forms of it before they develop the psychological competence required in false-belief tasks. In stark contrast, the behavior of children with autism characteristically remains almost totally devoid of any signs of spontaneous pretend play. The lack of pretend play, particularly the absence of role play and mime play with imaginary objects, is well known. Although studies have shown that many autistic children can, with appropriate prompting, engage in some forms of pretend play (Lewis and Boucher 1988, Ungerer and Sigman 1981), the play is characterized by lack of spontaneity and by stereotypical, inflexible, and repetitive patterns. What is most conspicuous is the absence of *other-regarding* pretending, typified by role play and joint pretend play, in which two or more children act on a shared pretense (Harris, forthcoming).

Might a faulty capacity for pretense, especially for other-regarding pretense, severely degrade a person's capacity to ascribe mental states? It would, according to the theory of psychological competence that we favor, the mental-simulation theory. This theory asserts that psychological competence fundamentally depends on the capacity to use one's own cognitive and motivational resources to simulate other people, a capacity that calls on no special theory of mental states.[5] For example, we often predict what another will decide to do by making a decision ourselves—a "pretend" decision, of course, made only in imagination—after making adjustments for relevant differences in situation and past behavior. According to our version of the simulation theory, such vicarious decision making also underlies our capacity to explain the behavior of others in terms of mental states, and probably also the very capacity to grasp the concepts of such states as belief and desire. If pretending is the key to making and understanding ascriptions of mental states then, of course, a developmental pathology, such as autism, that severely restricts the capacity to pretend should also severely restrict a child's capacity to make and understand such ascriptions, even if in other respects the child's intelligence is normal.

To help the reader understand how mental simulation can yield predictions and explanations of behavior, it will be instructive to examine the logical structure of pretend play. Children enter informal games of make-believe by initially pretending something to be true that they do not believe to be true. In pretense, they accept an initial premise (or premises), for example, that certain globs of mud are pies. By combining the initially stipulated premise with their existing store of beliefs and calling on their reasoning capacity, they are able to obtain answers to questions not addressed in the initial premise. In the mud-pie example, they would typically be able to answer the question "How many pies are there?" And where there is more than one player, their answers would typically agree: barring a stipulation to the contrary, the answer is the same as the number of (approximately pie-shaped) mud globs. "Which pie is biggest?" The biggest mud glob, of course, unless otherwise stipulated. This *productive* feature of many games of make-believe, pointed out by Kendall Walton, closely parallels our understanding of subjunctive conditionals, as Gareth Evans suggested.[6] Wondering if the bridge would have collapsed had there not been a heavy snowfall, we pretend that there wasn't a heavy snowfall, and then ask whether the bridge would have collapsed: this, with some amendments, is the so-called Ramsey test for evaluating subjunctive conditionals.[7]

But there is a *further* productive feature of games of make-believe. What the child *does* with the mud pies depends not only on the stipulated pretend facts, along with his existing *perceptions* and *beliefs*, but also on his existing *desires, values,* and *norms*. Together, these fix or at least constrain the child's answer to the question "What shall I *do* with these pies?" This *further* productive feature of games of make-believe parallels our typical understanding of conditionals concerning *our own actions* under hypothetical or counterfactual conditions.

Gordon makes the connection with pretense explicit in describing how one might predict what actions one would take upon hearing footsteps coming from the basement:

To simulate the appropriate practical reasoning I can engage in a kind of *pretend-play*: pretend that the indicated conditions *actually obtain*, with all other conditions remaining (so far as is logically possible and physically probable) as they presently stand; then—continuing the make-believe—try to "make up my mind" what to do given these (modified) conditions. I imagine, for instance, a lone modification of the actual world: the sound of footsteps from the basement. Then I ask, in effect, "What shall I do now?" And I answer with a declaration of immediate intention, "I shall now. . . . " This too is only feigned. But it is not feigned on a *tabula rasa*, as if at random: rather, the declaration of immediate intention appears to be formed in the way a *decision* is formed, *constrained* by the (pretended) "fact" that there is the sound of footsteps from the basement, the (*un*pretended) fact that such a sound would now be unlikely if there weren't an intruder in the basement, the (*un*pretended) awfulness of there being an intruder in the basement, and so forth. (1986, 160–161)

As in pretend play, an initial premise—here the hypothetical condition—is added to one's store of beliefs, desires, and other inputs to intention formation and decision making. In one important respect, however, this kind of simulation is unlike children's games of make-believe (and also unlike rehearsals and drills). Although the simulation may be accompanied by autonomic arousal and some expression of emotion, it stops short of overt action. One does not carry out the decision, say to call the police, even in overt pretend play. Our motivational, emotional, and decision making systems are running "off-line," as it were, disengaged from their natural output systems.

The simulation theory says that in predicting, explaining, and interpreting *another's* behavior, we likewise run the explanation or prediction through our own motivational and emotional systems, utilizing our own capacity for practical reasoning and decision making. In simulating another, however, it is often not sufficient to imagine being in the other's situation, that is, to employ our imagination merely to ask, "What would *I* do, believe, want, and feel were I in Smith's situation?" For this would leave open the further question "What about *Smith*: what does *Smith* do, believe, want, or feel in that situation?" Rather than simulate ourselves in Smith's situation, we must simulate *Smith* in Smith's situation (as it appears to Smith).

This is a further, more complex use of pretense. When one is predicting *one's own* actions or reactions in hypothetical conditions, the initial premise—for example, that there is a sound of footsteps coming from the basement—is simply stipulated. But when we explain or predict *another's* behavior in such a situation, one may, in addition, have to make adjustments of various kinds. These might be based on knowledge of the other's actual behavior in related situations in the past: one tries to become in imagination a person who might have acted as the other did in such situations. In false-belief tasks like those presented in Wimmer and Perner 1983 and Baron-Cohen, Leslie, and Frith 1985, the needed adjustment is a simple one: just *ignore* one or more of the facts, and then carry on as before. In the Maxi example, what one needs to ignore is the fact that while Maxi was outside, his candy was moved. That is, one need only undo the move in imagination, thereby restoring the candy to its previous location. Then, within the context of this pretense, one simply states where the candy is. One will then predict correctly that he will look for his candy not where it *actually* is but where it was before it was moved. Notice that instead of invoking a special folk-psychological principle that *people typically believe* that objects (to put it crudely) tend to stay put, one simply relies on one's own background assumption that objects tend to stay put. (For a more detailed account of the methodology of mental simulation, see Gordon 1992.)

Until and unless children develop the capacity and the motivation to make these imaginative adjustments, we should expect them to explain and predict as if everything they themselves count as fact were *accessible to the other* as a basis for action and emotion. We should also expect them to allow no *false* propositions into the other's data base, no false beliefs, in other words. Because people with autism are in general severely deficient in their capacity for pretense, particularly for other-regarding pretense, they should be unable to make the adjustments posited by the simulation theory. Therefore, the theory correctly predicts, these people will generally not succeed in the false-belief tasks, even where in other respects their intelligence is normal.

4 Pretending and the Theory-of-Mind Mechanism

We argued earlier that the theory theory is hard put to explain why children with Down's syndrome, who are generally poor theorists, have far more psychological competence than relatively intelligent children with autism, who are generally good theorists. The simulation theory would explain this in part by the fact that children with Down's syndrome, though poor theorists, spontaneously engage in complex, interactive forms of pretend play, whereas children with autism, though often good theorists, do not spontaneously engage in such play. But unlike the simulation theory, the theory theory does not hold that psychological competence depends on a capacity for certain kinds of pretending.

A further move, however, is available to theory theorists. They may argue that a theory of mental states differs in fundamental ways from theories in other domains, particularly in the nature of the concepts it employs. For one thing, it is a theory of intentional states, of states that are about something. And, it may be suggested, possession and use of a theory of intentional states requires a special cognitive mechanism and perhaps further that the same special mechanism is needed for pretense. This is proposed by one theory theorist, Alan Leslie, who posits a special computational mechanism, which he dubs the "Theory of Mind Mechanism," as requisite for overt pretend play as well as the understanding and recognition of intentional states (Leslie 1987, Leslie and Roth 1993). This proposal would parallel the simulation theorist's suggestion that both are implemented by off-line processing: utilizing systems that are normally dedicated to perception, cognition, motivation, emotion, and decision making, but using them in at least partial isolation from their normal input and output systems. The simulationist's idea is that the partial independence from input systems would explain, among other things, the freedom we have, in pretend play and in our representation of the content of others' mental states, to portray the world in contrary-to-fact ways, yet because output systems are not engaged in the normal way, this free play goes on within a "protected" context in which some of the normal consequences, especially but not only some of the behavioral consequences, do not actually ensue.

Leslie maintains that it is the theory-of-mind mechanism that makes this protected free play possible. What the mechanism does (to give a greatly simplified account of a rather complex theory) is to enable these systems to function at a higher semantic level: instead of manipulating object-level representations, as in their normal engagement with the world, they manipulate representations of representations, or "metarepresentations." The chief matter at issue between Leslie's hypothesis and the off-line hypothesis of the simulation theorist would seem to be this: do our systems operate at this higher representational level in pretense and in attribution of mental states, or do they operate in much the same way as in real-world engagements, but off-line? We believe Leslie's answer misrepresents the nature of pretense: the recognition and understanding of pretense might arguably involve metarepresentation, but not ordinarily the production of pretense. We also think the off-line hypothesis explains more, requires fewer specially dedicated resources, and comports better with evidence from other domains, such as imitation and mimicry. Although we briefly discuss mimicry in the following section, detailed discussion of Leslie's hypothesis would not be appropriate in a short essay on autism. We intend to discuss his hypothesis elsewhere, because it appears to be the only way the theory theory can be squared with the evidence that in the populations tested, psychological competence is better correlated with capacity for pretense than with capacity for theoretical understanding.

5 Simulation and Imitative Behavior

The capacity for simulation involves not only the deliberate procedure of putting oneself in the other's place but also a number of automatic, unconscious responses. For example, there is subliminal muscular mimicry of the bodily postures and especially the facial expressions of others. Where the other's face bears an expression of emotion, adopting of a similar expression tends to produce a similar emotion in oneself. Even when it does not produce a like emotional response, it at least gives the simulator the wherewithal to recognize the other's emotion. The automatic response to facial expressions is complemented by another mechanism. Like many other animals, human beings have an automatic tendency to direct their eyes to-ward the target of a conspecific's gaze. This mechanism automati-cally turns one's own attention from the other's response to its environmental stimulus: to the *object* of the other's attention or emo-tion (what it is *about*), or the *object* (aim, goal) of the other's action.[8] The tendency is activated particularly when another exhibits startle, terror, or some other strong reactive emotion, or shows attentiveness and interest. In normal children, all of this emerges in the first year. If psychological competence essentially depends on a capacity to sim-ulate others, these imitative mechanisms are important, perhaps even essential, stepping-stones to competence. In particular, they fa-cilitate finding the environmental explanation of another's action and emotion.

In the case of children with autism, there is strong evidence that at least the gaze-tracking response is largely absent, and some evi-dence of deficiency in the tendency to mimic emotional expression (Baron-Cohen and Ring 1993, Meltzoff and Gopnik 1993). Thus we should expect autistics to be deficient in both the tendency to search for reasons for (or objects of) action and emotion and the capacity to locate them in the environment. These problems are not likely to show up in the artificial tasks presented in most false-belief experi-ments. For such experiments call primarily for predictions of action rather than explanations and furthermore offer the subject only a narrative rather than a live, expressive protagonist. It is no surprise, then, that in the specific behavior tested in false-belief experiments, the autistic seems for the most part to resemble a normal 3-year-old. But where the task is one of explaining another's behavior in terms of an environmental stimulus or object, and the subject is allowed to see the other's facial expression or overt behavior and track the direction of the other's gaze, the simulation theory predicts that au-tistics will perform far below the level of normal 3-year-olds.

6 Conclusion

We claimed that the evidence suggests that the psychological compe-tence that normal children develop but autistic children do not de-velop is based not on a *theory* but rather on a *skill*. That skill, it appears, includes a capacity for egocentric recentering and a capacity to be engaged as an agent in a world imagined to deviate some-what from the actual world. These capacities appear to be intact in children with Down's syndrome but deficient in children with autism. Also deficient are some of the ancillary imitative mechanisms that would ordinarily facilitate simulation, particularly by producing emotional responses that copy those exhibited by others and by turning the simulator's attention toward the environmental causes and objects of other's emotions and actions.

This is the first philosophical paper we know of on the topic of autism. We have tried to bring to bear some recent philosophical thinking about the nature and acquisition of mental concepts and the nature of pretense. But we acknowledge that this is at most a small contribution toward understanding what is still a mysterious pathology.

Acknowledgments

We are indebted to Simon Baron-Cohen and Paul Harris for comments that were extremely helpful, especially in filling in some of the gaps in our knowledge of recent empirical research. Baron-Cohen kindly furnished preprints of some of the papers since published in Baron-Cohen, Tager-Flusberg, and Cohen 1993. We thank the editors for a number of suggestions that helped shape our presentation.

Notes

1. We prefer to speak of the child's "psychological competence," rather than the child's "theory of mind," to minimize the danger that descriptions of the phenomena to be explained will be skewed by intuitions associated with the term *theory*.

2. Most notable are Sellars's behavioristic "Rylean ancestors" (Sellars 1956), who (unlike autistic people) have no difficulty in speaking to one another about "the public properties of public objects" or even about the *meanings* of overt speech acts.

3. It should be noted, however, that other findings are not as consistently supportive as those of Wimmer and Perner 1983.

4. Baron-Cohen, Leslie, and Frith 1985 explicitly endorses Leslie's thesis, briefly discussed below, that the absence or deficiency of a certain computational mechanism explains the deficiencies of autistic children in pretend play and in

attribution of mental states. But the study grants that "the ability we have been testing could be considered as a kind of *conceptual* [as opposed to *perceptual*] perspective-taking skill," which suggests a view similar to the one we favor. A later paper, Baron-Cohen and Cross 1992 (173, n. 1), makes it clear that Baron-Cohen himself is not committed to the theory theory. This interpretation is further supported by personal communication from Baron-Cohen, in which he declares himself "still rather neutral" in the debate between the theory theory and the simulation theory.

5. For philosophical formulations and defenses of the simulation theory, see Gordon 1986, 1992, and Goldman 1989, 1992. For application to developmental issues, see Harris 1989, 1992. A double issue of the interdisciplinary journal *Mind and Language*, vol. 7 (Spring–Summer 1992) is devoted to the topic. The contents of this issue also appear, along with the earlier essays cited above and much new material, in Davies and Stone 1994.

The simulation theory has numerous historical precursors, including R. G. Collingwood's theory of historical reenactment and the nineteenth-century doctrine that the proper methodology of the human sciences is *Verstehen*, or empathetic understanding. Unlike these earlier views, however, simulation theory attempts to account for ordinary human competence, and it is concerned with prediction just as much as with explanation or understanding. Furthermore, it provides an account of our commonsense concepts of mind and various mental states and processes. In addition, the simulation theory is sensitive to experimental data concerning the normal development, and in autistic children the arrested development, of the capacity to understand, explain, and predict the behavior of others. Finally, the theory offers a speculative account of the way our knowledge of other minds is encoded in our brains.

6. The example and the thesis it exemplifies are taken from Walton 1973. The connection between Walton's thesis and counterfactuals was suggested by Evans (1982).

7. Ramsey 1978, 143. See also Stalnaker 1968. As in the case of conditionals, playing a game of make-believe requires that one solve the pragmatic problem of selecting *appropriate* "adjustments." For example, if these globs of mud are pies, then they are not globs of mud, since pies are made of edible stuff, whereas mud is not edible (or at least not palatable). But one could allow that these are indeed globs of mud if one pretended that pies are not made of edible stuff or that mud (or this kind of mud) is edible. Again, are the pebbles we encounter within these mud pies nuts or raisins or do they, perish the thought, remain pebbles?

8. Gordon offered the following speculation: "One possibility is that the readiness for practical simulation is a prepackaged 'module' called upon automatically in the perception of other human beings. One might even speculate that such a module makes its first appearance in the useful tendency many mammals

have of turning their eyes toward the target of another's gaze. Thus the very sight of human eyes might *require* us to simulate at least their spatial perspective—and to this extent, at least, to put ourselves in the other's shoes" (1986, 170). Commenting on this passage, Baron-Cohen and Cross say, "This quotation stands as a virtual prediction of the results presented in this paper" (1992, 183).

References

Baron-Cohen, S. 1988. "Social and Pragmatic Deficits in Autism: Cognitive or Affective?" *Journal of Autism and Developmental Disorders* 18:379–402.

Baron-Cohen, S. 1990. "Autism: A Specific Cognitive Disorder of 'Mind-Blindness.'" *International Review of Psychiatry* 2:81–90.

Baron-Cohen, S., and P. Cross, 1992. "Reading the Eyes: Evidence for the Role of Perception in the Development of a Theory of Mind." *Mind and Language* 7:172–186.

Baron-Cohen, S., A. M. Leslie, and U. Frith. 1985. "Does the Autistic Have a 'Theory of Mind'?" *Cognition* 21:37–46.

Baron-Cohen, S., A. M. Leslie, and U. Frith. 1986. "Mechanical, Behavioral, and Intentional Understanding of Picture Stories in Autistic Children." *British Journal of Developmental Psychology* 4:113–125.

Baron-Cohen, S., and H. Ring. 1993. "The Relationship between EDD and ToMM: Neuropsychological and Neurobiological Perspectives." In *Origins of an Understanding of Mind*, ed. P. Mitchell and C. Lewis. Hove, England: Lawrence Erlbaum Associates.

Baron-Cohen, S., H. Tager-Flusberg, and D. J. Cohen, eds. 1993. *Understanding Other Minds: Perspectives from Autism*. Oxford: Oxford University Press.

Davies, M., and T. Stone, eds. 1994. *Mental Simulation: Philosophical and Psychological Essays*. Oxford: Blackwell.

De Gelder, B. 1993. "Intentional Ascription, Autism, and Troubles with Content." In *Pragmatics at Issue*, ed. J. Verschueren. Amsterdam: J. Benjamins.

Evans, G. 1982. *The Varieties of Reference*. Ed. J. McDowell. Oxford: Oxford University Press.

Fodor, J. A. 1975. *The Language of Thought*. New York: Thomas Y. Crowell.

Fodor, J. A. 1978. "Propositional Attitudes." *Monist* 61:501–523. Reprinted in J. A. Fodor, *Representations*. Cambridge: MIT Press.

Fodor, J. A. 1987. *Psychosemantics*. Cambridge: MIT Press.

Frith, U. 1989. *Autism: Explaining the Enigma.* Oxford: Blackwell.

Goldman, A. I. 1989. "Interpretation Psychologized." *Mind and Language* 4:161–185.

Goldman, A. I. 1992. "In Defense of the Simulation Theory." *Mind and Language* 7:104–19.

Gordon, R. M. 1986. "Folk Psychology as Simulation." *Mind and Language* 1:158–171.

Gordon, R. M. 1992. "The Simulation Theory: Objections and Misconceptions." *Mind and Language* 7:11–34.

Harris, P. 1989. *Children and Emotion.* Oxford: Blackwell.

Harris, P. 1992. "From Simulation to Folk Psychology: The Case for Development." *Mind and Language* 7:120–144.

Harris, P. 1991. "The Work of the Imagination." In *Natural Theories of Mind,* ed. A. Whiten. Oxford: Oxford University Press.

Kanner, L. 1943. "Autistic Disturbance of Affective Contact." *Nervous Child* 2:217–250.

Leslie, A. M. 1987. "Pretense and Representation: The Origins of 'Theory of Mind.'" *Psychological Review* 94:412–426.

Leslie, A., and D. Roth. 1993. "What Autism Teaches Us about Metarepresentation." In *Understanding Other Minds: Perspectives from Autism,* ed. S. Baron-Cohen, H. Tager-Flusberg, and D. J. Cohen. Oxford: Oxford University Press.

Lewis, V., and J. Boucher. 1988. "Spontaneous, Instructed, and Elicited Play in Relatively Able Autistic Children." *British Journal of Developmental Psychology* 6:325–339.

Meltzoff, A., and A. Gopnik. 1993. "The Role of Imitation in Understanding Persons and Developing a Theory of Mind." In *Understanding Other Minds,* ed. S. Baron-Cohen, H. Tager-Flusberg, and D. J. Cohen. Oxford: Oxford University Press.

Newell, A. 1980. "Physical Symbol Systems." *Cognitive Science* 4:135–183.

Premack, D., and G. Woodruff. 1978. "Does the Chimpanzee Have a 'Theory of Mind'?" *Behavioral and Brain Sciences* 4:515–526.

Ramsey, F. P. 1978. *Foundations.* London: Routledge and Kegan Paul.

Sellars, W. 1956. "The Myth of the Given: Three Lectures on Empiricism and the Philosophy of Mind." In *The Foundations of Science and the Concepts of Psychology and Psychoanalysis,* ed. Herbert Feigl and Michael Scriven, Minnesota Studies in the Philosophy of Science, no. 1. Minneapolis: University of Minnesota Press.

Stalnaker, R. C. 1968. "A Theory of Conditionals." In *Studies in Logical Theory,* ed. N. Rescher. Oxford: Blackwell.

Stich, S., and S. Nichols. 1992. "Folk Psychology: Simulation or Tacit Theory?" *Mind and Language* 7:35–71.

Ungerer, J. A., and M. Sigman. 1981. "Symbolic Play and Language Comprehension in Autistic Children." *Journal of American Academy of Child Psychiatry* 20:318–337.

Walton, K. L. 1973. "Pictures and Make-Believe. *Philosophical Review* 82:283–319.

Wimmer, H., and J. Perner. 1983. "Beliefs about Beliefs: Representation and Constraining Function of Wrong Beliefs in Young Children's Understanding of Deception." *Cognition* 13:103–128.

Alcohol Addiction and Responsibility Attributions

Ferdinand Schoeman

The problems encountered by those who are alcohol-dependent share much with the critical personal problems we all face. The way we think about the alcohol-dependent person has implications for the way we think about human problems in general. Conversely, the more alcohol dependence shares with other problems, the more the factors that relate to those other problems relate to alcohol abuse. Appreciating this will help us put into context some of the puzzling features that long-term alcohol abuse poses.

Proponents of biochemical or genetic accounts of alcohol abuse have at times argued that their findings demonstrate that large classes of individuals have diminished control over their excessive-drinking patterns or over their behavior while under the influence. Several researchers who have been skeptical of biochemical accounts have wanted to discount the relevance of biology completely and argue that the cause of wrecked cars, families, or lives is wholly attributable to environmental forces. Proponents of these two perspectives—biomedical and psychosocial—concur, however, on seeing individual alcohol abusers as victims of forces over which little personal control can be exercised.

Among critics of these single-factor theories are to be found many who would argue that since every even remotely plausible theory of

This paper is a shortened version of a paper originally appearing in Mary Bockover, ed., *Rules, Rituals, and Responsibility* (Chicago: Open Court Publishing Co., 1991). Copyright of that article is in the name of the author.

abuse will have only a limited range of relevance and that issues of individual character and choice are nearly always relevant, there is no basis for mitigating the gravity of the harm to self or others that the alcohol abuser can be accused of inflicting. The options we seem to be left with are that the alcohol abuser either has radically diminished control or is fully accountable.

These polarized postures cannot reflect the perspective good judgment would bring to bear on the issue; good judgment eschews wholesale answers to recurring questions. Occasionally questions recur because the facts necessary to settle them are unavailable. In the case of alcohol abuse, however, the problem is deeper. Questions and approaches recur because there are real difficulties with all of the solutions that have been offered, stemming in part from an impoverished set of categories for conceptualizing the issue. Not only is there a dispute between those providing services to alcohol-dependent people, but there is also plenty of debate among those seeking scientific accounts of alcohol dependence and abuse. What this means is a somewhat disorderly state of understanding where patterns are not evident without careful elaboration of details about each case. My approach will be to plumb the divergent perspectives for insights that may provide the foundation for a comprehensive and coherent outlook.

It would be wrong to infer that recourse to particularized, detailed judgment is the result of the failure of science to provide an answer. In many ways, science has already provided us with illuminating information about alcohol-induced comportment and addiction. But what science provides is not enough to settle the moral questions. We would be mistaken in expecting that kind of answer from science in the first place, though often scientists assume, or are cast in, the role of being experts in just this sort of determination.

In this chapter I challenge a range of hard-line views about alcohol abuse, views that suggest that because there is no credible evidence of adequate single-factor causal accounts of alcohol abuse, patterns of alcohol abuse need not be seen as undermining or mitigating the abuser's responsibility for his or her behavior. But I also challenge the more compassionate view that because alcohol abuse undermines responsibility in many contexts, it undermines responsibility in all. I will begin by reviewing the majority opinion of a recent Supreme Court case and discussing the significance of diseases in attributing responsibility for behavior. I then examine the view that we are responsible for our own character in light of some recent medical uncoverings, in order to show that the implementation of the hard-line perspective on attributions of responsibility would turn our selves and society into entities bereft of humane understanding. Along the way I discuss some problems with thinking that people are responsible for choosing what cultural or traditional norms they should adopt and consider some commonsense considerations that attenuate or qualify attributions of responsibility. I conclude the paper by observing that the way we should think about responsibility for drinking patterns is not one issue but many, and answering it requires that attention still be paid to the context of the question.

1   *Traynor and McKelvey v. Turnage*

Let me begin this conceptual excursion by describing a line of reasoning evidenced in a recent Supreme Court ruling, *Traynor and McKelvey v. Turnage.* In this case Traynor and McKelvey sought extended benefits from the Veterans Administration on the grounds that their earlier problems with alcoholism constituted a handicap for which they were not responsible. Veterans are entitled to an extension of the period during which benefits can be provided if a handicap for which they are not responsible prevented them from utilizing their benefits within 10 years of being discharged. Justice White, writing for the majority, found that the Veterans Administration's rule of treating alcoholism as the result of willful misconduct was not unreasonable or arbitrary in light of the substantial body of medical evidence supporting that outlook. Citing Fingarette 1971, White reasoned that alcoholism that is not the result of an underlying psychiatric disorder is not so entirely beyond the agent's control as to undermine the willfulness of the drinking and thus the condition. White claimed that it is controversial whether alcoholism is properly regarded as a disease, and that even if it is a disease, this does not mean that there is no element of culpable willfulness on the part of those alcohol-dependent people who continue to drink. He concluded by suggesting that no basis could be found for judging this sort of alcohol-dependent person to be devoid of all control for excessive drinking. For the purposes of this case, alcoholism could therefore be considered a willfully incurred disability.

With this line of reasoning in mind, I want to point out some phenomena that challenge our ordinary notions of when agents are responsible for their conditions, choices, and qualities of character. The significance of these challenges for these notions and for our judgment will be developed below.

2 The Relevance of Disease to Attributing Behavior

An examination of the notion of disease in our culture will help us become clearer about the problem. To be in a diseased state is normally to be in a condition of impaired functioning, to have one's overall capacities or some specific functioning incapacitated. Characteristically, we regard failures to perform up to normal levels as excusable in someone with diminished abilities. The reason for this dispensation is that it is unfair to expect of a person a level of performance that he or she cannot achieve without unusual costs being borne.

What standard or standards are invoked in deciding whether costs borne are unfair? Even if I put a much higher value on undisturbed sleep than do most people, the unusual costs involved for me in attending to my choking baby at night are not of the sort that counts in this moral calculus. However much I prefer my sleep to my children's lives, this sort of consideration carries no moral weight. To take another example, in defense to a criminal charge, I can plead that I succumbed to coercion when the threat was serious damage to my arm, but not when the threat was serious damage to my violin, even if I care more for my violin than for my arm (Fingarette 1985, 1981; *Model Penal Code*, sec. 209). The central point here is that the notion of an act's being voluntary involves value judgments about what behavior is fitting in particular contexts.

We cannot always be at our best, and inevitably we cannot always be minimally adequate. Why do we hold people to a standard of performance even though we know that everyone has periods when they cannot actually perform up to that level? One response is that ideally we would only hold people to a standard that they can at the time meet but that evidentiary problems beset personalizing a public standard to an individual's particular and momentary inabilities. This difficulty may account for the difference between social standards and legal standards, the former being more tailored to individual conditions.

Alternatively, it could be that we hold people to standards they cannot at times meet because we would be wrong to suppose that having standards can involve anything less demanding (Adams 1985). The problem for this perspective is that we do recognize inability as excusing one some of the time, and in light of this we need an account of why it is appropriate some times but not others.

A third possibility is that we hold people to a standard we know they cannot meet at times, because we think that having this standard helps people locate the resources to perform better than they otherwise would. The standard itself is a factor determining whether people will succeed in conforming to certain expectations. Having a less forgiving standard pushes individual motivations in a direction favorable for a desired outcome.

Having discussed standards and disabilities in general, I now shift to disabilities that are in some sense self-inflicted. If a potentially excusing impairment is self-inflicted, then though the agent cannot function at full throttle, the diminished capacity itself is attributable to the agent, and whatever failures the impairment effects, these too are attributable to the agent.

Various attitudes are attendant upon our characterization of behavior as resulting from an impaired condition. Problematic behavior that results from a nonblamable impairment, like an epileptic seizure, a narcoleptic nap, an abusive swearing associated with Tourette's disorder, are characteristically met with sympathy and consolation rather than with criticism and rebuke.

Recognizing this leads us to a problem. As we learn about how individual choices make impairments more or less likely, we tend to have less sympathy for those who are stricken with a disease attributable to personal habits or decisions. The familiar quip "Smoking cures cancer" reflects an emergent callousness toward those we think accountable for their frightful condition. In the same vein, those who acquire AIDS as a result of their own risky sexual practices or drug abuse are thought by many to be getting just what they deserve. As we learn more about how diet, exercise, patterns of relaxation, and other habits of life make one more or less prone to diseases of certain sorts, and how qualities of character make recovery variably likely, fewer and fewer afflictions come to be seen as completely out of personal control. Accordingly, we tend to show less compassion for the condition we regard as controllable.[1] As more about impairments comes to be connected to choice, less about a person will seem like a visitation and more will seem like the consequences of a blameworthy character defect. The upshot of this is to radically attenuate the conditions under which we will afford sympathetic responses to human suffering.

3 Some Unnerving Discoveries

Some recent discoveries portend attributions of responsibility for many conditions that have been thought purely matters of fate. It was reported in the *New York Times* that new studies of people with multiple personalities suggest some fascinating prospects. For ease of description, let us say that body *b* is home for personalities *x, y,* and *z*. Personality *x*, we are told, may be highly allergic to certain substances and develop a rash or hives when these substances are ingested or present in the environment. But if personality *y* emerges in *b*, the allergic reaction may readily dissipate. Given that allergies are generally not thought to be mind-mediated, this result is intriguing.

Reactions to drugs also may vary from personality to personality within the same body. Drugs that make *y* sleepy may have no effect on *z*. Finally, even the curvature of the eye may change from personality to personality. A prescription for corrective lenses for *x* may be completely inappropriate for *y* or *z*, these personalities requiring a prescription tailored to their individual cases. Again, who would have thought that brains or minds exercise control over reactions to drugs or the shape of the eyes? To know that these things occur is not yet to know how to control these phenomena, but it leaves open the prospect that someday allergies, reactions to drugs, and who knows what else, may be controllable by the agent affected.

Another recent study reported that people prone to cynical, hostile, and angry responses are more likely to suffer premature death from coronary and other causes (Blakeslee 1989). People so disposed are said to have "toxic personalities," probably traceable to biological characteristics present at birth.

There are studies that show the effect of confidence on the course of malignancies in people. Those convinced that they will lick the disease as a result of an optimistic and confident outlook are more likely to survive the disease than those whose outlook is more glum.

Of course, knowing that confidence about achieving a cure will help does not imply that it is within the person's control to place him or herself in the lower-risk group. Many, if not most, of us would be terrified by the diagnosis of a malignancy and find gratuitous and heartless the claim that if only we could have a bright outlook, we would have a fighting chance to survive (Sontag 1977).

Something similar to the bright-outlook factor just described is known about alcohol-abuse rehabilitation. Among problem drinkers, those with the outlook that their condition is one that they cannot control are less likely to control it than those who confront the problem with a different frame of mind about alcohol consumption.

Social-cognitive models of alcoholism maintain that alcoholics' expectations and self-conceptions will influence how they respond to a single drink. Alcoholics who are convinced that there is no alternative after having a drink other than embarking on a binge will be more likely to undergo this chain of events. . . .

The drinker's self-conception of being an alcoholic also affects the course of drinking problems. Subjective beliefs about the disease of alcoholism and about the nature of the person's drinking problem can be more important than objective levels of dependence for selecting treatment goals. Those who believe in the disease theory and that they are alcoholics have a poorer prognosis for controlled drinking. (Peele 1984, 1342–1343)

Researchers are finding that qualities of character, cognitive beliefs, and directions of cultural identification are significant factors in the body's reaction to different kinds of assault or conditions and in the person's ability to dig himself out of a troubling situation.

Not all qualities of character have an impact for the same kind of reasons or even in roughly similar respects, but a body's reaction still turns out to be mediated by character, directly or indirectly. What is significant about this is that, as Aristotle informed us thousands of years ago, our character is itself something for which we are accountable. Once we have reached a mature age, we are assumed to have had ample opportunity to have dealt with those aspects of character that present problems. This outlook does not presuppose that people are not biologically or culturally disposed to be a certain way, but only that character is plastic enough to modify if one begins early to form the right habits. And though we may not have succeeded in extinguishing qualities we regard as undesirable or in nurturing those we deem admirable, we tend to see ourselves and others as responsible for whatever degree of success or level of failure achieved at any given time. Very little short of outright thought control or wholesale moral corruption insulates a person from accountability for the kind of adult he or she has become.

4 Consequences of the Responsible-for-Character View

These comments about character are unexceptionable, but they do have implications. If the qualities of our character give us some measure of control over our reaction to environmental chemicals, disease agents, and diseased conditions, and if we use the standard criterion of having a measure of control to calibrate a level of accountability, then many of the things we regard as unattributable to agents may strictly be so attributable. The social function of the notion of a disease in mitigating moral blameworthiness becomes greatly attenuated.

We cannot rest content with the attenuation of sympathy and support for problems that result in part from qualities of character or choice. What must constitute a part of our outlook is a standard of reasonableness: what is it fair to expect of a person? It is not enough to demonstrate item by item that with attention and motivation, an individual could have improved each quality had he so chosen. For even if he could have changed each, he surely could not have improved *all* of his characteristics had he so chosen.

We also know that not all people face the same hurdles in developing their characters along certain lines. Some may find certain changes rewarding, while others find them continually at odds with something pressing inside of themselves. Some may find that just at the time they recognize the need for change, the stresses in their lives prevent them from being able to address life constructively.

Some may find external support for important changes, while others encounter discouragement for the same efforts at redirection. In his impressive attack on the disease notion of alcoholism and his reconceptualization of heavy drinking as a central activity of life, Herbert Fingarette observes, "One cannot simply and without consequences forsake a central activity, abandon a preferred coping strategy, or disable a defense mechanism—however costly it has proven to be" (1988, 122). A few pages later he continues, "But, as the data show, heavy drinkers who are motivated to change and who are persistent in the face of setbacks can change *if they are given* the appropriate tools and strategies for reshaping their lives" (1988, 128). These passages suggest that the degree to which change is possible, even for those highly motivated, will in many cases depend on factors over which a long-term heavy drinker will have limited or no control. Having a supportive family, economic opportunities, or alternative role models—these are not resources easily accessible to many. Not everyone has within reach the appropriate tools and strategies for restructuring life.

Two related cautionary themes, which I will develop below, emerge from this discussion. (1) The fact that a characteristic is not the result of a disease does not mean that the individual is in control of the trait. (2) Qualities of character are in varying and unstable degrees attributable to the individual.

5 Culture and Choice of Values

There is a tendency to think that if biological explanations of alcohol abuse are only one aspect of the problem, with cultural and individual factors looming large, it is simply up to the individual to control drinking patterns. Once we introduce cultural factors, matters become complicated in ways that I do not think are widely enough recognized or appreciated. Cultures and traditions have a strong influence over how a person will frame his or her experiences of the world. Cultures and traditions will also impose values, loyalties, and directions on its members. Although we like to say that people are responsible for the values they adopt from the cultures they occupy, there is something peculiar about this. The peculiarity lies in omitting consideration of the authority that the culture and traditions have over people. And having authority means that individuals are not, and do not see themselves as, entirely free to pick and choose from among its norms those worth embodying. Three reasons can be offered to support this claim. (1) Many alternatives to an outlook are never presented. We cannot say that people deliberately reject options not visible on their horizon. (2) Some options that upon consideration may seem preferable may not be real options. For instance, one might say that a prescientific outlook is preferable, because more humanly centered, to our outlook. Recognizing this does not make this alternative possible for us. (3) If people approach a tradition in the spirit of selective and reasoned embrace and rejection of what is taken as settled in the tradition, the culture or tradition is at best one of several overlapping cultures they feel part of and is one that has attenuated authority for them.

Some points deserve elaboration here. First, because we think that people should situate themselves within a culture, we must accept that they will come to accept some behavior or styles that people outside the culture find troublesome or misguided. We recognize that they will not approach all issues as ones to be settled by an objective, culturally neutral perspective. Second, even if people recognize that cultural values conflict with widely held norms, it is not clear that it is the saliently rational norms that should dominate whenever there is conflict. Let me illustrate. John Wideman (1984) makes clear in an autobiographical account that his rejection of ghetto values during adolescence came with enormous costs, since it cut him off from the vision, riches, and pains identified as the African-American experience, and thus from himself. As we learn more about the role of cultural identification, I believe we will also appreciate the limited authority an ethical scheme has over people's lives.

Learning is based on trust in certain formal and informal authorities: parents, teachers, community leaders, elected officials, religious leaders, role models, and the "successful" behavior patterns one sees around oneself. These paradigms of social learning, belonging, and participation, and thereby of moral being, are indispensable. Our cognitive and moral economies require that we rely on such authorities for the bulk of our everyday judgments.

Solomon Asch (1961) suggests an interpretation of the observed shift of the individual's view of authoritative or peer assessment when there is a discrepancy—an interpretation involving a critical piece of social dynamics. Asch points out that conformity has been seen by psychologists as either the result of an effort to avoid social punishment or achieve social rewards on the one hand or as the effect of manipulation by those with power or authority on those without these qualities on the other hand. Either of these perspectives presupposes that the shift occurs in only one direction. Asch questions this presupposition, suggests that the shifts are bidirectional, and proposes that conformity can be seen as a group process that has the character of a group achievement. Conforming should not be judged as a distortion of individual rationality but as an essential factor in promoting social being.

In a speculative essay on social evolution, Donald Campbell (1975) suggests that a universal tendency for conformity to the opinions of prestige figures and others may be essential to the human capacity to retain socially adaptive customs and not the character defect typically discovered in those conforming. Campbell points out that for this mechanism to have succeeded in retaining adaptive social customs, the mechanism would have to "operate blindly, without regard to apparent functionality." This suggests that some strategies connected with sociability and traditions serve a role ignored by rational philosophical reconstructions that stress individual autonomy in value orientation.

6   Attributing Alcohol-Consumption Patterns

In the case of alcohol-consumption patterns, considerable effort has been expended on assessing whether the most potent causal determinants to drinking are genetic, social, contextual, or individual. On the basis of what is currently known about alcohol use, I take it that, despite being strongly favored by treatment centers and some funding agencies, the genetic and the corresponding disease account of alcohol abuse are no longer uniquely strong contenders when it comes to explaining most troublesome drinking patterns. In contrast, cultural and contextual factors are now regarded as important in understanding alcohol abuse. To quote Peele again,

Field studies have found demographic categories to play an important role in alcoholism. Cahalan and Room [974] identified youth, lower socioeconomic status, minority status (black or Hispanic), and other conventional ethnic categories (Irish versus Jewish and Italian) as predicting drinking problems. Greeley, McCready, and Theisen [1980] continued to find "ethnic drinking subcultures" and their relationship to drinking problems to be extremely resilient and to have withstood the otherwise apparent assimilation by ethnic groups into mainstream American values. . . . Vaillant [1983] found Irish Americans in his Boston sample to be alcohol dependent (i.e., alcoholic) seven times as often as those from Mediterranean backgrounds (Greeks, Italians, and Jews), and those in Vaillant's working class sample were alcohol dependent more than three times as often as those in his college sample. (Peele 1984; 1339–1340)

Vaillant also found that return to moderate drinking versus abstinence was not a function of having alcoholic relatives but was related to the cultural group of the alcohol abuser. (Peele 1984, 1346–1347)

There are a number of tempting inferences related to this discussion that are important to identify and discuss critically. The first of these is that if alcoholism is not a disease, then it is up to individuals to control their drinking.

What excuse does an individual have who transgresses legal or social norms while under the influence, or for drinking in the first place? The defense of blaming one's culture doesn't have much appeal in either a court of law or the court of public consciousness. This moral inference (no disease means individual responsibility) is also manifest in the majority Supreme Court opinion of *Traynor and McKelvey v. Turnage*, discussed above, which argued that if the cause of habitual drinking is not genetic or in other respects medical, the drinking behavior itself is "willful misconduct" and the habit a "willfully incurred disability."

In a dissenting opinion, Justice Blackmun argued that the plaintiffs deserved a particularized evaluation of the degree to which their alcoholism was voluntary, and therefore the Veterans Administration erred in making the presumption of voluntariness irrebuttable (*Traynor and McKelvey v. Turnage*). Blackmun pointed out that both Traynor and McKelvey began drinking at an early age: eight or nine in the case of Traynor and thirteen in the case of McKelvey. Alcohol dependence was widespread in McKelvey's family. In light of these facts, I think that we would want to follow Justice Blackmun by saying that even if alcoholism is not a disease in the classic sense, there are cases in which we would not want to hold the alcohol-dependent person blamable for his condition.

The focus on the presence or absence of disease in alcohol studies points to a restrictive set of alternatives. As indicated above, we tend to respond to people differently if we think that their behavior or demeanor is the result of a disease rather than the result of, what, something that is not a disease? If their behavior is the outcome of a disease, we will be supportive. If not, we will be critical if the behavior has transgressed some norm. But are these the only options: disease and support on the one hand and health and condemnation on the other? What if we know that someone is having a hard time for any of a variety of reasons and that there is a good prospect that, with the support and encouragement of others, this soul can muster the courage or effort or self-confidence to improve? Does the fact that he or she is not diseased require us to withhold our support and to insist that success, if it comes, will have to come without the encouragement of others? Or what if we believe that even with support, this person will fail for any of a variety of reasons? Is it clear, then, that we should be condemning?

We have a spectrum of responses available. Our thinking about what is fair to expect of people must respect the ambiguities implicit in our understanding of what individuals can do even if they are not diseased. Let me begin with a neutral example before turning to the alcohol-related context.

A runner will run faster in a race than when practicing. It is not that the runner will just try harder in a race but that there is added endurance, drive, and excitement, and hence capacity for running. This suggests that what abilities a person has depend at times on external factors. Furthermore, we know that confidence is an important factor in both creative and competitive contexts. It is uncontroversial to say that people will perform better, exhibit enhanced abilities, if they have confidence in themselves. Of course, we can say that in some situations, having confidence in one's ability is a function of having reasonable beliefs and certain character traits, that both these beliefs and traits are the responsibility of a mature individual, and that fault lies in underestimating what patterns of change are possible.

What we know about the effect of beliefs and objective contexts
on abilities in the realm of sports also applies to the struggle with
alcohol. We might find fairly reasonable the abject outlook a person
adopts. He may see that his own efforts at change have thus far been
unsuccessful. He may see that most of those around him have not
managed any better. He may put stock in a cultural outlook that
predicts failure for those like him. He may be aware of statistical
studies that show that people with his profile fail at a rate of 70 percent or higher. Finally, he may find respected therapists substantiat-
ing his own dismal estimate of his native capacity to modify a bad
habit.

The kind of understanding we afford people who have fallen short
of our social ideals is often taken to be an ideological issue, pitting
those who advocate hard-line views of responsibility against those
who encourage compassion. But viewing it this way is a mistake. We
all want our attributions of responsibility to reflect just standards.
The question we must address is what does applying this standard
require of us. Does it require us to ignore the individuating features
of an individual's past, including socialization? Does it require us to
ignore barriers, social and psychological, that stand in the way of
many well-intentioned addicts' efforts at recovery? The issue is not
one between justice and some more compassionate stance but between different visions of justice. What we learn from the history of
this debate is that socially acceptable resolutions display features that
reflect both objective and subjective conceptions of just attribution
(Allen 1981, 69–71). Researchers err in thinking that new developments will radically change this mixture toward an illness model just
as law-and-order visionaries err in thinking that the mixture will shift
radically to the objective standard because we cannot scientifically
prove that either socialization or biochemistry is the last word on
patterns of alcohol abuse.

Alcohol abuse is a human problem unlikely to yield to straightforward scientific or moral analysis. This means that our moral attitudes
and social policies are destined to fall on all sides of the issues. We
will be forced both to insist on the responsibility of the heavy drinker
and to afford rehabilitative services and prevention programs that to
many, including those being serviced, suggest diminished accountability. It is not unusual now for alcohol abusers to be deemed re-

sponsible by a court and then sentenced to participate in programs that tell the abuser that he or she is not accountable for continuing patterns of drinking. However incoherent this compound picture strikes one as being, we don't have available a more satisfactory picture. Insisting on a coherent picture at this point may require us to ignore important considerations.

In thinking about the implications of the foregoing discussion, it might be useful to focus on an example that is less constrained by legal or constitutional complexities than was the case with which I began. Ralph Tarter described a dilemma for those who make decisions about liver transplants. Many people need liver transplants, but alcohol abusers are represented among this group out of proportion to their percentage in the general population. Should the fact that a person's liver became diseased through alcohol abuse be regarded as relevant when allocating the few livers that become available for transplant?

Here we might be tempted to finesse the issue by observing that a person with a record of abuse is a poor transplant prospect for medical reasons alone. (What will keep him from ruining the next liver with his uncontrolled drinking?) But in first considering the issue, without considering its being medically counterindicated, I confess to thinking that it is unfair to allocate scarce resources to someone who caused a problem when the same resources could be used to help someone who is innocent in the relevant sense. My second thought, though, was that this response is oblivious to most of what I have been worrying over in this paper. To the extent that we cannot make a determination of who is and who is not blameworthy for having ruined his or her liver, we must not use alcohol abuse as a morally disqualifying factor.[2] But as a social policy, should we put the same resources into seeking cures and treatments for diseases that are in some sense largely self-inflicted and those that are not, with everything else constant? I suggested above that we do not know where such a policy would lead in light of discoveries about character and diseases. On the other hand, we have a general, and probably salutary, attitude that discounts suffering on the part of people who knowingly enough risk behavior that is not regarded as socially valuable.

For medical treatment, we might want to argue that if choices must be made, they should be made on the basis of need, not desert, even though this *could* mean disregarding previous drinking patterns.[3] For allocating resources for development of cures, we might legitimately use avoidability as a criterion along with other criteria, like the number of people directly affected, the number of parties indirectly affected, the comparative efficiency of expenditures along given lines, etc. But the criterion of avoidability would have to apply to nearly all sufferers of a given malady, and it is very unlikely that we could fairly come to such a judgment.

7 Concluding Thoughts

So what should we think? We should feel perplexed about our practices of attributing responsibility even as applied to as widespread and historically common a phenomenon as alcohol consumption. We should not think that science has failed us in not answering this question for us. We should appreciate that it is the community's responsibility to set standards of accountability that reflect and respect the limits and strengths of human nature.

Among the realizations we may come to is that the question of the responsibility of the heavy drinker for his or her behavior is not one issue but a range of issues; answers suitable in one domain may not be appropriate in another. Factors relevant to deciding what should be covered by standard medical-insurance plans are not necessarily those to be used in settling cases at law governing what benefits the Veterans Administration should be required to supply. Taking a public posture to reform social expectations about the degree of control drinkers should exercise may not prove helpful in addressing what to do with someone who for thirty years, has believed that drinking is not a matter of self-control.

Deciding as an individual or a society to be supportive and understanding toward someone burdened by alcohol abuse may not at all stem from a belief that the behavior patterns were outside anyone's control. One might think that a given individual's drinking problems are not attributable to anyone else but that there are so many tragic challenges this person has had to face that it is no wonder that his drinking is uncontrolled.

We may think no one else is to blame for a person's drinking problems but nevertheless regard the society as disqualified from making a moral judgment. For instance, one might argue that it is hypocritical for a society that socializes people to drink as a way of alleviating anxiety, expends enormous resources in advertising the desirability of alcohol consumption, and structures tax incentives to consumers who do this in a business setting, to then condemn people who drink excessively while facing real problems. Or one might think that a culture that neglects to offer services to a high percentage of troubled children cannot legitimately complain when these same children adopt nonconstructive patterns of coping with these problems, patterns that become entrenched character traits. Alternatively, policy considerations might well lure us into treating alcohol-dependent people as accountable though we know that some significant percentage of these are unfairly blamed. A range of factors relevant to some of these determinations may well be irrelevant to others.

Depending on the setting, there may already be in place a deliberative body able to make an individualized assessment of the degree to which an individual is blameworthy for his alcohol dependency. In the context of a criminal trial, there already is such a body. In the case of a potential recipient for an organ transplant, there also already is a body that can try to make an individualized determination of the potential recipient's accountability for his or her condition. In the case of extensions of veterans' benefits for alcohol-dependent people, we may ask how much it would add to the administrative costs of the Veterans Administration to allow veterans who want to claim that their drinking is involuntary to be provided with a forum for evaluating this claim.

In conclusion, let me point to some considerations that can help explain our conflicting attitudes about the alcohol-dependent person, exemplifying a whole range of human problems and resolving practically what our responses to such issues should be. In my discussion of disease and responsibility thus far, I have been assuming that there is one level of ability or competence such that, whatever is at stake in the context, if the individual meets that level, he is accountable, otherwise not. If we look at how we generally attribute responsibility for behavior, seeing when we say that the act was the agent's and when not, we find no one level of competence satisfying all behavior contexts.

We generally attribute responsibility for behavior to an individual when we do not find some aspect of the environment, external or internal, "overwhelming." The assessment of when pressures are overwhelming, however, cannot be made in terms of the levels of the pressures by themselves. This point can be illustrated with reference to the notion of coercion. The concept of coercion is relevant here because it is used as a way of gauging whether a person's behavior reflects, or is an expression of, the person's will. An intricate array of reasons is relevant to assessing whether an agent is to be regarded as the author of her action. Compare the following two situations: I agree to sell you my house for $10,000 because you threaten to slash my face unless I do so. During a recession when I lose my job and have no prospect of another, I agree to sell my house for one tenth its value ($10,000) so that I can afford to keep myself and family from starvation. Though the prospect of death by starvation is more fearsome than the prospect of a scarred face, the latter agreement is regarded as more binding than the former, less an undermining of the agent's real will. If a policeman subtly pressures a suspect in a custodial setting, a resulting confession is regarded as forced and hence not the product of the defendant's will, while if a doctor tells me that unless I submit to a procedure I will die of natural causes, my consent to the procedure is regarded as voluntary and representing my real (very scared) self.[4]

Recognizing that there is a variable standard of accountability and attribution helps us see first of all why we may have conflicting attitudes in thinking about alcoholism and similar problems. An impairment, like fatigue, is serious enough that for most contexts, the impairment counts as an excuse from accountability, but in some very serious contexts, like driving or sentry duty, it does not. By and large, then, we have reason to be supportive and forgiving toward the person who falls below the standard in most contexts, but not toward people who fall below it in some contexts. In the case of the alcohol-dependent person, we can be forgiving and supportive for some behavior but not for behavior that seriously endangers others.

Let me illustrate with a recent affair: Brozan 1989. Hedda Nussbaum acquiesced in the abuse and eventual murder of her adopted daughter. Nussbaum herself had been the victim of repeated, serious abuse. Does her own victimization excuse her from accountability for her daughter's death? One can coherently say that suffering abuse would excuse her from a lot of personal failings but not for standing by while her daughter is killed.

In cases such as the one described, *up to a point* we would be supportive, compassionate, and, if necessary, forgiving toward Hedda Nussbaum, because of what she had to endure. Her situation calls for compassion and understanding, and these emotions and attitudes toward her are apposite. It would also be odd to suggest that we can just turn these emotions off at the threshold where we judge her condition no longer excusing. We feel that she does deserve our sympathy, even if she deserves a harsher response too. Though these responses conflict, they are not contradictory or ungrounded. And this is my first point. We have an explanation for conflicting attitudes: sympathy and support for conditions that excuse for many contexts, and resentment for violating norms that even disadvantaged people should not violate. (After all, it cannot be that only nondisadvantaged people can do wrong. If there are normal people who are cowardly or lack integrity, why should there not also be condemnable cowards and scoundrels among the disadvantaged?)

To return to the alcohol-dependent person, we can be sympathetic, understanding, supportive, and forgiving for a wide variety of behaviors without precluding legitimate expressions of resentment for some serious or important failings. We are not limited to one response. The alcohol-dependent person, the abused spouse, the disadvantaged—all deserve our support, sympathy, and constructive endeavors on their behalf. But they, like the rest of us, also live in a community with values that can be more demanding for some ranges of behavior than for others. We can and should be supportive when something we can do addresses a human problem. We can and should be resentful when someone, even with a problem, doesn't show enough judgment or restraint.

How do we tell when asking something of a person is asking too much? Without thinking that I can answer this question, I want to emphasize that this is a moral or social question for which biological and psychological data are relevant but not decisive (Fingarette 1972). All I can offer here is the observation that what we often take to be conflicting outlooks toward heavy drinking are more appropriately seen as reasonable responses to separate objective aspects of a perplexing problem.[5]

Acknowledgments

A special expression of appreciation is due to Herbert Fingarette, not only for published pieces that provoked many of the thoughts contained in this chapter but also for especially gracious and elaborate suggestions lavished on an earlier version of it. I also wish to thank Elizabeth Patterson, Frank Zimring, Pat Hubbard, Nora Bell, William McAninch, George Schroeder, Natalie Kaufman, Mary Bockover, and Kaye Middleton Fillmore for valuable comments on an earlier version of this paper. I am also indebted to the National Endowment for the Humanities for financial support during the time that this paper was written and to the Earl Warren Legal Institute at the University of California at Berkeley and the Law School at the University of South Carolina for providing ideal academic environments.

Notes

1. This does not pertain just to vulnerability to diseases. It is a human tendency to regard increasing one's vulnerability to harm from any source as a fault and as attenuating the sympathy others should address to one. If I leave my bicycle or house unlocked when I go for a vacation, there will be less sympathy for my loss than if I had secured these and was robbed anyway. Similarly, if I am robbed while walking through Central Park at 3:00 A.M. with $100 bills pinned to my shirt, few will be sympathetic to my plight.

2. Jane Jacobs reported that it is common to find families of continual drinkers adopting the attitude that the drinker has no choice and families of binge drinkers adopting the view that if the person does in fact resist drinking most of the time, then the drinker does have control over those times when the drinking recurs. My own predilection is for trusting the attitudes of those who (have to) live with people with problems.

3. In *Allen v. Mansour*, Allen, a 27-year-old suffering from end-stage liver disease caused by consumption of alcohol, wanted Medicaid to pay for a liver transplant. At this time Allen had abstained from drinking for four months, but the authorizing body had a policy of not authorizing transplants for liver disease for alcohol-dependent people who had not been abstemious for at least two years.

Speaking for the court, Chief Judge Pratt found that the two-year policy was arbitrary. Although the court granted Allen his injunction, by the time it was issued, his condition deteriorated to the point that he could no longer be operated on. Cases like this are tragic, and whatever one's principles are, they seem to melt before the facts of a person's desperate yet treatable condition.

4. Not all rightful threats fail to count as coercion, as is evidenced in the centrality of legal coercion to criminal law (Wertheimer 1987).

5. I want to thank Herbert Fingarette for suggesting the line of thinking that I pursue in this concluding section.

References

Adams, Robert. 1985. "Involuntary Sins." *Philosophical Review* 96:3–32.

Allen v. Mansour. 681 F. Supp. 1232 (E.D. Mich. 1986).

Allen, Francis. 1981. *The Decline of the Rehabilitative Ideal: Penal Policy and Social Purpose.* New Haven: Yale University Press.

Asch, Solomon. 1961. "Issues in the Study of Social Influences on Judgment." In *Conformity and Deviation,* ed. Irwin Berg and Bernard Bass. New York: Harper and Brothers.

Blakeslee, Sandra. 1989. "Cynicism and Mistrust Linked to Early Death." *New York Times,* January 17, p. 21.

Brozan, Nadine. 1989. "Unresolved Question: Is Nussbaum Culpable?" *New York Times,* January 24, p. 15.

Calahan, D., and R. Room. 1974. *Problem Drinking among American Men.* New Brunswick, N.J.: Rutgers Center for Alcohol Studies.

Campbell, Donald. 1975. "On the Conflicts between Biological and Social Evolution and between Psychology and Moral Tradition." *American Psychologist* 30:1003–1126.

Fingarette, Herbert. 1971. "The Perils of Powell: In Search of a Factual Foundation for the Disease Concept of Alcoholism." *Harvard Law Review* 83:793–812.

Fingarette, Herbert. 1972. *The Meaning of Criminal Insanity.* Berkeley: University of California Press.

Fingarette, Herbert. 1981. "Legal Aspects of Alcoholism and Other Addictions: Some Basic Conceptual Issues." *British Journal of Addiction* 76:125–132.

Ferdinand Schoeman

Fingarette, Herbert. 1985. "Victimization: A Legalist Analysis of Coercion, Deception, Undue Influence, and Excusable Prison Escape." *Washington and Lee Law Review* 42:65–118.

Fingarette, Herbert. 1988. *Heavy Drinking: The Myth of Alcoholism as a Disease.* Berkeley: University of California Press.

Greeley, A. M., N. C. McCready, and G. Theisen. 1980. *Ethnic Drinking Subcultures.* New York: Praeger.

Model Penal Code and Commentaries. 1985. Philadelphia: American Law Institute.

Peele, Stanton. 1984. "Cultural Context of Psychological Approaches to Alcoholism." *American Psychologist* 39:1337–1351.

Sontag, Susan. 1977. *Illness as Metaphor.* New York: Farrar, Straus, and Giroux.

Traynor and McKelvey v. Turnage. 108 S. Ct. 1372 (1988).

Vaillant, G. E. 1983. *The Natural History of Alcoholism: Causes, Patterns, and Paths to Recovery.* Cambridge: Harvard University Press.

Wertheimer, Alan. 1987. *Coercion.* Princeton: Princeton University Press.

Wideman, John. 1984. *Brothers and Keepers.* New York: Holt, Reinhart, and Winston.

Value, Illness, and Failure of Action: Framework for a Philosophical Psychopathology of Delusions

K. W. M. Fulford

Delusion is in many respects the paradigm symptom of mental illness. Yet standard textbook accounts of its psychopathology are in important respects sharply at variance with its clinical characteristics.

In this chapter I argue that the standard account is not so much wrong as incomplete. It proceeds from an essentially scientific model, the so-called "medical" model, in which disease concepts are defined by reference to what are taken to be objective norms of bodily and mental functioning. This model thus excludes, or at best marginalizes, the evaluative element in the conceptual structure of medicine. It is a heuristically powerful model, not least in respect of psychopathology—it explains the cognitive impairments of dementia, for instance. But it fails to give an account of delusions and related psychotic symptoms.

Recognizing the evaluative logical element in medicine, on the other hand, leads to what amounts to a "full-field" model, as distinct from a "science-half-field" model. In a full-field model, the patient's primary experience of illness is as important as medical knowledge of disease; and the analysis of this experience in terms of incapacity, or failure of action, is as important as the analysis of disease in terms of failure of function. The additional elements of a full-field psychopathology—value, illness, and failure of action—we will find are necessary for an adequate account of delusion, and thus, given the central importance of delusion in the map of psychiatry, for psycho-pathology in general.

The chapter is divided into two main sections. Section 1 details some of the limitations of the standard account of delusions. Particu-larly important here is the failure of this account to explain the par-ticular kind of loss of insight by which not only delusions but also other psychotic symptoms are characterized. Section 1 ends with a checklist of the logically relevant features of these symptoms, that is, the features that any philosophical account of their psychopathology must seek to explain. In section 2, I show that the additional re-sources of a full-field psychopathology explain each of these features. I outline the significance of this for the future development of philo-sophical psychopathology in a brief concluding section.

1 The Standard Account of Delusions

The central place of delusions as the paradigm symptom of mental illness has long been recognized (Jaspers 1963). Delusions are seri-ous symptoms; they are as reliably identifiable as the symptoms of physical illness (Wing, Cooper, and Sartorius 1974), and they are cross-culturally stable (Wing 1978). Along with certain closely related symptoms, such as hallucinations, they form the core of that whole group of disorders, the psychotic disorders, in which, as the modern counterpart of the traditional "mad" or "insane," the patient charac-teristically lacks insight into his or her condition. This lack of insight, moreover, has given these disorders a particular ethical and medico-legal significance. At least since classical times, the insane have been regarded as not responsible for their actions, and hence both in need of protection, if necessary amounting to involuntary treatment (Fulford 1990a), and excused from liability under the law (Walker 1985).

The particular kind of loss of insight involved here (psychotic loss of insight) is crucial to understanding the psychopathology of delu-sions. As a number of authors have noted, insight is a complex no-tion carrying, even in medicine, several different meanings (David 1990, Markova and Berrios 1992). In respect of a number of these, the insight of the deluded patient may be entirely normal. Thus with delusions the patient is perfectly *aware* that there *is* a problem (in contrast to the patient with asymptomatic cancer, say). Similarly, he is aware that it is *his* problem (in contrast to, for instance, the patient with a parietal-lobe lesion leading to "visual neglect," who is incapable of recognizing that the paralyzed arm lying on the bed belongs to him). Again, he is aware that the problem may have *serious consequences* (in contrast to the alcoholic, for example, who denies that his marriage is breaking up and his job at risk as a result of his drinking). The deluded patient, it is true, does lack insight into the *psychological nature* of the problem. But so also, for example, does the patient with a hysterical paralysis who believes that he really is paralyzed.

The loss of insight involved in delusions is thus different from all of these. We will be looking at this in detail in a moment. But a core feature of the psychopathology of delusions, the datum of clinical observation, is that the deluded patient fails to recognize his or her delusion as a *symptom* of illness at all. With a delusion of persecution, for example, the patient's belief is construed by everyone else as a symptom of mental illness, while from the patient's perspective what is wrong is simply that he is being persecuted. Similarly, with a delusion of guilt, what is wrong from the patient's perspective is not that he is ill but that he has done something terribly wrong. Hypochondriacal delusions make the point neatly. With a delusion of cancer, say, the patient shares with everyone else the belief that there is something medically wrong. But where the patient believes that what is medically wrong is that he *has* cancer, everyone else takes the patient's *belief* that he has cancer to be an indication that what is medically wrong is that he is mentally ill.

In the textbooks this feature of delusions is often brought out by comparing them with other similar, but nonpsychotic, symptoms. Thus the thought that one has cancer may take the form of an obsessional symptom—a repeated thought that, like a bad case of getting a tune stuck in your head, simply will not go away. With obsessional thoughts, however, the patient's insight is characteristically intact. Hence the patient may complain to his doctor about the repeated *thought*, much as he might about any other symptom. But with a delusion of cancer, the patient really *believes* he has cancer. Hence it is of this that he complains, not of the thought. The difference here can be practically important. Thus obsessions are common in severe depression, but as the depression deepens, an obsession may become converted into a delusion (the ridiculous thought that one has cancer becomes the firm belief that one has cancer). As Gittleson (1966) has shown, this is associated with a sudden increase in risk of suicide. This radical misconstruction of what is wrong, as a specifically psychotic loss of insight, is thus at the heart of the psychopathology of delusions.

Definition and Use of the Concept of Insight

Despite its phenomenological significance, psychotic loss of insight has turned out to be particularly resistant to definition within the framework of traditional psychopathology. The difficulties here go back to the work on insight of one of the founders of modern scientific psychiatry, Aubrey Lewis. In a carefully argued paper rich with clinical examples, he suggested that at least to a first approximation, insight could be defined as a "correct attitude to a morbid change in oneself" (1934, 333). Yet as he showed, by this definition, however carefully it is elaborated, many patients with nonpsychotic disorders, not to mention many with physical disorders, lack insight, while at least some patients with psychotic disorders have rather good insight.

There are two possible interpretations of this observation: either the notion of insight as the defining characteristic of psychosis is otiose; or the suggested definition of insight is wrong. Aubrey Lewis considered only the former. He concluded that, central as the notion had been to traditional psychopathology, the psychotic/nonpsychotic divide represented a distinction without a difference and should be abandoned in a properly scientific psychiatry.

This has been the official line ever since. So much so that the distinction has been progressively downgraded in successive classifications of psychiatric disorders, the intention (openly acknowledged, World Health Organization, 1978) being that it should disappear. But the difficulty for the official line is just that fifty years after Aubrey Lewis the distinction still persists. Moreover, it persists not only in everyday psychiatric usage (in such expressions as "antipsychotic drug" and "puerperal psychosis") but also in academic journals, in the continuing forensic significance of psychotic disorders, and, not least, in the latest editions of our official classifications.

Both *DSM* III (American Psychiatric Association, 1980) and *ICD* 10 (World Health Organization, 1992), although claiming to have given up the distinction, include a range of psychotic disorders and even a category for psychotic disorders "not elsewhere classified." Indeed, the use of the psychotic/nonpsychotic distinction in both these classifications can be shown to be strictly equivalent to its use in earlier more traditional editions (Fulford, forthcoming).

The continued use of the psychotic/nonpsychotic distinction thus suggests, contrary to Aubrey Lewis, that it is his (prima facie plausible) definition that is at fault rather than the concept of psychotic loss of insight. If the distinction really were otiose, then like the distinction between endogenous and reactive depression, for example, it should have disappeared. But despite all efforts at eradication, it persists. It is true that what the distinction consists in is not immediately obvious. But this means only that the concept of psychotic disorder (like the concept of time, for example) is useful, even essential, in ordinary usage, despite the lack of a clear, unambiguous, and widely agreed-on explicit definition.

Particular Psychotic Symptoms

In partial recognition of this, the standard line has been to fall back on individual psychotic symptoms: hallucination, certain kinds of thought disorder, and, crucially, delusion. The idea is that while the broad notion of psychotic loss of insight may be difficult to pin down, at least we know how to define particular psychotic symptoms. This was how the British Butler Committee, a government committee set up to review the treatment of the mentally ill in law, sought to circumscribe the kinds of disorder that could appropriately be considered to be legal excuses (Butler 1975). It is also the line taken more or less explicitly in many textbooks (Gelder, Gath, and Mayou 1983).

At first glance, this approach is persuasive. Thus a hallucination, for example, is generally straightforwardly defined as a perception in the absence of a stimulus (Harre and Lamb 1986). As we will see later, not all hallucinations are psychotic. A psychotic hallucination is one in which the hallucinatory percept, reflecting a psychotic loss of insight, is believed to be real. So hallucination, in respect of insight, rests on delusion. And delusion, so the standard line continues, is definable, again more or less straightforwardly, as a "false belief, held despite evidence to the contrary, and one which is not explicable in terms of the patient's educational and cultural background. It is held with complete conviction and cannot be shaken by argument" (Harre and Lamb 1986).

As psychiatrists (Mullen 1979), psychologists (Hemsley and Garety 1986) and philosophers (Flew 1973) have all pointed out, there is a good deal wrong with at least the subsidiary clauses of this definition: conviction is no mark of pathology, many delusions are culturally congruent (e.g., delusions of cancer), and the evidential grounds of perhaps a majority of our normal beliefs are at best uncertain. Yet the central plank of the definition—the idea that delusion is a false belief—seems at first glance, at least, uncontentious. From a medical point of view, moreover, it has the advantage of providing apparently objective norms for the diagnosis of delusion and is thus consistent with the scientific self-image embodied in the conventional medical model of disease. Philosophers too have emphasised the importance of falsity of belief in the standard definition. Glover (1970) and Quinton (1985) both made this feature crucial to their accounts of the irrationality of the insane. Similarly, Flew (1973) emphasised the objective falsity of delusions as the one sure defence against the misuse of diagnoses of mental illness as a means of political coercion.

That delusions can be objectively false beliefs—often, as both Glover (1970) and Flew (1973) require, bizarrely so—is an important feature of their psychopathology. Among the nihilistic delusions associated with severe depression, for example, the patient may believe that his or her body has been wholly replaced with a cancer. Compared with more commonplace delusions, such beliefs are not merely unlikely to be true; they are contingently impossible. And approaching the logically impossible are some delusional beliefs in which identity breaks down: Capgras's syndrome, for instance, in which a near relative is believed to have been replaced by an impostor identical with the real relative, and other delusions of misidentification (Spier 1992); and Cotard's syndrome, in which one may believe oneself never to have been born (Sims 1988).

Hence delusions, as symptoms of mental illness, as the central symptom of the central kind of mental illness (psychosis), may be false—objectively false—beliefs. The standard definition is thus right to the extent that it emphasizes this as a feature of delusions. The difficulty, however, is that delusions, as symptoms of psychotic mental illness, are not necessarily *false* beliefs at all.

Delusions Are Not Always False Beliefs

The most obvious sense in which delusions may not be objectively false beliefs is when they turn out to have been true all along, for example, the patient with delusions of persecution who turns out to be under investigation by the tax authorities. However, a second and more fundamental sense in which delusions may not be false beliefs is when they are known to be true even at the time the diagnosis is made. In such cases there is clearly *something* wrong with the patient's beliefs, but so far at least as the content of their beliefs is concerned, this is known by the person making the diagnosis to be essentially *con*cordant rather than *dis*cordant with the facts.

The standard clinical example of delusions being in this second sense true beliefs is provided by the Othello syndrome of delusions of infidelity. There have been a number of case reports of this syndrome (Shepherd 1961). The core feature of the condition is a delusional belief in the infidelity of one's sexual partner. This is a belief that (like normal jealousy) may be all-consuming; moreover, it may be supported on grounds that are apparently bizarre. But as has been pointed out in the literature (Vauhkonen 1968), whatever the diagnosis depends on, it is not that the patient's belief is, with regard to the plain facts, false.

There is perhaps room in cases such as these for arguing that the patients concerned, if not wholly wrong (in the way required by Glover [1970] and Flew [1973], for instance), were nonetheless mistaken—they had, say, exaggerated to the point of error. There is, however, a third and even more fundamental sense in which delusions may not be false beliefs, namely that for some patients this would present us with a paradox.

I have reported one such case that occurred in Oxford (Fulford 1989, chap. 10). The patient, a 43-year-old man, was brought to the Accident and Emergency Department following an overdose. He had tried to kill himself because he was afraid he was going to be "locked up." However, this fear was secondary to a paranoid system at the heart of which was the hypochondriacal delusion that he was "mentally ill." He was seen by the duty psychiatrist and by the consultant psychiatrist on call, neither of whom were in any doubt that he was deluded. Indeed, both were ready on the strength of their diagnosis to admit him as an involuntary patient. Yet had their diagnosis depended on the falsity of the patient's belief, as in the standard definition, they would have been presented with a paradox: if the patient's belief that he was mentally ill was false, then (by the standard definition) he could have been deluded, but this would have made his belief true after all. Equally, if his belief was true, then he was not deluded (by the standard definition), but this would have made his belief false after all. By the standard definition of delusion, then, his belief, if false, was true and, if true, was false.

Evaluative Delusions

Cases of the kind just described are not common. They can be important clinically because the syndromes in which they occur may carry a definite risk of harm, either through suicide or, as in the Othello syndrome, homicide (Vauhkonen 1968). Their logical significance, of course—what they tell us about the meaning of the clinical concept of delusion—is not tied to the seriousness of their practical implications, still less to the frequency with which they occur. There is, however, yet a fourth sense in which delusions may not be false beliefs, or at any rate objectively false beliefs, as assumed in the standard definition—a sense that brings us back to the everyday of clinical practice. Delusions commonly and uncontentiously may not be beliefs about matters of fact at all, whether true or false, but value judgments. This is not just in the sense that many delusions are strongly value-laden. It is rather that the actual content of a delusional belief may be a value judgment (Fulford 1991).

Examples of this occur commonly in the affective psychoses, with negative value judgments in psychotic depression and (usually) positive value judgments in its elevated-mood counterpart, hypomania. In depression, for example, delusions of guilt are common: these may be factual in form (the patient believing, say, that they are responsible for some famine or earthquake), but they may also be evaluative. Thus one patient had forgotten (he *had* forgotten) to give his children their pocket money, and he believed this was "the worst sin in the world," that he was "worthless as a father," and that his children would be "better off if he were dead." Similarly, a lady with hypomania believed she was Mary Magdalen reincarnated (mixed factual and evaluative judgment), that certain minor charities she had performed were "of great and enduring moral worth" (moral-evaluative judgment), and that her reams of chaotic poetry were of "unparalleled literary merit" (aesthetic judgment).

Such delusions are not confined to affective disorders. They occur in schizophrenia, for example, and in paranoid psychoses (psychotic disorders with predominantly delusional symptomatology, as in the Othello syndrome). An interesting example of this is delusional dysmorphobia, in which the patient delusionally perceives himself or herself to be ugly (Thomas 1984). Some of the symptomatology of anorexia nervosa may possibly be of this kind. But the commonest and clearest examples of evaluative delusions occur in the affective psychoses.

Evaluative delusions are remarkable philosophically not least because, despite being clinically commonplace, they have been largely overlooked. Fact and value, whatever one's philosophical views about the logical relationship between them (Warnock 1967), are in many respects conceptual chalk and cheese, so evaluative delusions should have been of interest to philosophers (I return to this in section 2). Similarly, in psychiatry, delusions are classified by content (persecutory, grandiose, etc.), by some aspects of their form (e.g., simple, as in dementia, versus elaborate), and even by their relationship to other pathologies (secondary delusions, e.g., secondary to depression, as against primary delusions, which appear to come "out of the blue"). But they are not differentiated into factual and evaluative. Evaluative delusions are included among the examples given in psychiatric textbooks: in the *Oxford Textbook of Psychiatry* (Gelder, Gath, and Mayou 1983), for example, and in Leff and Isaacs's *Psychiatric Examination in Clinical Practice* (1981). Evaluative delusions are that common. Yet they are not explicitly differentiated from factual delusions.

The clinical reason for this is obvious enough, namely that it makes no difference to treatment whether a patient's delusions are factual or evaluative. With depression complicated by delusions of guilt, for example, decisions about treatment, even about whether involuntary treatment is appropriate, are not influenced by whether the content of the patient's delusions are factual or evaluative. But this makes evaluative delusions even more remarkable philosophically. For it means that these two quite different conceptual species—fact and value, philosophical chalk and cheese—have identical implications. Different meanings, then, but the same implications. Yet this feature of delusions has been neglected as much by philosophers as by clinicians.

Delusions and Impaired Cognitive Functioning

The logical range of delusions, as symptoms of mental illness, is thus much wider than has generally been recognized. Even so, it is still possible to retain an essentially scientific medical model of the meaning of delusion by shifting the definition from "false" to "unfounded" belief. This is how delusions are defined in the *Oxford Textbook*, for instance (Gelder, Gath, and Mayou 1983). The medical model, as noted earlier, is based on the analysis of disease in terms of impaired functioning. Hence the shift from "false" to "unfounded" implies a disease model of delusion in which delusion is taken to involve some impairment specifically of intellectual or cognitive functioning, "cognitive" being used here as in psychiatry and psychology to denote such particular intellectual functions as orientation, attention, memory, and general IQ. According to this view, delusions would normally be false but could, by chance, happen to be true, or indeed paradoxical, or even evaluative, all these being conceptually epiphenomenal to the underlying disturbance of cognitive functioning.

There are both empirical and philosophical difficulties with this account, however. The empirical difficulty is simply that, despite the best efforts of the cognitive psychologists, no impairment of cognitive functioning specific to delusions has yet been identified (Hemsley and Garety 1986). Such impairments are characteristic of a number of conditions in which delusions occur: in dementia above all but also in hypomania (extreme distractibility) and depression (extreme slowing of thought). But all these actually *impair* delusional-belief formation, just as they impair the formation of normal beliefs. The best-quality delusions—elaborate, well sustained, ingeniously defended—occur in monosymptomatic delusional disorders (like the Othello syndrome), in which there is little if any other pathology at all.

It is, of course, possible that the discovery of some subtle disturbance in cognitive functioning specific to delusions is waiting around the corner. But this would still leave the philosophical difficulty. This difficulty arises from the fact, noted earlier, that an important feature of the clinical psychopathology of delusions is that delusions are the *central* symptom of the *central* kind of mental illness (psychosis). We should thus expect the relevant disturbance of functioning to be relatively transparent rather than relatively obscure. It needn't be, of course, but we should expect it to be. Hence, as even so staunch a philosophical advocate of the medical model as Boorse (1975, 1976) has noted, disturbed-function accounts as a whole fail to do justice to the central place of delusions in the conceptual map of psychiatry.

The Logically Relevant Features of Delusions

In this section we have seen that the standard medical model fails to account for a number of important features of the psychopathology of delusions and other psychotic symptoms. These include (1) the particular kind of loss of insight by which psychotic symptoms in general are marked out from nonpsychotic symptoms; (2) the remarkable logical range of delusions, occurring as they do not only as false beliefs but also as true factual beliefs and as value judgements; (3) the central clinical importance of delusions as the paradigm symptom of mental illness, including (4) their central ethical and medicolegal significance; and (5) the fact that the clinical implications of delusion are identical for each of its very different logical forms.

It could, of course, be said, Well, so much the worse for delusions. Just as Aubrey Lewis rejected the concept of insight because he could not make it fit his definition, so we might reject, say, evaluative delusions, or we might refuse to acknowledge the central ethical significance of psychotic disorders. This is a possible response. Even as a negative response, however, it stands to be tested by the above features of the psychopathology of delusions just as surely as any positive account. For these features represent criteria by which *any* conceptual theory of delusion, even a skeptical theory, is measured. A prodelusion theory must explain why the clinical concept of delusion is as it is. An antidelusion theory must explain why the concept merely appears as it does.

The standard account has thus far failed either way. It has neither explained the conceptually significant clinical features of delusions and related psychotic symptoms nor explained them away. In the next section I will explore these features from the perspective of a model of the medical concepts that differs in important respects from the standard model. I have described this model in detail elsewhere (Fulford 1989). In the concluding section of this chapter I will return to the implications of the model for philosophical psychopathology generally. The essential characteristic of the model is that it provides a more complete view of the conceptual structure of medicine. The standard model, as we have seen, focuses on facts, disease theory, and failure of function. The new model incorporates these elements but adds to them values, the experience of illness, and the analysis of this experience in terms of incapacity, or failure of action. In this sense, then, as illustrated in figure 1, it is a full-field model rather than a half-field model. As we will find, the additional elements of a full-field model are required to explain the psychopathological features of delusions and other psychotic symptoms.

2 Delusions in a Philosophical Psychopathology

In this section I will be drawing on the general features of a full-field psychopathology to explore the clinical phenomenology of psychotic disorders. I will focus particularly on the elements added to the conventional medical model, looking first at the experience of illness, then at the significance of the evaluative logical element in medicine, and finally at the notion of failure of action. As just noted, we will find that these are essential to understanding insight and delusion. In focusing on these elements, however, we should not lose sight of the fact that the elements traditionally emphasized—disease theory, fact and failure of function—are equally important to a complete psychopathology.

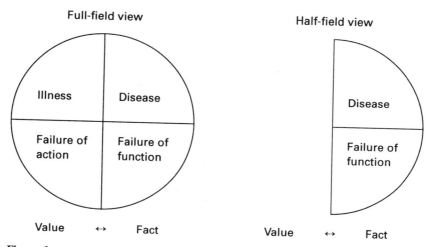

Figure 1
The full-field view and science-half-field view of the conceptual structure of medicine. As described more fully in the text, the standard model of the conceptual structure of medicine can be understood as a half-field view. The half-field view emphasises facts—disease and failure of function—but at the expense of values: the experience of illness and failure of action. These latter elements (the left half of the full-field view) are shown in this chapter to be necessary for an adequate account of delusions and related psychotic symptoms. Both halves of a full-field view, however, are required for a complete psychopathology.

The Experience of Illness

In section 1, I noted that the concept of psychotic loss of insight had proved so difficult to define in terms of the science-based disease theories of Aubrey Lewis and his successors that strenuous attempts have been made to exclude the distinction from our classifications. In a full-field psychopathology, by contrast, a single feature of the experience of illness is sufficient to provide an account of psychotic loss of insight. Indeed, it is sufficient to generate complex differential diagnostic tables for each of the three main types of psychotic symptoms: thought disorder, hallucination, and delusion.

Consider, then, the primary experience of illness. This involves (among other things) a two-way distinction. For example, suppose that my hand suddenly stops moving across this page. The experience of this as something *wrong with* me is distinct from the experience of my not moving my hand (something I *do*) and equally from that of my hand being restrained by someone else (something *done to* me). A similar two-way distinction helps to demarcate pain as a symptom. Pain is a sensation, and it is thus something we do something about rather than (like movement) something we do. But pain experienced as something wrong with me is different both from my being hurt by someone or something and from my hurting myself (sitting on a pin, say). Much the same is again true of the symptoms of mental illness. For example, difficulty remembering things, as something wrong with me, is different both from being distracted (done to) and from simply not bothering to remember (done by), and anxiety as a symptom is different both from being frightened by something (done to) and from frightening myself (by, e.g., voluntarily going hang-gliding).

There is thus a three-way distinction here, done-by/wrong-with/ done to, a distinction that can be shown to be a very general feature of the primary experience of illness, both physical and mental (Fulford 1989, chaps. 7 and 8). There are, of course, other (better recognized) elements of the experience of illness: intensity and duration, for instance. Thus a phobia is, inter alia, a disproportionate fear (World Health Organization, 1978). Moreover, the three-way distinction itself invites further analysis (Fulford 1989, chap. 12). But it is at least a very general feature of the experience of illness. And when it comes to psychotic disorders, this feature provides a way of analyzing the particular kind of loss of insight by which such disorders are characterized.

The key idea here is that psychotic loss of insight involves the misconstrual of an experience across the three-way distinction by which illness generally is defined. This is different from simply failing to recognize the psychological origin of a symptom (remember the example of hysterical paralysis in section 1). It is rather an active relocation of the experience in question to one or another side of the three-way distinction. The schizophrenic symptom of "thought insertion" (one of a range of specifically psychotic disorders of thinking) provides a good illustration of this. With thought insertion, the patient has thoughts in his own head—thoughts that in this sense he is

Table 1
A differential diagnosis of hallucinations drawing on illness theory

Perception	Construction					
	By patient			By others		
	Done by	Wrong with	Done to	Done by	Wrong with	Done to
Normal perception	+		+	+		+
Illusion			+ +			+ +
Eye damage			+ +			+ +
Eye disease		+ +			+ +	
Psychotic hallucination	+		+		+ +	
Imagination	+ +			+ +		

thinking yet that at the same time he experiences as the thoughts of some other person or agency. Mellor (1970) reports how one patient described this experience: "The thoughts of Eamonn Andrews [a TV presenter] keep coming into my head. There are no other thoughts there, only his. He uses my mind like a screen."

Thought insertion is thus very odd experientially. Having *other* people's thoughts in your head is quite different from the many ways in which your *own* thoughts may be influenced by others. It is also quite different from your own thoughts running on more or less automatically. It is different again from other kinds of pathological thought: obsessional thoughts, for instance, especially if violent or sexual in nature, are sometimes described by the patient as not their own, but what they mean by this is only that they are not thoughts that they would normally think (Sims 1988). Yet, odd as thought insertion is, it stands out immediately in left-field terms as a misconstrual along the done-by/wrong-with/done-to distinction (Fulford 1989, chap. 10). Ordinary thoughts are construed by the patient and everyone else as things we do. Nonpsychotic pathological thoughts, such as obsessional thoughts, are construed by the patient and everyone else as something wrong. Only thought insertion is construed by everyone else as something wrong with the patient while the patient experiences it as something that is done *to* him (Eamonn Andrews is using my mind).

The three-way distinction by which illness is defined is capable of generating more complex differential diagnoses for more complex phenomena. This is illustrated for hallucinations in table 1. In this table several different kinds of perceptual experience are located across the done-by/wrong-with/done-to distinction as construed by the patient (left-hand side of the table) and others (right-hand side). The elements of the standard medical model (the right-field of figure 1) fail to differentiate psychotic from nonpsychotic symptoms. In left-field terms, however, psychotic symptoms stand out straightforwardly as involving a misconstrual along the done-by/wrong-with/ done-to distinction, by which the primary experience of illness is partly defined. This is represented in the table by an asymmetry between the patient's construal of his perceptual experience and others' construal of it. Thus illusions (e.g., being tricked by sleight of hand) and eye damage (e.g., a blow to the eye) are both symmetrical done-to experiences. Imagery, on the other hand, which is under voluntary contol (Gelder, Gath, and Mayou 1983), is a symmetrical done-by experience. And ordinary eye disease is a symmetrical wrong-with experience. Perception is more complicated than thought because it is partly something done by us (it is active; it makes sense to tell someone to "look carefully," for example) but also something done to us (by the environment). Only hallucinations are asymmetrical: from the patient's perspective, like normal perceptions, they are partly done-by experiences and partly done-to experiences, while from everyone else's perspective, they are something wrong. Hence the differential diagnosis of hallucinations is more complex than that of thought insertion. But the essential point is the same: that only for true hallucinations, the full psychotic symptom, does the patient's construal across the three-way distinction by which illness is defined differ from everyone else's.

Tables of this kind (I have elsewhere called them "differential-illness-diagnosis tables" [Fulford 1993]) illustrate the importance of illness theory, as opposed to disease theory, for psychopathology, the importance of focusing directly on the features of the actual experience of illness in seeking to clarify our psychopathological concepts. Whereas disease theory (as in Aubrey Lewis's work) wholly fails to differentiate psychotic from nonpsychotic symptoms, a single element of the primary experience of illness is sufficient to generate these detailed differential-diagnosis tables.

A full-field psychopathology, then, explains the first feature of delusions noted at the end of section 1. So-called "normal hallucinations," however, remind us that, powerful as these differential-illness-diagnosis tables are, they are not in themselves sufficient to give a full characterization of psychotic symptoms. An example of a normal hallucination would be the tired intern who hears the telephone ring as she is dropping off to sleep, only to be reassured by the switchboard operator that she must have dreamed it. A corresponding symptom for thought insertion is the forced thoughts that may occur as part of the aura of temporal-lobe epilepsy. These have all the experiential features of inserted thoughts, except that the patient is readily persuaded by the doctor that they are part of the patient's epilepsy and hence, in the terms of the table, something wrong (Lishman, personal communication).

So the hallmark of true psychotic symptoms is not solely a misconstrual along the three-way distinction by which illness is defined. It is a *sustained* misconstrual. Moreover, it is a misconstrual which is sustained with something of the determination of a *delusional* misconstrual. Thus a psychotic patient, when shown that there is no one in the room from whom they heard a voice coming, rather than accepting that they must have imagined it, will claim that a microphone was used or that the person has jumped out of the window or even that the person speaking is invisible. This indeed is sometimes called delusional elaboration (Wing, Cooper, and Sartorius 1974).

Observations such as these support the claim of traditional psychopathology, noted earlier, that delusions are the root symptom of psychotic disorder. Further analysis of delusion, as we will see later, requires a shift from the experience of illness as such (the upper-left quadrant of the full-field view in figure 1) to an interpretation of this experience in terms of loss of agency or failure of action (the lower-left quadrant). Before considering this in detail, however, we need to look first at a key feature of delusions themselves: their dual presentation as statements of fact and as value judgments.

Value Judgments

In the standard medical model, as developed by Boorse (1975), for instance, the evaluative element in medicine, if recognized at all, is marginalized and hence tends to be ignored. I have argued elsewhere that this evaluative element is important in medicine generally as well as in psychiatry (Fulford 1989, chap. 11), and in relation not only to psychopathology but to classification and diagnosis (Fulford 1994), medical jurisprudence (Fulford and Hope 1994), and psychiatric ethics (Fulford 1993b).

The significance of this evaluative element, however, depends on the view taken of the logical relationship between facts and values. A descriptivist account, in which values may be entailed by facts (Warnock 1971), leaves it open for the value element in medicine to be reduced to the factual. The theories of Boorse and others can indeed be understood, not as establishing *value-free* scientific accounts of the concepts of disease and dysfunction, but rather as descriptivist *moral* theories of these concepts (Fulford 1989, chap. 3). There is certainly something of this evident in medical thinking about delusions. *DSM* III is one of the few medical texts in which evaluative delusions are mentioned explicitly. Here, though, it is said that such delusions should not be diagnosed unless the belief in question is so obviously mistaken as to be *objectively* false (American Psychiatric Association, 1990, my emphasis). Moreover, of the two examples given, one is a genuine good/bad evaluation, but the other is not—it is concerned with the patient's perception of her body size.

In *DSM* III, then, evaluative delusions are in effect reduced to factual delusions. As a form of moral descriptivism, this would certainly explain why evaluative and factual delusions have the same implications. Moreover, the very existence of evaluative delusions might seem to support descriptivism. A standard objection to nondescriptivist theories is that they make *any* value judgment possible in principle (Warnock 1967). If, in Hume's phraseology, there is no "ought" from an "is," if evaluative conclusions require an evaluative premise, then there is no logical limit to the ways in which a given state of affairs may be evaluated. Yet with evaluative *delusions*, it seems that there are value judgments that are not only false but false in a sense so close to the sense in which factual delusions are false that the two have not generally been distinguished.

This line of argument, however, fails to take into account the full logical range of delusions. For as we have seen, delusions may also be true factual beliefs. Thus, while there is clearly *some* sense in which delusions are false beliefs, the sense in question is not that of objectively false factual beliefs, and hence this sense does not support the existence of objectively false evaluations. On the contrary, the full logical range of delusions supports the nondescriptivist position. For it suggests that for a value judgment to be false it has to be false in a sense (the sense of psychotic loss of insight) that is *different* from the ordinary empirical sense in which factual beliefs may be false.

There are, of course, many other arguments for and against both descriptivist and nondescriptivist positions, the so-called "is/ought" debate in ethical theory. If the medical concepts are evaluative through and through, these arguments indeed are important to the development of a philosophical psychopathology (Fulford 1994). But the point for now is that the clinical psychopathology of delusions is itself a barrier to the reduction of values to facts, and hence of evaluative to factual delusions. Any account of delusions must therefore take seriously the dual presentation of the symptom in two logically distinct (though, of course, not unrelated) forms: as fact *and* as value. We will see in the next section that in a full-field account it is just this feature of delusions that is the key to their psychopathology.

Failure of Action

As to their content, delusions fit neatly across the done-by/wrong-with/done-to distinction by which illness is defined (Fulford 1989, chap. 10): delusions of guilt, for example, are construed by the patient as something they have done; delusions of persecution, on the other hand, are construed as something being done to the patient. Even the occasional delusion about matters apparently remote from the patient, e.g., the coast of England melting (Wing, Cooper, and Sartorius 1974), is invested with deep personal significance.

However, it is not the content but the form of a belief that is relevant to its status as a delusion. This was recognized by Jaspers (1963) and is emphasized in textbooks of psychiatry (Gelder, Gath, and Mayou 1983). And it is consistent with the second feature of delusions noted at the end of section 1, namely that as symptoms of psychotic mental illness, they may be true as well as false factual beliefs. This fact is also consistent with the existence of the paradoxical delusion of mental illness—this is paradoxical just to the extent that textbook definitions of delusion require us to look at the content of the delusional belief to see whether it is true or false. If, however, we combine these facts with the further observation that delusions, as symptoms of psychotic mental illness, may not be beliefs at all (at least as to matters of fact) but rather value judgments, we are pointed beyond traditional psychopathology to the idea that we should understand the form of delusional thinking in terms not of impaired cognitive functioning but of impaired reasons for action. This is because reasons for action share with delusions the remarkable property of being expressible either as matters of fact or as value judgments.

Consider the following example. I am driving along the road and turn right. My passenger asks why I turned right. I reply either "This is the way to Oxford" (fact) or "I want/need, etc., to go to Oxford" (value). Either kind of reply would be appropriate; either would be taken as an account of my reasons for the (simple) action of turning right. Hence there is a correlation between the philosophical chalk and cheese of delusions, which may be expressed as facts or values, and a similar philosophical chalk and cheese of reasons for action, which may also be expressed as facts or values.

A correlation is not in itself proof of a substantive relationship. But this correlation does mean that a failure-of-action account of illness maps directly onto the second feature of the psychopathology of delusions listed at the end of section 1. It also maps onto the third feature, namely the central place of delusions in the map of psychiatry. To see this, we need to know more of the background illness theory. The basic idea is that whereas disease is naturally analyzed in terms of failures of the functioning of bodily and mental parts and systems, the experience of illness is naturally analysed in terms of incapacity, or failure of action (Fulford 1989, chaps. 7–10). This is to say, to be a patient, as Toulmin (1980) has pointed out, is no longer to be fully an agent. Within a theory of this kind, different kinds of illness are marked out as failures at different points and in different ways in what Austin (1956–1957) called "the machinery of action": movement has a different place in action from sensation, appetite is different again, and so on. Hence if illness is, generically, failure of action, different kinds of illness, involving different symptoms, will be represented by different kinds of failure of action in a full-field psychopathology.

In all this variety, however, reasons can be shown to have a special place (Fulford 1989, chap. 10). For there is a sense in which reasons actually *define* what is done. Driving along the road, I turn right. This involves volition, control, perception, coordination, and other parts of the machinery of action. But *what* I am doing, my *action*, depends on my reasons for turning right—to head for Oxford (as above), or to avoid a horse, or to demonstrate turning right to a learner, and so on. Reasons, then, are a constitutive element, rather than merely an executive element, of the machinery of action. Hence if the experience of illness generally, physical as well as mental, involves failure of action, then defective reasons for action amount to a failure of a particularly profound kind. In all other failures there is a well-defined action but some executive difficulty of performance (paralysis, obsession blocking volition, depression-induced lack of drive, etc.). But if the reasons themselves are defective, there is a constitutive failure rather than merely executive failure. Thus no reason means no action at all. With defective reasons, then, there is a *central* failure of action, which, in the terms of the theory, accounts for delusion's being the *central* symptom of mental illness.

This in turn explains the fourth feature of delusions: their central ethical and medicolegal significance. This is most transparent for the status of psychotic mental illness as an excuse in law (Fulford 1993b), though the same point justifies compulsory psychiatric treatment (Fulford 1990a). Most legal excuses, traditionally conceived, involve lack of intent—as in accidents, inadvertence, duress, and mistake (Hart 1968). In each of these cases, the person concerned does not intend what they do. Each is thus a case of no action. If I reach across the table because I want the sugar but inadvertently knock over the salt, my *action* (as defined by my reasons) is not knocking over the salt but reaching for the sugar. However, this has meant that on conventional accounts of delusion, it has been something of a mystery

why insanity too should be an excuse. The insane are not unconscious (like the automaton); they do not lack intellectual understanding (like the mentally defective); they are not out of control
(like the epileptic); they are not even acting under duress (like the
addict). On a failure-of-action account, on the other hand, delusions
are automatically assimilated to the list of traditional excuses. For on
this account, as we have just seen, there is, as with other excuses, no
action, as defined by the reasons of the person concerned.

At least as a hypothesis, then, the idea that the irrationality of delusions is an irrationality of reasons for action, rather than of conventional cognitive functioning, explains a number of key features of
their clinical psychopathology. The explanation of the remaining
feature—feature 5, that factual and evaluative delusions have the
same implications—requires a little more setting out. However, it is
worth quickly running through this feature because it shows how the
account extends the traditional understanding of the psychopathology of delusions and thus connects psychopathology to philosophical
work on the concept of mind.

Extending Traditional Psychopathology

The explanation for the identical practical implications of factual
and evaluative delusions in a failure-of-action psychopathology depends on the observation that although reasons may take the form
of facts or values, the status of a given fact or value *as* a reason depends on a background structure that includes other facts and values
(Fulford 1989, chap. 10). In the example above, "This is the way to
Oxford" is a reason for me to turn right only if "I want to go to
Oxford," and vice versa. And both these in turn depend on other
facts and values: Oxford is a nice place to go, I work in Oxford, etc.
But what this means is that the significance of a fact or value *as* a
reason depends on this background structure rather than solely on
the content of the fact or value itself, or even on whether this content
is true or false, eccentric or conventional. In all these respects, then,
reasons are again mirrored by delusions. For if, ex hypothesi, delusions are defective reasons for actions, the defects must be in this
background structure. By noting the analogy of the classical paradox

of the liar, with the paradoxical delusion of mental illness, one can see this directly (Fulford 1989, chap. 10). Hence the significance of delusions (including their clinical implications) will be largely independent of their content.

The way in which this account extends traditional psychopathology can be illustrated in terms of the distinction between form and content. Traditionally, as noted earlier, it is form rather than content that is the key to the definition of delusion as a symptom of mental illness. Form and content are not absolute, however, but nested, as it were. In "This is a chair," for example, "chair" is part of the content of a statement that is descriptive in form, but the descriptive statement itself becomes the content of, say, the order "Tell him this is a chair." In traditional psychopathology it has been assumed that "content" refers primarily to the subject matter of delusions (it being recognized that delusions, although more likely to be concerned with some subjects other than others, *can* be concerned with anything at all) and that "form" refers to falsity of belief (with one or more qualifications, as outlined earlier). What is shown by the present account is that falsity of belief itself is nested in a background structure and that a defective form of this structure makes a belief a delusion.

A failure-of-action account of psychotic phenomena thus gives a good fit with their clinical psychopathology (the features summarized at the end of section 1) and thus by bringing out the embedded structure of these and other psychotic symptoms, extends the traditional understanding of them. Of course, at this stage of its development, the account is a framework for research rather than a fully worked out theory. That it is a promising account is shown by its natural fit with the prima facie features of psychotic phenomena. But as yet nothing substantive has been said, in particular, about the (putative) background structure upon which the status of a value judgment or statement of fact as a reason depends, and nothing can be said, therefore, about the (also putative) defects in this background upon which, according the views advanced here, the status of a value judgment or statement of fact as a delusion depends.

It is at just this point that a failure-of-action account of psychopathology makes contact with recent work in the philosophy of mind on the intentionality of action (Fulford 1993c). Whether this contact will prove fruitful it is still too early to say, but it looks promising. There are a growing number of philosophers who, following Austin's (1956–1957) lead, are starting to explore abnormal psychological phenomena as a resource for philosophy. Much work in this area is too general in nature to allow cross-references with the rich field of psychopathology. But Searle's (1983) theory of intentionality, for example, although not developed with delusions in mind, is detailed and specific, and suggests a number of possible connections with the phenomenology of delusions. Searle's analysis could suggest new ways of exploring the background thinking that psychotic delusions and other psychotic symptoms reflect. And conversely, background thinking, the range of types of phenomena that can figure in delusions, and the other ways in which beliefs may be irrational all provide crucial data for philosophical research in this area.

3 Conclusions

It has several times been noted, and is worth repeating, that the approach to psychopathology outlined in this chapter is not antiscientific. Just as full-field models of illness and disease are additive, adding value to fact, illness to disease, and action to function, so in psychopathology what is needed is the addition of philosophy to science. There is no real conflict here, of course. Psychiatry, it must be said, remains somewhat embattled behind distinctly positivist barricades. But a mature understanding of science itself recognizes the importance of conceptual as well as empirical inquiry, and sociologists of science have long emphasized the nexus of personal and social values within which scientific research necessarily proceeds (Hesse 1980). Moreover, it is at precisely those points where scientific advance is most dramatic that the conceptual may be as prominent as the empirical, as in quantum theory at the present time (d'Espagnet 1976). It is here that Kuhn's (1962) paradigm shifts occur. So the emergence of a new philosophical psychopathology at this time could presage just such a shift.

What the vehicle of the shift will be we can know only with hindsight. The ideas drawn on in this chapter are broadly in the

Anglo-American tradition of analytical philosophy. There are other promising approaches. There is already a good deal of detailed work in the Continental tradition into the bizarre existential features of early schizophrenia (Spitzer, Uehlein, and Schwartz 1993). This too is timely. After all, notwithstanding its modern empiricist self-image, psychopathology is a descendant of continental phenomenology: and the central problem that Jaspers (1974) himself identified for psychopathology—that of reconciling causal and meaningful accounts of mental illness—is as likely to be successfully addressed in these terms as in any other. Moreover, it is fashionable nowadays in some philosophical circles to be disparaging about the linguistic-analytical method. Still, focusing, as it does, on the actual use we make of our concepts, this method is particularly well tuned to the problems with which clinical psychopathology is concerned (Fulford 1990b). And to the extent that these problems, arise from a too narrow or restricted view of psychopathology, as in the case of the psychotic/nonpsychotic distinction, it is from an enlarged or full-field view that we should expect new understanding to emerge.

The particular ideas set out here may, of course, turn out to be wrong. But the general links between philosophy and psychiatry illustrated by the psychopathology of delusions could prove fruitful for both disciplines. They could prove fruitful for psychiatry, because the abstractions of formal philosophy generate models for future research in psychopathology, which in turn have significance for such areas as diagnosis, classification, medical jurisprudence, and perhaps even for the new "hard" sciences of neuroimaging (Harrison 1991). They could prove fruitful for philosophy because the oddity and diversity of psychopathological phenomena represent, as Austin (1956–1957) anticipated, a rich resource for philosophical research. We have had indications of this here in the significance of evaluative delusions for our understanding of the logical relationship between facts and values: and delusional and other abnormalities of belief are relevant more widely in philosophy, for example, to theories of intentionality (Fulford 1993c). There is thus the potential for a two-way trade between philosophy and psychiatry, a trade that, if pursued vigorously, will ensure that philosophical psychopathology turns out to be no less productive than its scientific counterpart.

Acknowledgments

I am grateful to the editors of this volume for their advice and support during the preparation of this article.

References

American Psychiatric Association. 1980. *Diagnostic and Statistical Manual of Mental Disorders*, 3rd ed. Washington: American Psychiatric Association.

Austin, J. L. 1956–1957. "A Plea for Excuses." *Aristotelian Society Proceedings* 57:1–30. Reprinted in *The Philosophy of Action*, ed. A. R. White (Oxford University Press, 1968).

Boorse, C. 1975. "On the Distinction between Disease and Illness." *Philosophy and Public Affairs* 5:49–68.

Boorse, C. 1976. "What a Theory of Mental Health Should Be." *Journal of the Theory of Social Behaviour* 6:61–84.

Butler, R., chairman. 1975. *Report of the Committee on Mentally Abnormal Offenders.* Cmnd. 6244. London: Her Majesty's Stationery Office.

David, A. S. 1990. "Insight and Psychosis." *British Journal of Psychiatry* 156:798–808.

D'Espagnat, B. 1976. *Conceptual Foundations of Quantum Mechanics*, 2nd ed. Reading, Mass.: W. A. Benjamin.

Flew, A. 1973. *Crime or Disease?* New York: Barnes and Noble.

Fulford, K. W. M. 1989. *Moral Theory and Medical Practice.* Cambridge: Cambridge University Press.

Fulford, K. W. M. 1990a. "The Concept of Disease." Chap. 6 in *Psychiatric Ethics*, 2nd ed., ed. S. Bloch and P. Chodoff. Oxford: Oxford University Press.

Fulford, K. W. M. 1990b. "Philosophy and Medicine: The Oxford Connection." *British Journal of Psychiatry* 157:111–115.

Fulford, K. W. M. 1991. "Evaluative Delusions: Their Significance for Philosophy and Psychiatry." *British Journal of Psychiatry* 159:108–112; suppl. 14, *Delusions and Reality.*

Fulford, K. W. M. 1993a. "Thought Insertion and Insight: Disease and Illness Paradigms of Psychotic Disorder." In *Phenomenology Language and Schizophrenia*, ed. M. Spitzer, F. A. Uehlein, M. A. Schwartz, and C. Mundt. New York: Springer-Verlag.

Fulford, K. W. M. 1993b. "Value, Action, Mental Illness, and the Law." In *Criminal Law: Action, Value, and Structure*, ed. K. Gardner, J. Horden, and S. Shute. Oxford: Oxford University Press.

Fulford, K. W. M. 1993c. "Mental Illness and the Mind-Brain Problem: Delusion, Belief, and Searle's Theory of Intentionality." *Theoretical Medicine.*

Fulford, K. W. M. 1994. "Closet Logics: Hidden Conceptual Elements in the *DSM* and *ICD* Classifications of Mental Disorders." In *Philosophical Perspectives on Psychiatric Diagnostic Classification*, ed. J. Z. Sadler, M. Schwartz, and O. Wiggins. Baltimore: Johns Hopkins University Press.

Fulford, K. W. M. Forthcoming. "Completing Kraepelin's Psychopathology: Insight, Delusion, and the Phenomenology of Illness." In *Insight and Psychosis*, ed. X. F. Amador and A. S. David. Cambridge: Cambridge University Press.

Fulford, K. W. M., and R. A. Hope. 1994. "Psychiatric Ethics: A Bioethical Ugly Duckling?" In *Principles of Health Care Ethics*, ed. G. Raanon. New York: John Wiley and Sons.

Gelder, M. G., D. Gath, and R. Mayou. 1983. *Oxford Textbook of Psychiatry*. Oxford: Oxford University Press.

Gittleson, N. L. 1966. "The Effect of Obsessions on Depressive Psychoses." *British Journal of Psychiatry* 112:253–259.

Glover, J. 1970. *Responsibility*. London: Routledge and Kegan Paul.

Harre, R., and R. Lamb, eds. 1986. *The Dictionary of Physiological and Clinical Psychology*. Oxford: Basil Blackwell.

Harrison, P. J. 1991. "Are Mental States a Useful Concept? Neurophilosophical Influences on Phenomenology and Psychopathology." *Journal of Nervous and Mental Disease* 179 (6): 309–316.

Hart, H. L. A. 1968. *Punishment and Responsibility: Essays in the Philosophy of Law*. Oxford: Oxford University Press.

Hemsley, D. R., and P. A. Garety. 1986. "The Formation and Maintenance of Delusions: A Bayesian Analysis." *British Journal of Psychiatry* 149:51–56.

Hesse, M. 1980. *Revolutions and Reconstructions in the Philosophy of Science*. Brighton, England: Harvester Press.

Jaspers, K. 1963. *General Psychopathology*. Trans. J. Hoenig and M. W. Hamilton. Manchester: Manchester University Press. First published in 1913.

Jaspers, K. 1974. "Causal and 'Meaningful' Connections between Life History and Psychosis." Chap. 5 in *Themes and Variations in European Psychiatry*, ed. S. R. Hirsch and M. Shepherd. Bristol: John Wright and Sons. First published in 1913.

Kuhn, T. S. 1962. *The Structure of Scientific Revolutions*, 2nd ed. Chicago: University of Chicago Press.

Leff, J., and A. D. Isaacs. 1981. *Psychiatric Examination in Clinical Practice*, 2nd ed. Oxford: Blackwell.

Lewis, A. J. 1934. "The Psychopathology of Insight." *British Journal of Medical Psychology* 14:332–348.

Markova, I. S., and G. E. Berrios. 1992. "The Meaning of Insight in Clinical Psychiatry." *British Journal of Psychiatry* 160:850–860.

Mellor, C. S. 1970. "First Rank Symptoms of Schizophrenia." *British Journal of Psychiatry* 117:15–23.

Mullen, P. 1979. "Phenomenology of Disordered Mental Function." Chap. 2 in *Essentials of Postgraduate Psychiatry*, ed. P. Hill, R. Murray, and A. Thorley. London: Academic Press.

Quinton, A. 1985. "Madness." Chap. 2 in *Philosophy and Practice*, ed. A. P. Griffiths. Cambridge: Cambridge University Press.

Searle, J. R. 1983. *Intentionality: An Essay in the Philosophy of Mind*. Cambridge: Cambridge University Press.

Shepherd, M. 1961. Morbid Jealousy: Some Clinical and Social Aspects of a Psychiatric Syndrome. *Journal of Mental Science* 107:687–704.

Sims, A. 1988. *Symptoms in the Mind: An Introduction to Descriptive Psychopathology*. London: Bailiere Tindall.

Spier, S. A. 1992. "Capgras' Syndrome and Delusions of Misidentification." *Psychiatric Annals* 22 (5): 279–285.

Spitzer, M., F. A. Uehlein., and M. A. Schwartz. 1993. "Phenomenology, Language, and Schizophrenia: Introduction and Synopsis." In *Phenomenology Language and Schizophrenia*, ed. M. Spitzer, F. A. Uehlein, M. A. Schwartz., and C. Mundt. New York: Springer-Verlag.

Thomas, C. S. 1984. "Dysmorphophobia: A Question of Definition." *British Journal of Psychiatry* 144:513–516.

Toulmin, S. 1980. "Agent and Patient in Psychiatry." *International Journal of Law and Psychiatry* 3:267–278.

Vauhkonen, K. 1968. *On the Pathogenesis of Morbid Jealousy, with Special Reference to the Personality Traits of and Interaction between Jealous Patients and Their Spouses*. Copenhagen: Munksgaard.

Walker, N. 1985. "Psychiatric Explanations as Excuses." Chap. 9 in *Psychiatry, Human Rights, and the Law*, ed. M. Roth and R. Bluglass. Cambridge: Cambridge University Press.

Warnock, G. J. 1967. *Contemporary Moral Philosophy*. London: Macmillan Press.

Warnock, G. J. 1971. *The Object of Morality*. London: Methuen and Co.

Wing, J. K. 1978. *Reasoning about Madness*. Oxford: Oxford University Press.

Wing, J. K., J. E. Cooper, and N. Sartorius. 1974. *Measurement and Classification of Psychiatric Symptoms*. Cambridge: Cambridge University Press.

World Health Organization. 1978. *Mental Disorders: Glossary and Guide to Their Classification in Accordance with the Ninth Revision of the International Classification of Diseases*. Geneva: World Health Organization.

World Health Organization. 1992. *Mental Disorders: Glossary and Guide to Their Classification in Accordance with the Tenth Revision of the International Classification of Diseases*. Geneva: World Health Organization.

Problems with the *DSM* Approach to Classifying Psychopathology

Jeffrey Poland, Barbara Von Eckardt, and Will Spaulding

Within the communities of psychiatry and clinical psychology, the dominant framework for conceptualizing psychopathology is codified in the *Diagnostic and Statistical Manual of Mental Disorders* (*DSM*) of the American Psychiatric Association. In this framework, psychopathology is classified in categories (e.g., schizophrenia, major depression) defined in terms of clinically identifiable features of individuals (e.g., flat affect, depressed mood, hallucinations, delusional beliefs). Although this approach to classification was first systematized by the nineteenth-century psychiatrist Emil Kraepelin, it continues to play an extensive role in guiding clinical and research activity involving psychopathology. In addition, *DSM* categories play pivotal roles in financing mental health care, maintaining hospital and clinic records, administering research funds, and organizing educational materials and curricula concerned with psychopathology.

Our view is that *DSM* constitutes a faulty conceptualization of the domain of psychopathology and that it interferes with optimal pursuit of clinical and scientific purposes. Indeed, there has been a decade of widespread complaint regarding *DSM*, but such complaint has been largely ineffective in stemming the impact of the approach. One reason for this ineffectiveness is the absence of a well-developed alternative that can play the roles currently served by *DSM*. As Kuhn (1970) has stressed, scientific revolutions do not occur, despite manifest problems with a reigning paradigm, until a viable alternative appears on the scene. The primary purpose of this chapter is to characterize some of the most severe shortcomings of *DSM* in a way that suggests directions for the development of a viable alternative.

The plan for the chapter is as follows. In the first section, we make some preliminary points about purposes of classification in the domain of psychopathology, and we briefly characterize a number of different approaches to such classification. In section 2 we outline the *DSM* approach to classification. And in sections 3 and 4 we formulate arguments demonstrating the inadequacy of *DSM* in a way that identifies what we take to be its most serious flaws. In the final section we clarify some implications of the discussion with respect to the development of an alternative approach to classifying psychopathology.

1 Purposes and Types of Classification Schemes

Purposes of Classification

On our view, there are two primary purposes of a classification scheme in the domain of psychopathology. Such a scheme ought to enhance the effectiveness of clinical activity, and it ought to promote scientific research programs concerned with psychopathology and its treatment.

One useful way of understanding the role of classification in clinical activity is to see it as reducing clinical uncertainty. That is, a classification scheme ought to contribute significantly to answering such questions as the following: What is wrong? What intervention strategies and techniques are likely to help? What is likely to happen over time? Is the current strategy or technique effective? Are the predictions about the course of a problem coming true? In other words, a useful classification scheme ought to contribute to an understanding of clinical problems in a way that promotes the design, implementation, and assessment of useful intervention strategies. A classification scheme can promote such understanding when it allows practitioners to identify what portions of their knowledge and what elements in their armamentarium of strategies and techniques are relevant on any given occasion, and when it directs a clinician's attention to variables that need to be monitored to assess clinical problems and clinical change.

There are at least two ways in which a classification scheme ought to promote scientific research programs concerning psychopathology and its treatment: it ought to promote scientifically *acceptable* research, and it ought to promote *productive* research. Thus such a scheme should contribute to the design and implementation of quantified and well-controlled studies, and it should promote formulation of research questions that lead to the development of more precise, reliable, and substantial bodies of knowledge that are well integrated within the larger framework of scientific understanding of human functioning. To be productive, a classification scheme must play a significant role in integrating the study of psychopathology with the empirical findings and theoretical developments in such areas as developmental psychology, cognitive science, and neuroscience. It should both inform and be informed by developments in these other scientific research programs.

Types of Classification

By an approach to classification of a domain, we mean an approach to representing the phenomena within that domain in a way that characterizes those phenomena and makes discriminations among them relevant to certain purposes. There are two general types of approachs to classification that have been employed in the domain of psychopathology: categorical and dimensional. And within each of these types there are various subtypes.[1]

A *categorical* approach to classification is a nonquantitative approach that locates the individuals in a domain within some set of categories. A *strict* categorical approach involves disjoint categories, while a more *lenient* categorical approach allows for some overlap.[2] Categorical systems of classification can also differ with respect to the types of criteria employed for placing individuals into categories. *Monothetic* criteria for category inclusion are sets of individually necessary and jointly sufficient conditions. Within a purely monothetic approach each category is associated with a single set of criteria. On the other hand, *polythetic* criteria for category inclusion are sets of jointly sufficient but not individually necessary conditions. Within such a framework, each category can be associated with several sets of criteria sufficient for inclusion. Thus individuals in the same category need not satisfy all of the same criterial conditions. Finally, a *mixed* approach can involve categories with either monothetic or polythetic criteria, and it can allow for overlapping polythetic criteria sets that include some necessary conditions (i.e., criteria that are included in every set).

Standing in contrast to categorical approaches to classification are *dimensional* approaches, which involve one or more dimensions of quantitatively measurable attributes along which individuals in the domain of interest can be located. There are two subtypes of dimensional approaches. On the one hand, a *pure dimensional* approach locates individuals within an n-dimensional space according to the values that characterize the individual on each of the n dimensions selected for the purposes of classification. In dimensional systems the number of dimensions have typically been small (see, e.g., Eysenck 1986), but such a restriction is not necessary. The purposes of classification and the nature of the domain determine how many and which dimensions are most appropriate. On the other hand, a *process-oriented dimensional* approach involves characterizing individuals in terms of several attribute dimensions and an identification of pertinent causal structure (i.e., a representation of how attributes causally combine with each other). Thus a process-oriented dimensional approach to classification is quantitative rather than qualitative, multidimensional in character, and concerned with process rather than simple attributions of states or traits to individuals.[3]

2   The *DSM* Approach to Classification

The history of classifying psychopathology has been frequently reviewed (e.g., Spitzer and Williams 1983, Blashfield 1984, Millon 1986, Kirk and Kutchins 1992). For our purposes, the main points are as follows. It is generally agreed that prior to the implementation of *DSM* III in 1980, psychiatric classification was not clearly conceived, probably not very reliable, not significantly related to important variables (e.g., course, outcome, responsiveness to treatment), and not grounded in a scientific understanding of the domain of psychopathology.[4] As a consequence, such classification had limited clinical utility with respect to understanding, treating, and making predictions about the problems from which individuals suffered. And it did not contribute significantly toward advancing scientific knowledge of psychopathology.

In response to the dismal record of prior classification schemes, an effort was made to upgrade the scientific quality, and hence the clinical and research utility, of psychiatric classification. This effort culminated in the publication of *DSM* III (American Psychiatric Association, 1980), which was heralded as a major scientific advance in the description of psychopathology. Yet despite the fanfare and initial enthusiastic acceptance of *DSM* III by many psychiatrists, there was much criticism and debate regarding its features and its utility for clinical and research purposes. Typical objections were that the *DSM* III system is not reliable, that it has no demonstrated validity with respect to key-criterion variables, that its "atheoretical"[5] stance is no virtue at all, that the process whereby *DSM* was developed was quasi-scientific at best, and that, statements to the contrary notwithstanding, the *DSM* III system is not atheoretical and the theory it embodies is false in the domain of psychopathology.[6]

In an effort to respond to some of the criticism and to update the *DSM* system in the light of evolving scientific knowledge, a revised version of *DSM* III was developed and published in 1987. Unfortunately, although some changes were made, *DSM* III R (American Psychiatric Association, 1987) does not offer any substantial improvements with respect to key validation issues, nor does it involve any deep substantive changes in the structure of the taxonomy. At present another major revision effort is underway and should culminate in the publication of *DSM* IV. There is considerable talk (Widiger et al. 1991) about stepping up the effort to validate various categories (i.e., to demonstrate significant relationships to key variables and to theories of etiologies). However, it is not evident that there will be any significant changes in the basic structure of the classification scheme or in the fundamental approach toward comprehending psychopathology that it embodies. Nor do the efforts at revision appear responsive to either the validity problems or the reliability problems faced by earlier versions of *DSM*.[7] As a consequence, what we say below most likely applies to *DSM* IV as well as to its two immediate predecessors.

Jeffrey Poland, Barbara Von Eckardt, and Will Spaulding

Features of the *DSM* Approach: Claims and Realities

Structure

DSM embodies a mixed monothetic/polythetic, lenient, categorical approach to the classification of psychopathology. That is, it is a categorical approach involving categories defined in terms of polythetic criteria, typically with some necessary conditions of inclusion, and it allows for overlap of category membership.[8] This means that, for most categories, individuals need not share all of their criterial features with other members of the same category, an aspect of the approach that is supposed to reflect the idea that mental disorders can be manifested in clinically diverse ways.

Operationalized criteria

A highly touted virtue of all criteria employed in defining *DSM* categories is that they are "operationalized" in terms of readily observable clinical attributes and other conditions, and hence that they are allegedly more scientific than the criteria employed in earlier diagnostic systems. It should be noted, however, that many of the criteria are highly inferential in character (e.g., hallucinations, delusions, loss of interest, depressed mood) and that there are few objective measures for assessing their presence or absence. Most key assessments are based on self-reports, subjective ratings, third-person reports, and chart reviews. It should also be noted that the language and concepts employed for describing clinical phenomena are not based on theory but are drawn from commonsense, "folk-psychological," or protoscientific clinically based understanding (e.g., "delusion," "self-esteem," "hallucination," "loosening of associations").

Atheoretical categories

Another highly touted feature of the *DSM* III system is that it is "atheoretical" in character, which means that the categories do not explicitly involve or presuppose any particular theory of etiology or pathology (American Psychiatric Association, 1987, xxiii). Rather, they are supposed to be clinically defined categories that are theoretically neutral and that provide structure within which clinicians and researchers can employ their favored theoretical hypotheses. Thus the *DSM* III approach assumes that it is possible to individuate psychopathological conditions on the basis of directly observable clinical manifestations [9] and that, given such information, clinicians can agree on the identification of psychopathological conditions without agreeing on how they come about (American Psychiatric Association, 1980, 7). The *DSM* III system is supposed to be a "purely descriptive" classification system that mirrors a theoretical taxonomy based on (as yet unknown) etiologies and pathologies.[10]

However, contrary to its alleged atheoretical status, the system very definitely embodies a theory concerning the domain of psychopathology (Millon 1991, Carson 1991), namely, the view that there exist what we will refer to as "syndromes with unity." These are clusters of associated clinical attributes that exhibit such dynamic characteristics as typical course, outcome, and responsiveness to treatment, and that are related to underlying pathological conditions and etiological factors of development (e.g., genetic and environmental factors). The view also involves the idea that clinical criteria, when polythetically combined, are sufficient for defining the psychopathological conditions that exhibit these properties and relations. As we understand them, the operationally defined categories within the *DSM* system are supposed to be *natural kinds* with a characteristic causal structure (i.e., a core pathology) that underwrites the various lawful regularities characteristic of the disorder (e.g., association of criterial features, dynamic properties of the syndrome).[11] The various efforts aimed at validating the *DSM* categories are specifically concerned with identifying the nomological relations of association, progression, and causation that unify the syndromes.

Management of variability
The recent *DSM*s also have a number of features aimed at reining in the manifest variability of individuals who fall within given diagnostic categories. From the *DSM* perspective, such variability represents the many ways in which a disorder can be expressed at the clinical level or, alternatively, the many factors relevant to treatment design and implementation, case management, and prognosis. As noted earlier, one such feature is the polythetic character of the criteria. In addition, the *DSM* approach makes allowances for variation in noncriterial features of an individual (features that are not among those determining which category is applicable). Thus the system is

"multiaxial" in the sense that it not only locates individuals within diagnostic categories of mental disorders but also involves representation of additional information about an individual that is deemed necessary for adequately understanding and treating that person. Such information includes relevant physical conditions, severity of identifiable psychosocial stressors, and assessments of the individual's level of adaptive functioning. With such information, clinicians are supposed to gain a broader appreciation of the context within which a person has been functioning and within which they will be treated.

Furthermore, in the *DSM* system a person can be assigned to more than one diagnostic category, which allows the representation of different pathologies exhibited by a person. And the system includes a number of "mixed categories" (e.g., schizoaffective disorder) that apply to individuals exhibiting cardinal features of more than one purer disorder. Finally, it includes a number of "residual categories" (e.g., depressive disorder not otherwise specified, psychotic disorder not otherwise specified) that allow for conditions not meeting the criteria for a given category but sufficiently similar to deserve a related diagnosis. Thus the categorical approach embodied within *DSM* is not strict, and it includes a number of hybrids and "wastebasket" categories that increase its coverage of individuals exhibiting psychopathology.

Clinical role
As a tool for managing clinical uncertainty, *DSM* structures the collection of information by leading the clinician to focus on those features that are criterial for various diagnostic categories within the system. The aim is to identify those categories (if any) whose criteria are satisfied. Once a diagnosis is made, one brings to bear background knowledge of the category (or categories) and the person in order to design and implement a treatment plan that targets the identified disorder(s). Over time, one assesses the effectiveness of the plan in terms of clinical changes (i.e., changes in the clinically salient features of the disorder[s]).

It is important to note that within the *DSM* approach as currently conceived and implemented, virtually all diagnostic assessment and assessment of change is conducted in dyadic psychiatric interviews, sometimes in accord with a structured interview protocol whose purpose is to insure full, unbiased, and balanced coverage with respect to relevant clinical information.[12] Virtually all of the assessment is based on clinical judgment concerning the presence or absence of clinically identifiable features and on subjective ratings of their severity. The exceptions are historical or contextual information provided by written records or other persons. There are no laboratory tests that routinely play a role in a *DSM*-oriented diagnostic assessment.

Research role
The research agenda emanating from the *DSM* approach is organized around each of the diagnostic categories (e.g., schizophrenia research, depression research, etc.). Research efforts are typically aimed at answering questions concerning

• optimal diagnostic criteria for each category,

• an optimal set of diagnostic categories and subtypes,

• developmental etiological factors, including vulnerability factors, environmental factors, and genetic markers,

• underlying pathology that constitutes the core of the disorder,

• dynamics of the syndrome that are criterial for a category (e.g., likely treatment response, course, outcome),

• various epidemiological features (incidence, prevalence, gender or racial associations, familial associations).

In the language of research methodology, current research is concerned with "validating" the categories by demonstrating that each is defined by features of clinical or natural history that are contemporaneously or dynamically related and that are each lawfully related to other significant causal or noncausal variables.

3 Problems with the Clinical Utility of the *DSM* Approach

In a nutshell, the *DSM* approach to classification of psychopathology does not effectively serve clinical purposes, because it is largely uninformative and irrelevant with respect to the problems faced by clinicians. The following argument expresses these concerns in a more detailed way.

1. To effectively reduce clinical uncertainty, a *DSM* diagnostic assessment must yield either a set of categories exhibiting nomological unity (i.e., a set of valid categories) or a body of information sufficient for characterizing clinically important features of individuals.

2. The categories do not exhibit the sorts of nomological unity (i.e., validity) called for by the approach.

3. The data collected when performing *DSM*-oriented assessments are highly limited and do not adequately characterize clinically important features of individuals.

4. Thus a *DSM* diagnostic assessment does not yield either the required set of categories or the required body of information.

5. Thus a *DSM* diagnostic assessment does not effectively reduce clinical uncertainty.

The Goals of a Classification Scheme

The first premise concerns the goals of a classification scheme with respect to clinical utility. There are two ways in which a *DSM*-oriented assessment potentially characterizes what is wrong, how best to respond, how to assess change, and how to predict the future. The first is to identify *DSM* categories with nomological properties that suffice for each of these purposes. Thus once an individual's pathology is classified, knowledge of the lawful characteristics of the relevant categories (i.e., nomological clustering of features and relations to etiology, pathology, and clinical dynamics) puts the clinician in a position to more confidently address key clinical issues. Alternatively, one might allow that even if the categories lack sufficient nomological structure, a *DSM*-oriented approach to assessment leads to the collection of information about the clinical state of the individual and associated environmental and other background variables that can be used, in the light of other background knowledge, to manage clinical uncertainty.

Failure of Nomological Unity

Our second premise is that the *DSM* categories simply do not exhibit the sorts of nomological unity called for by the approach. One reason for thinking this is that existing evidence does not support the view that the domain of psychopathology is best conceived in terms of syndromes (i.e., regularly associated clinically salient features) that are nomologically related to etiological or pathological conditions and are characterized by lawful dynamics (i.e., course, outcome, responsiveness to treatment). This is, of course, an empirical claim requiring support from a review of the research to date (which is beyond the scope of this chapter). But it appears to be generally acknowledged that the categories remain largely unvalidated.[13] In addition to such considerations of existing evidence, however, we shall argue below (section 4) that there are also principled reasons (based on features of the domain of psychopathology) for thinking that the categories are not likely to be validated by future research and that there are few (if any) "syndromes with unity."

Inadequate Data Base

The data collected for the purposes of making a *DSM*-oriented diagnostic assessment, the various "signs and symptoms" that constitute the criteria for *DSM* categories, are drawn from a highly restricted domain of information about a person. Specifically, the data are limited to what can be collected in a psychiatric interview, by a chart review, by casual observation of a person in a setting, or by interview of third parties. Such data include self reports concerning personal states and experiences, behavioral observations, and subjective ratings of signs and symptoms by the clinician. The data also include family history, demographics, and chronology (e.g., duration of symptoms, changes in symptoms over time, previous occurrences of symptoms). The thrust of our third premise is that there is good reason to question whether these kinds of information suffice for making an adequate clinical assessment.

There are two sorts of consideration that lead to this doubt: the character of the data (i.e., its quality and scope) and the character of clinically relevant features of individuals (i.e., the nature and distribution of the features). We contend that the data collected in a *DSM*-oriented diagnostic assessment is not adequate for characterizing clinically important features of individuals because (1) the data is of poor quality and limited scope and (2) the clinically relevant features of individuals are of many sorts and are highly variable across individuals within the same (or different) *DSM* category.

To begin with, the data is of essentially poor quality. It is, for the most part, subjective, unquantified, and substantially biased. Insofar as identification of symptoms and assessment of severity is based on the clinician's judgment and ratings, rather than more objective measurement procedures, it suffers from deeply seated *subjective variability* across time, setting, and rater.[14] The inferential character of many of the criteria (e.g., from delusional speech it is inferred that a person has corresponding beliefs) means that, in the absence of theoretical and empirical constraints, symptom identification is based on highly fallible intuitive judgments. And the absence of more objective procedures of measurement means that the data are essentially qualitative and *unquantified*. As a result, there is only marginal discriminatory power in assessments employing such data (e.g., there cannot be controlled measurements of the degree of severity of clinical features that can play a serious role in the assessment of change). Furthermore, the data are often significantly *biased* because it is typically collected in an emotionally charged setting in which power relations are highly salient and hidden agendas abound. And since a *DSM*-oriented assessment focuses in upon criterial signs and symptoms, it is entirely pathology oriented and hence fails to provide a balanced view of an individual's functioning.

Moreover, the quality of the data is compromised by the use of *vague and imprecise concepts*. The behavioral and psychological attributes expressed by the clinical descriptions developed within the *DSM* approach are conceived in protoscientific terms derived from commonsense and informal clinical understandings of psychological functioning, rather than in terms derived from scientific psychology and neuroscience. For example, attention, as conceived within the *DSM* approach, is unrelated to any sophisticated understanding of selectivity, vigilance, attentional capacity, and types of attentional systems. Similarly, thought disorder, which has been removed from usage in *DSM* III R, has been replaced by several conceptualizations that focus primarily on speech patterns and do not reflect cognitive processes concerning reasoning, judgment, decision making, problem solving, etc. (i.e., thought processes). Thus the quality of the data developed within a *DSM*-oriented assessment is flawed in that it fails to reflect important theoretical distinctions and refined conceptualizations of psychological phenomena.

In addition to problems with the quality of the data, there are also significant problems regarding its scope. The sorts of assessments promoted by the *DSM* approach fail to sample many domains relevant to understanding and intervening in psychopathology. The emphasis on easily identifiable, clinically salient signs and symptoms ignores information concerning several significant levels of analysis, for example, information regarding *elemental* cognitive deficits (e.g., deficits in preattentional processing, cognitive flexibility, memory, conceptual processing), deficits in more molar cognitive and behavioral skills (e.g., deficits in problem-solving capacity, social skills, metacognition), and problematic patterns of interaction with other individuals and groups. Neither structured psychiatric interviews nor casual observations in a milieu nor psychiatric records containing past information of this same sort provide the kind of detailed, multilevel, multidomain, longitudinal, and cross-situational sampling of information required for a sophisticated and revealing analysis of the structure of an individual's psychopathology.

For example, a *DSM*-oriented assessment does not yield information required for identifying subtle properties of a functional deficit (e.g., phasic properties of elemental cognitive processes) or for gathering quantified data on the frequency of certain types of behavior across settings with different contextual parameters. Nor does it provide the sorts of information required for making the numerous differential assessments (e.g., competence deficits versus performance deficits, psychotic exacerbations versus complicated role performances, normal functioning versus highly compensated functioning) essential for refined clinical understanding of a person. Thus the information omitted from a *DSM*-oriented assessment does not fit easily into the category of, and cannot be dismissed as, useful *auxiliary* information bearing on case management, since it can, and usually does, contribute essentially to an understanding of a person's psychopathology.[15]

The inadequacy of the data collected in a *DSM*-oriented diagnostic assessment is revealed not only by its limited quality and scope but also by the wide-ranging intracategory variability of individuals with respect to clinically important variables. Most of this variation is not represented by the limited data collected in a *DSM*-oriented assessment, and it is masked by DSM categorical labels, even when several are employed. Nor is such variation represented along the various axes of the multiaxial approach advocated in *DSM*. There are many sources of such intracategory variation that need to be recognized.

First, because virtually all *DSM* categories involve numerous unquantified criterial attributes, many clinically relevant attributes are lumped togther under a single diagnostic label (e.g., major depression involves cognitive, affective, motivational, and physiological attributes). And since there is no serious quantified parceling of the levels of these attributes,[16] individuals who fall within a category may well differ on precise measures of them (e.g., frequency of hallucination, intensity of mood). As a result, very different patterns of attributes may be present in individuals receiving the same diagnosis on the basis of the same grossly conceived criteria.

In fact, the situation is yet worse than this. Not only is there likely to be unmeasured variation in *levels* of the criterial attributes *shared* by individuals in a particular diagnostic category, but also, given the polythetic character of *DSM* criteria, very different symptom profiles, at the clinical level, can be grouped together as manifestations of the same disorder (e.g., Clarkin et al. [1983] point out that there are 56 different ways to satisfy the criteria for borderline personality disorder). The consequence of this form of intracategory variation is that individuals within the same category can differ substantially with respect to the structure of their clinically identifiable deficits even if the focus is limited to criterial features. For example, according to *DSM* criteria for depression, individuals need *not* experience depressed mood, so long as they do exhibit a reduction in levels of interest in regular activities. Such differences potentially signal very different deficit structures, and they potentially have enormous impact upon the choice of intervention strategies and tactics as well as upon an individual's responsiveness to such interventions. Moods, for example, can be exceedingly powerful in their impact upon an individual's cognitive functioning, and they are substantially different from the impact of diminished levels of interest in activities.

Unfortunately, the unrepresented variability of individuals within a typical *DSM* diagnostic category does not stop here. The *context* of an individual's problems and deficits is also inadequately represented within the *DSM* approach. Two points should be made in this regard. First, the means for explicit representation of context is a crude subjective-rating scale (axis IV) concerning the severity of psychosocial stressors in the person's environment that likely played a role in causing recent occurrences of an individual's problems. Such a scale is typically based upon self reports or second-hand reports, and it is not detailed, objectively quantified, comprehensive, or strategically assessed. As a consequence, such a scale does not isolate relevant contextual factors in a precise, discriminating, or quantitatively usable way. Second, it appears to be a feature of the *DSM* approach that "context" means the extraorganismic (social or physical) environment. But this is surely an arbitrary stipulation. A more appropriate conception of the context of a deficit includes intraorganismic attributes as well. However, the *DSM* approach makes no provisions for representing the internal *psychological* context (e.g., the contexts of functioning with respect to memory, attention, perception, reasoning, problem solving), which may have a significant impact upon what deficits a person exhibits as well as upon how a person responds to interventions.

There is yet one more dimension of variability that leads to intracategory heterogeneity. The *DSM* approach provides no representation of the underlying biological, psychological, or environmental processes that constitute the pathology of a given mental disorder. The explicitly avowed "atheoretical" approach and the exclusive focus upon clinical features mean that information about such processes is conveyed neither by a "diagnosis" nor by the assessment data that led to it. As a consequence, there is room for massive "process heterogeneity" (Corning and Steffy 1979) within diagnostic categories. Such potential variation means that classification within a *DSM* category does not really shed any light on what an *individual's* pathology is or on whether or how pathology dynamics can be managed. As long as *DSM* remains atheoretical with respect to pathology, it will continue to fail to represent the causal processes operating within an individual and will very likely continue to classify within the same category individuals who exhibit superficial similarities but differ significantly on underlying process.

To sum up, there is very likely massive *unrepresented* heterogeneity across individuals falling within the same *DSM* diagnostic category. Unfortunately, the features involved in this unrepresented variation (i.e., the structure of an individual's deficits and capacities, the context of their functioning, and the causal processes involved) make potentially significant differences with respect to both understanding the pathology and its treatment. Thus, given the limited scope and quality of the information collected, a *DSM*-oriented diagnostic assessment does not produce adequate information on clinically important features of the *individuals* it classifies.

Consequences

The three premises just reviewed imply that a *DSM*-oriented diagnostic assessment does not issue in either a set of categories or a body of information that adequately serves clinical purposes. Because of the lack of nomological unity of the categories, the poor quality and restricted scope of the data collected, and the massive, unrepresented intracategory heterogeneity with respect to clinically important variables, a *DSM*-oriented assessment leaves the clinician in a weak position for effectively saying what is wrong with a given person, what is likely to be most effective in helping him or her, and what is likely to happen over time. Thus such an assessment is not sufficient for reducing clinical uncertainty. Simply including a patient within one or more *DSM* categories is not enough, because of their lack of validity and the massive, unrepresented intracategory heterogeneity that they exhibit. And the sort of information collected—being subjective, nonquantitative, and restricted to the protoscientifically conceived clinically observable traits of a person—is not sufficient, because it is of poor quality and leaves too many variables unassessed. As a consequence, clinicians must go well beyond the parameters of the *DSM* approach if they are to gain a handle on clinical uncertainty.[17]

4   Problems with the Research Utility of the *DSM* Approach

We turn now to a discussion of the role of *DSM* in research on psychopathology. Recall that we identified two major purposes that a system of classification ought to serve with respect to such research, namely, to promote scientifically acceptable research (i.e., quantified and well-controlled studies) and to promote productive research that is well integrated within broader scientific research programs concerned with human functioning. In our opinion, the *DSM* approach to classification does not serve either of these purposes very effectively.

Failure to Promote Scientifically Acceptable Research

To begin with, the *DSM* approach to classification does not promote scientifically acceptable research programs. Our argument for this claim is predicated on the various features of *DSM* categories discussed above, i.e., they involve numerous unquantified criterial attributes and they are protoscientifically conceived, polythetic, and massively heterogeneous with respect to criterial clinical attributes, underlying processes, and other attributes of individuals and their environments. In the typical study in which diagnostic categories function as independent variables, these features of the categories mean that there are many unrepresented and uncontrolled potential confounds and sources of experimental error. As a consequence, such studies are not well-controlled research, and they tend to yield uninterpretable findings. For example, depression research that employs *DSM* criteria for creating experimental and control groups is essentially confounded by the polythetic character of the criteria for major depression. Such criteria allow that individuals will count as depressed if they exhibit either depressed mood or loss of interest in regular activities, *and* they exhibit any four symptoms from a list of seven other cognitive, physiological, or emotional variables. To the extent that this sort of variability is not measured and taken into account, the results of such research are uninterpretable and of questionable value.[18]

Jeffrey Poland, Barbara Von Eckardt, and Will Spaulding

Failure to Promote Productive Research

In addition to not being scientifically acceptable, *DSM*-oriented research programs are also not likely to be productive. As described earlier, such research programs focus upon clinically salient signs and symptoms (i.e., attributes at highly molar levels of organization and function), and they aim at identifying syndromes that are nomologically related to etiological and pathological processes and that exhibit characteristic dynamic features at the clinical level of expression (e.g., course, outcome, treatment responsiveness). However, there are strong reasons to believe that such "syndromes with unity" do not exist to be discovered, and hence that this approach toward research in psychopathology is in serious trouble.

The first reason is that, as noted earlier, the existence of such syndromes has not been well supported by past research. The validation of *DSM* categories is quite generally acknowledged to be an unpaid debt. In addition, a more principled reason for believing that syndromes with unity do not exist, and hence that *DSM*-oriented research is not likely to be productive, is that the domain of psychopathology exhibits two features that, when taken together, undermine the likelihood of there being much (if any) nomological structure at the clinical level of description.

The first such feature is the massive *heterogeneity* of the various diagnostic categories discussed earlier, i.e., the wide-ranging, intracategory variation with respect to biological, psychological, behavioral, and environmental variables that potentially have impact on what clinical features are exhibited, how they relate to each other, and how they evolve over time. The second crucial feature is the significant amount of *context dependence* exhibited by psychological attributes and processes at the clinical and other levels of analysis. That is, psychological attributes and processes at many, perhaps all, levels are not entirely encapsulated, and hence their expression, interrelations, and dynamical properties will vary, depending on what else is going on in the system.

For example, whether or not an individual exhibits a deficit in selective attention will depend on numerous variables concerning, inter alia, memory, thought processes, cognitive resources, interpersonal strategies, and emotional responsiveness. Failure to attend to and process relevant stimuli may be due to a memory lapse, intrusive thoughts, a limitation of attentional capacity, an interpersonal strategy, or an emotional response to other aspects of a situation. Adequate attention, on the other hand, can be the product of normal cognitive functioning or of highly compensated functioning that masks a cognitive deficit (e.g., when metacognitive strategies or environmental structures compensate for disruptive thought processes). Thus the clinical expression of pathology or normalcy depends upon the interaction of multiple processes and is inevitably sensitive to intra- and extraorganismic contexts.

If these two features of intracategory heterogeneity and context sensitivity are indeed characteristic of psychopathology, then there will be heterogeneous mixes of interacting and context-sensitive variables in individuals receiving the same *DSM* diagnosis, and these will lead to differences in the expression, interrelations, and dynamics of attributes at the clinical level. As a consequence, tight nomological relations directly involving clinically salient attributes are unlikely to exist. If this is so, then questions stimulated by the *DSM* approach, focusing as they do on clinical phenomenology, are likely to direct attention away from the loci of nomological structure in psychopathology, and thus research programs addressing such questions are likely to be unproductive.[19]

Two clarifications should be emphasized. The first is that we are not saying that there *cannot* be syndromes of the sort hypothesized by the *DSM* approach. We are saying that if there are any, they are rare, and they require that special conditions obtain. In particular, the existence of well-defined clinical syndromes exhibiting nomic relations to underlying pathology and other variables requires low levels of both intracategory heterogeneity and context sensitivity of the processes and attributes involved. Such processes and attributes must be substantially uniform across individuals and encapsulated relative to other attributes and processes.[20] The second clarification is that we are not claiming that no individual clinical features are nomologically related to other variables (e.g., underlying psychological or biological variables). Again, however, the conditions under which a tight nomological relation exists between a highly molar clinical feature and some other variable are rare and specific (in that they are homogeneous and context-sensitive).

Finally, if, as we have argued, the *DSM* approach to classification of psychopathology embodies a false theory of the domain (i.e., the theory of syndromes with unity) and hence tends to promote unproductive research, then it fails to effectiviely contribute to scientific knowledge concerned with human functioning. In addition, because of its "atheoretical" stance with respect to causal processes and its exclusive focus upon protoscientifically conceived clinical phenomenology, it fails to draw on the basic sciences of mind, brain, and behavior for the purposes of conceptualizing psychopathological phenomena. As a consequence, the *DSM* approach neither informs nor is informed by these other sciences, and hence it fails to integrate the study of psychopathology within the larger framework of scientific research.

5 Implications of the Discussion and Outlook

The main reasons for the failure of the *DSM* approach to effectively serve clinical and research goals are that, as noted, it involves a false theory of the domain of psychopathology, and it involves a faulty model of scientific rigor, as reflected in both its approach to measurement and its nonquantitative, protoscientific, and "atheoretical" conceptualization of the categories. It appears *unlikely* that the domain of psychopathology is best conceived of in terms of syndromes with unity or that natural kinds will be discovered at the level of clinical phenomenology. There is simply no reason to suppose that the features of clinical phenomenology that catch our attention and are the source of great human distress are also features upon which a science of psychopathology should directly focus when searching for regularities and natural kinds (see Corning and Steffy 1979, Cromwell 1982). Human interests and saliencies tend to carve out an unnatural domain from the point of view of nomological structure. Hence the relations between the scientific understanding of psychopathology and clinical responsiveness to it may be less direct than is commonly supposed. In insisting that classification be exclusively focused on clinical phenomenology, *DSM* not only undermines productive research but also undermines the development of effective relations between clinical practice and scientific understanding.

The current situation, therefore, involves a crisis: the dominant approach to classifying psychopathology is deeply flawed and not doing the work it should be doing. As we see it, there is a need for an alternative approach to classification that embodies a better model of scientific rigor and a more accurate theory of the domain of psychopathology. Such an alternative needs to place less emphasis on clinical phenomenology in classification and give more balanced attention to processes at all levels of analysis. And it needs to get a handle on the massive interindividual variation with respect to attributes and functioning, as well as their evident context sensitivity. Furthermore, it is especially important that an alternative be based on a more intimate relationship with basic science than is *DSM*.

This, then, is the challenge facing researchers in the area of psychopathology: to develop an approach to classification that is responsive to the purposes of classification and that overcomes the obstacles and problems undermining the *DSM* approach. Whether *DSM* can itself be responsive to this challenge is something we doubt. But, of course, the pressure is on skeptics to produce the required alternative. This task must await another time.[21]

Notes

1. See Blashfield 1984 and Millon 1991 for detailed discussions of categorical and dimensional approaches to classification of psychopathology. Although our presentation is largely consistent with these presentations, we extend the taxonomy of types of approaches. See also Beckner 1959 and Sokal and Sneath 1963 for seminal discussions of the various approaches to classification.

2. We ignore, for now, the possibility of *hierarchical* categorical frameworks, in which the set of categories is structured by relations of subordination and superordination.

3. Space does not allow a fuller elaboration of this approach in the present chapter. It constitutes a significant extension of the standard taxonomy of classification systems, and it is an approach that is implicit in the practice of many clinicians and researchers.

4. But see Blashfield 1984 and 1991 and Kirk and Kutchins 1992 for critical discussions concerning reliability studies of psychiatric classification.

Jeffrey Poland, Barbara Von Eckardt, and Will Spaulding

5. The authors of *DSM* advocate a purely descriptive, atheoretical approach to the definition of diagnostic categories. Thus criteria for the categories make no reference to etiology or underlying pathology.

6. These objections are formulated in many of the papers included in Millon and Klerman 1986. See also Carson 1991 and Kirk and Kutchins 1992. Several of these critical themes will be echoed and elaborated in the discussion below.

7. Indeed, it appears that the problem of the reliability of the diagnostic categories has not been solved to date, despite the many affirmative claims made by proponents of the *DSM* approach. Efforts to enhance reliability (e.g., the use of structured interviews) do so only at the expense of creating new problems (e.g., undue restriction of the data collected for a diagnostic assessment). See below for further discussion of these issues.

8. The *DSM* approach has been variously described as "hierarchical" (American Psychiatric Association, 1980) and "prototypal" (Cantor and Genero 1986). Neither of these variants impact significantly on the thrust of what follows.

9. Along with, perhaps, other collateral information regarding onset; course; outcome; familial, racial, and gender associations; and base-rate data concerning incidence and prevalence.

10. An issue we must bypass here is whether *DSM* is concerned with purely syndromal classification or whether, as we suggest in the text, it is concerned with viewing syndromes as reflections of underlying pathological processes. Indeed, the literature concerning *DSM* reflects both of these ways of understanding the significance of syndromes. Neither view, however, spares the approach from the problems discussed below.

11. In the language of *DSM* III R, a syndrome is considered to be "a manifestation of a behavioral, psychological, or biological dysfunction in the person" (American Psychiatric Association, 1987, xxii). It appears to be an assumption of the *DSM* approach that for each category of mental disorder, there is a core or essential pathology that exhibits itself in various ways at the clinical level and that can be distinguished from the variety of other, potentially clinically relevant features of individuals and their environment.

12. Structured interview protocols, such as the Schedule for Affective Disorders and Schizophrenia, or SADS (Endicott and Spitzer 1978), are tools for organizing a diagnostic interview in a way that strategically gathers information about signs and symptoms for formulating a *DSM* diagnosis.

13. See the *DSM* III R itself (American Psychiatric Association, 1987, xxiv), Kendall 1989, and Widiger et al. 1991 for representative acknowledgments of this point by those within the psychiatric community. In the "schizophrenia community" a consensus exists that there is widespread variability with respect to symp-

tom clustering, treatment responsiveness, course, and outcome. And there are no generally accepted etiological or pathological accounts. Comparable claims can be made regarding virtually every other *DSM* category. An exception to this gloomy picture might be bipolar affective disorder. But data bearing on validity need to be assessed *on a category-by-category basis*. Validation of one category does not mean that other categories are ipso facto valid as well.

14. For example, consider that judgments of "prominance" of a symptom in a symptom picture are reguired for many diagnoses (e.g., bipolar disorder, schizophrenia). These are unquantified judgments vulnerable to contextual and individual variation that is not mitigated by the *DSM* "operationalization" of the criteria involved.

15. Assessing such matters is time consuming, it sometimes requires specific technology, and it requires special assessment skills. Thus, although it is essential, such assessment is well beyond the scope of a typical *DSM*-oriented diagnostic assessment, which focuses exclusively upon highly molar behavior and speech. The *DSM* approach to classification, in our opinion, tends to promote the idea that sophisticated assessment of psychopathology can proceed efficiently and effectively while ignoring the basic tenets of sound scientific assessment strategy and procedures and, as a result, while ignoring the complex structure of psychopathological deficits. Both the polythetic categorical structure of the *DSM* classification system and its focus on informally conceived clinical phenomena promotes an unquantified and nondiscriminating checklist approach to assessment, which undermines clinical understanding.

16. Such levels are typically assessed, if at all, on the basis of clinical judgment (i.e., subjective rating of symptoms).

17. Of course, there is a sense in which the use of *DSM* categories reduces uncertainty: by increasing the confidence with which a clinician proceeds. But given the points made in the text about masking variance, this is false confidence at best and potentially quite harmful as a result.

One predictable reply to this argument is that *DSM* provides a starting point for clinical diagnostic assessment and that it is part of the *DSM* approach to incorporate whatever other information is necessary for management of a disorder. However, there are two things wrong with this reply. First, what is the point of calling something a "diagnosis" if it leaves the major part of the assessment undone? If it is true that once the *DSM* categories applicable to a person's pathology have been identified, there is still room for massive variation in the structure of the deficits, the context of functioning, the underlying pathological processes, and the interventions likely to be effective, then it is grossly misleading to label the result of such an assessment a "diagnosis." Indeed, it is quite misleading to identify a *DSM* diagnosis as a meaningful starting point for assessment if, rather than reducing clinical uncertainty, it increases such uncertainty by introducing categorical distinctions that mask wide-ranging variation of crucial features across individuals. Second, the suggestion that all of the unaddressed information bears only on the management of the identified disorder(s) and not on an understanding of the pathology itself is, in our opinion, a misreading of the significance of that information. Collecting such information (e.g., quantified measures of criterial attributes, molecular and molar cognitive attributes, and environmental attributes) are potentially relevant to an understanding of what the structure of the pathology is in a given case. It is precisely the information not identified by *DSM* criteria that must be collected if a person's pathology is to be comprehended at all; in many cases, clinically salient attributes are misleading noise.

18. Comparable arguments based on the unquantified, protoscientifically conceived, and heterogeneous character of the categories contribute further to scepticism about the value of research structured by *DSM* categories.

19. It is very implausible that this problem can be dealt with by more elaborate reconfiguration of the clinical variables that enter into the criteria for the various categories. The problem is intimately involved with *DSM*'s exclusive focus on the descriptive phenomenology of psychopathology. In research contexts, this means that the more we search for specific nomological relations characteristic of syndromes defined in such terms, the less success we are likely to have. Thus the planned efforts to "validate" the *DSM* IV categories are very likely going to be futile insofar as they are predicated on identifying optimal criteria sets at the clinical level of description for each disorder. In general, the *DSM* approach has stimulated research questions and lines of inquiry that are leading up blind alleys.

20. See Fodor 1983 for a discussion of the idea of "informational encapsulation" and its significance for the existence of lawful relations among psychological variables.

21. In a companion to this paper (Poland, Von Eckardt, and Spaulding 1992), we outline what we take to be a version of a "process-oriented dimensional approach" that is responsive to the various problems outlined in the text, and which is gaining wider acceptance within the clinical and research communities despite the apparent ubiquity of *DSM*. Such an approach is multidimensional, idiographic, process-oriented, and rooted in basic science. Many clinicians and researchers, while paying lip service to *DSM*, conduct their work in a more sophisticated way.

References

American Psychiatric Association. 1980. *Diagnostic and Statistical Manual of Mental Disorders*, 3rd ed. Washington, D.C.: American Psychiatric Association.

American Psychiatric Association. 1987. *Diagnostic and Statistical Manual of Mental Disorders*, 3rd ed., rev. Washington, D.C.: American Psychiatric Association.

American Psychiatric Association. 1994. *Diagnostic and Statistical Manual of Mental Disorders*, 4th ed. Washington, D.C.: American Psychiatric Association.

Beckner, M. 1959. *The Biological Way of Thought*. New York: Columbia University Press.

Blashfield, R. 1984. *The Classification of Psychopathology: Neo-Kraepelinian and Quantitative Approaches*. New York: Plenum Press.

Blashfield, R. 1991. "Models of Psychiatric Classification." In *Adult Psychopathology and Diagnosis*, 2nd ed., ed. S. Turner and M. Hersen, pp. 3–22. New York: John Wiley and Sons.

Cantor, N., and N. Genero. 1986. "Psychiatric Diagnosis and Natural Categorization: A Close Analogy." In *Contemporary Directions in Psychopathology*, ed. T. Millon and G. Klerman, pp. 233–236. New York: Guilford Press.

Carson, R. 1991. "Dilemmas in the Pathway of the *DSM-IV*." *Journal of Abnormal Psychology* 100:302–307.

Clarkin, J., T. Widiger, A. Frances, S. Hurt, and M. Gilmore. 1983. "Prototypic Typology and the Borderline Personality Disorder." *Journal of Abnormal Psychology* 92:263–275.

Corning, W., and R. Steffy. 1979. "Taximetric Strategies Applied to Psychiatric Classification." *Schizophrenia Bulletin* 5:294–305.

Cromwell, R. 1982. "Eight Decades' Focus on Symptom Classification Is Enough: A Discussion." In *Preventive Intervention in Psychopathology: Are We Ready?* ed. M. Goldstein. Washington, D.C.: U.S. Government Printing Office.

Endicott, J., and R. Spitzer. 1978. "A Diagnostic Interview." *Archives of General Psychiatry* 35:837–844.

Eysenck, H. 1986. "A Critique of Contemporary Classification and Diagnosis." In *Contemporary Directions in Psychopathology*, ed. T. Millon and G. Klerman, pp. 73–98. New York: Guilford Press.

Fodor, J. 1983. *The Modularity of Mind*. Cambridge: MIT Press.

Kendall, R. 1989. "Clinical Validity." In *The Validity of Psychiatric Diagnosis*, ed. L. Robins and J. Barnett, pp. 305–323. New York: Raven Press.

Kirk, S., and H. Kutchins. 1992. *The Selling of "DSM": The Rhetoric of Science in Psychiatry*. New York: Aldine De Gruyter.

Kuhn, T. 1970. *The Structure of Scientific Revolutions*. Chicago: University of Chicago Press.

Millon, T. 1986. "On the Past and Future of the *DSM*-III: Personal Recollections and Projections." In *Contemporary Directions in Psychopathology*, ed. T. Millon and G. Klerman, pp. 29–70. New York: Guilford Press.

Millon, T. 1991. "Classification in Psychopathology: Rationale, Alternatives, and Standards." *Journal of Abnormal Psychology* 100:245–261.

Millon, T., and G. Klerman, eds. 1986. *Contemporary Directions in Psychopathology*. New York: Guilford Press.

Poland, J., B. Von Eckardt, and W. Spaulding. 1992. "Classifying Psychopatholgy: A Process-Oriented Approach." Unpublished.

Sokol, R., and P. Sneath. 1963. *Principles of Numerical Taxonomy*. San Francisco: W. H. Freeman.

Spitzer, R., and J. Williams. 1983. "Classification of Mental Disorders." In *Comprehensive Textbook of Psychiatry*, ed. H. Kaplan and B. Sadock, pp. 591–613. Baltimore: Williams and Wilkins.

Widiger, T., A. Frances, D. Pincus, W. Davis, and M. First. 1991. "Toward an Empirical Classification for the *DSM*-IV." *Journal of Abnormal Psychology* 100:280–288.

The Effectiveness of Psychotherapy: Epistemological Issues

Edward Erwin

There are now approximately 400 different types of psychotherapy (Kazdin 1986), but there is no consensus about which are effective in treating specific types of clinical problems. Indeed, with the possible exception of some behavioral and cognitive treatments, there is still disagreement about whether *any* are effective in treating *any* problems.

In one of the most influential reviews of psychotherapeutic outcomes—one that still serves as the basis for many of the more optimistic assessments of the field—Smith, Glass, and Miller (1980) conclude, on the basis of a meta-analysis of over 400 studies, that psychotherapy is generally and consistently effective, providing benefits on a par with other expensive interventions, such as schooling and the use of medicine. One of the authors of this review interprets the evidence as showing, subject to certain qualifications, that the average person receiving psychotherapy is better off at its termination than 80 percent of those not undergoing psychotherapy (Glass and Kliegel 1983). This optimistic verdict contrasts sharply, however, with the conclusion of Prioleau, Murdock, and Brody, who also used meta-analysis but excluded from their review studies of behavior therapy:

Thirty years after Eysenck (1952) first raised the issue of the effectiveness of psychotherapy, twenty-eight years after Meehl (1955) called for the use of placebo controls in psychotherapy, eighteen years after Brill et al. (1964) demonstrated in a reasonably well done study that the psychotherapy effect may be equivalent to the placebo effect, and after about 500 outcome studies have been reviewed—we are still not aware of a single convincing demonstration that the benefits of psychotherapy exceed those of placebos for real patients. . . . Given the absence of convincing contradictory data, and considering the partial support (at least) that the available research literature provides, we regard it as likely that the benefits of psychotherapy do not exceed those of placebo in real patients. (1983, 284)

Obviously, the way to answer Prioleau, Murdock, and Brody is to find convincing evidence of effectiveness. Many proponents of psychotherapy, including Freud himself, have sought such evidence in uncontrolled, clinical case studies. Others have placed their bets on "the definitive study": one that would include proper experimental controls and demonstrate, not with certitude but convincingly, that psychotherapy is at least sometimes effective. In the 1980s a great deal of money was spent in executing such studies, the most ambitious and presumably the best study of psychotherapy outcomes being the National Institute of Mental Health Treatment of Depression Collaborative Research Program. Two forms of psychotherapy and a drug were compared to a sugar pill for the treatment of depression. Preliminary results were quite encouraging, but the announcement of the final tabulation at the 1989 meeting of the Annual Association for the Advancement of Behavior Therapy appeared to shock many members of the audience: it was announced that the sugar pill had won (or rather had tied the two psychotherapies). This verdict is somewhat overstated: there were a few encouraging results, although even these may be found to be transient once follow-ups are completed. As of this writing, however, the "Collaborative Study" does not appear to be the definitive study that was anticipated.

The idea of one study demonstrating the effectiveness of psychotherapy now seems naive and may be abandoned. One of the reasons why meta-analysis was introduced is that some investigators had concluded that only the combined results of many studies would yield firm evidence of effectiveness. However, the use of meta-analysis has itself generated much controversy (see, e.g., Erwin 1984, Wilson 1985).

The fact that disagreement persists does not automatically translate into zero evidence of psychotherapeutic effectiveness. Perhaps the skeptics are misinformed or are too ideological to concede an obvious point. Yet when leading researchers in the field continue to disagree about the effectiveness of any type of psychotherapy, with the possible exception of cognitive behavior therapy, this is a sign that the evidence remains soft. Furthermore, suppose that *some* types of psychotherapy (in addition to cognitive behavior therapy) have been shown to be effective for some problems and types of patients. Still, claims of effectiveness for most of the 400 or so types of psychotherapy rest on nothing more than speculative clinical theories and uncontrolled single case studies. For these types of psychotherapy, at least, there is considerable disagreement—and not merely the sniping of a few recalcitrant critics—about their effectiveness. It is worth reflecting a moment on why this lack of consensus persists.

It may be that what the field needs most is better treatments; if a few stunningly powerful techniques were available, the case for an extreme skepticism might quickly vanish. A second thing that is needed is better science: more and higher quality empirical evidence and more satisfactory clinical theories. A third thing missing is philosophical agreement about the proper epistemological standards for evaluating claims of therapeutic effectiveness. This chapter deals with some of the persisting issues about such standards.

1 Experimental Evidence

By what standard or standards do we determine whether a particular therapeutic intervention caused or at least contributed to a given outcome? In particular, do we need to meet an *experimental* standard? The question is somewhat vague, if only because not all psychotherapists mean the same thing by "experimental." For example, some contrast experiments with case studies, but others treat case studies as themselves being "miniexperiments." In what follows, I will mean by "experiment" roughly what Campbell and Stanley (1963) mean in their classic monograph. To qualify as "experimental," a study must involve the manipulation of an independent variable and also employ some sort of comparison.

Another element of vagueness concerns the sort of cases in which we need experimental evidence. Are we asking if it is always needed in assessing therapeutic efficacy, or just sometimes? For the moment,

I will assume that the issue is whether experimental evidence is needed *generally*, and not whether it is needed in every single case. Later I will try to make this a bit clearer. Vague or not, there appears to be widespread disagreement about the issue. Cognitive behavior therapists generally agree about the need for experimental testing of therapeutic claims, and so do some psychoanalysts, but others, in the psychodynamic, hermeneutical, and humanistic traditions, often question the need for experiments. For example, one leading analyst, Robert Michaels (1986), contends that in the absence of controlled experiments, we can rely on "clinical wisdom." The authors of the recent report of the American Psychoanalytic Association (Bachrach et al. 1991) apparently agree that experimental evidence is not necessary. None of the studies they review qualify as experiments, yet the authors rely on them to show that patients suitable for psychoanalysis derive substantial benefits from their therapy. Finally, since most psychotherapies have not been studied experimentally and their proponents nevertheless advocate their use, it is a reasonable guess that many supporters of various types of therapy reject the need to meet an experimental standard.

One philosopher who has discussed the need for experiments in psychology is Charles Taylor (1985). He claims that two rival epistemologies divide American psychologists. One is the classical view, which, Taylor claims, is dominant among experimentalists; the other is a hermeneutical view. The classical view, he contends, includes at least two principles. The first requires that hypotheses be "intersubjectively univocal," by which Taylor means (p. 117), that they be based on "brute data" (1985, 117). To qualify as brute data, the statement of them must be certain in at least the sense that they must be *beyond dispute* arising from any personal interpretation or discernment (1985, 121). The second requirement of the classical model is that the auxiliary assumptions linking data to a hypothesis be free of interpretation (1985, 118). Psychoanalysis, on Taylor's view, does not meet the requirements of the classical model, but that is a problem with the model, not with psychoanalysis. Disputes in its domain cannot be settled by appeal to brute data, he argues, but instead turn on the plausibility of rival interpretations (1985, 123). Psychoanalysis, then, is an example—the "most obvious case," according to Taylor (1985, 148)—of a hermeneutical science.

Taylor does not reject the classical model of science altogether; rather, he objects to the attempt to extend it to all areas of psychology. I would go further, however, and object to its use in any area of science. Given how Taylor defines "brute data," it is appropriate to demand such data only if it is appropriate to demand certitude. I assume, as most epistemologists and philosophers of science do, that anyone making the latter demand is setting evidential standards at too high a level. What I question is whether most experimentalists accept Taylor's classical epistemological model (he does not show that any do). Even if most were to accept it, I suggest that they need not do so. The demand for experimental evidence, at least in assessing psychotherapeutic outcomes, can be based on firmer grounds. The grounds I have in mind are partly philosophical and partly empirical.

The philosophical part concerns the nature of empirical confirmation, at least if "Hypothesis h is confirmed" entails that there is some epistemic (and not merely pragmatic) reason to think that h is true, or approximately true. Harvey Siegel and I have argued that genuine confirmation requires that a "differential" condition be met (Erwin and Siegel 1989). Evidence e *differentially* confirms h just in case e plus our background evidence provides at least some reason for believing h to be true (or approximately true) and does not afford equal or better reason for believing some incompatible rival that is at least as plausible as h. This standard is likely to appear very obvious to many experimentalists, but it is implicitly denied by epistemologists, who insist that any increase in the probability of a hypothesis is sufficient to confirm it to some degree. It is also implicitly rejected by those who deny the need to rule out all plausible rivals to a tested hypothesis (e.g., Fine and Forbes 1986). And it is ignored by those who support the efficacy of certain psychotherapies but see no need to discount known plausible rivals to their therapeutic explanations of outcome data.

The empirical part of the grounds for demanding experimental evidence concerns plausible rivals to claims of therapeutic efficacy. If the patient improves, there is generally a plausible explanation available in addition to the therapist's: spontaneous remission took place (i.e., events occurring outside of the therapy session caused all or most of the improvement). A second, often plausible, rival hypothesis is that placebo factors made the difference. Whether this second hypothesis needs to be eliminated is controversial; I will take up this later.

Even if the possibility of spontaneous remission (and perhaps the operation of placebo factors) needs to be ruled out, do we always need experimentation to do this? Not necessarily. As Adolf Grünbaum points out (1984, 259), even in physics, our background evidence can sometimes serve as the probative equivalent of a control group, thus eliminating the need for experimental confirmation of a causal hypothesis. Which psychotherapy cases are of this sort? We have no algorithm for identifying them, but there are some general features of such cases that can be isolated.

According to Alan Kazdin's (1981) useful analysis, there are primarily five features that account for the evidential weaknesses of case studies. One is the use of anecdotal reports, such as the client's or therapist's uncorroborated report that improvement has taken place. A second is the use of one-shot or two-shot assessments, which increases the risk that therapeutic change resulted from testing. Third, in many clinical cases, the problem being treated is acute or episodic. Fourth is the presence of gradual, weak-outcome effects, in contrast to so-called "slam-bang" effects. Fifth is the fact that a case study involves only one individual.

Kazdin points out that to some extent the epistemic weaknesses of case studies can be diminished without transforming them into experiments. I am not sanguine that this can be done in many cases (see Erwin 1988, 210–215), but Kazdin's illuminating analysis provides a way of categorizing the cases that can provide evidence of therapeutic effectiveness despite their being nonexperimental: they are those in which most or all of the five epistemic vices that he cites have been eliminated (although placebo factors may also have to be considered).

One other factor should be mentioned. Often people who undergo psychotherapy receive some obvious benefits while in therapy, or even before therapy commences. They experience an increase in morale, for example, or they benefit from having a dispassionate observer listen to their problems. We might call these benefits "process effects," as opposed to benefits that arrive toward the end of the therapy (outcome benefits). In arguing for the need for experimentation, few would argue that it is necessary to do a controlled study to determine the cause of these process benefits. We are discussing, rather, ascertaining the possible causal connections between therapies and *outcome benefits*.

I conclude that to make the case for *normally* requiring experimental evidence in assessing therapeutic claims, we do not need to assume the defective so-called "classical model" criticized by Taylor (1985). Instead, it is sufficient first to show that confirmation is differential (Erwin and Siegel 1989) and then to argue on empirical grounds that this differential standard is generally not met where experimental controls are missing. However, there are so many different types of psychotherapy and possible therapeutic benefits that it is difficult to state a precise general rule. Given the complexities, it might be better to treat each therapy separately. If we need to state a general rule, then perhaps the following will do, but only if interpreted as a rule of thumb: in assessing psychotherapeutic claims of efficacy, experimental evidence is generally required except where most or all of the standard epistemological defects of case studies have been eliminated. We can then make the rule more informative by listing the standard epistemological defects, including the five identified by Kazdin and any that needed to be added to his list.

2 Placebo Controls

A different sort of issue about standards concerns the kind of experimental design that should be used in studying psychotherapeutic outcomes. In cases where experimental evidence is necessary, do we need a placebo control to establish effectiveness? Prioleau, Murdock, and Brody (1983) and Eysenck (1983) argue that we do. Their position has been widely adopted in the behavior-therapy literature since the publication of Paul's (1966) influential review, but it has also been questioned lately by many researchers, including leading behavior therapists (e.g., Kazdin 1986, Cordray and Bootzin 1983, O'Leary and Borkovec 1978).

One philosopher, P. Binns, questions the feasibility of using a placebo control, at least in studying the efficacy of psychoanalysis. His objection is this: "To exclude what Freudian therapy consists of—including such things as beliefs, attitudes, etc.—from our control group, the latter clearly must not believe that the placebo they are being given is curative of anything" (1990, 534). I do not see the cogency of this objection. Research has shown that if the placebo subjects do not believe in the efficacy of their treatment, the placebo controls are decidedly inadequate (Erwin 1978), for if those in the treatment group show greater improvement than those receiving the placebo, this might plausibly be attributed to their greater confidence in the (nonplacebo) treatment. So, to design a proper experiment, we should do just the opposite of what Binns recommends: we should insure that the placebo subjects *do* believe that the placebos are effective treatments. Would that defeat our purpose? Only if we were trying to show that beliefs and attitudes make no difference in psychoanalytic therapy. Why, however, would we want to show *this*? What we are trying to test is the hypothesis that belief in the therapy and other placebo factors make most or all of the therapeutic difference, that working through emotional conflicts, using free associations, dream interpretation, and the resolution of transference neurosis matters little or not at all. To test this hypothesis, we can compare psychoanalysis to a believed-in placebo lacking psychoanalytic ingredients, such as a sugar pill.

A second reason for questioning the need for placebo controls is conceptual. Kazdin (1986, 201), for example, finds the transfer of the concept of placebo controls from medical to psychotherapy research problematic, if not altogether inappropriate. The defining characteristic of a placebo, he argues, is that it be known to be inert for the problem to which it is applied, but psychotherapy "placebos," he points out, are not inert in this respect. It can be replied that pharmacological placebos are not inert either; they are *physiologically* inert for the problem being studied, but they may be effective for psychological reasons. However, if we define a placebo as a treatment that works only for psychological reasons, then we encounter a different problem. *All* effective psychological treatment will qualify as placebos.

There are other approaches to analyzing the placebo concept besides defining it in terms of psychological inertness, but almost all of them have serious problems of their own. The exception is Adolf Grünbaum's explication (this volume): his analysis is clear, precise, and free from the difficulties infecting other accounts. His result allows us to objectively use a single placebo concept in both medicine and psychotherapy, for his explication serves to distinguish placebos from nonplacebos *within psychological* therapies no less than it makes that distinction within somatic treatments. Suppose that a certain therapeutic theory specifies that therapy t's characteristic treatment factors f_1, and f_2, and f_3 are remedial for disorder d. On Grünbaum's analysis, therapy t is a placebo for d if and only if none of the characteristic factors f is remedial for d. So if confidence in the therapy typically explains all of the therapeutic gains of psychoanalysis in treating d, then relative to psychoanalytic theory, these gains are placebogenic in treating d. If we use the concept of a placebo in this way, then we are not forced to say that all psychological therapies are "placebos" merely because their effective ingredients, if any, are psychological in nature. I believe that Grünbaum's analysis solves the conceptual problems that Kazdin (1986) and others have raised.

A third reason for challenging the use of placebo controls concerns the potency of certain placebos. To require that a therapy outperform a placebo, the argument runs, is to set too high a standard: if the placebo used in a given study is itself effective for a certain disorder, then the therapy that ties it is effective as well. Although the potency of certain placebos is worth stressing, the main lesson is that failure to outperform a placebo is not necessarily a guarantee of ineffectiveness. For reasons to be given shortly, the inference that placebo controls are unnecessary, however, is unwarranted. Before getting to these reasons, we should consider a fourth, widely mentioned reason. Cordray and Bootzin (1983, 286) accuse Prioleau et al. (1983), when they insist on a placebo control, of confusing designs appropriate for answering questions about theoretical mechanisms with designs used to demonstrate effectiveness. Credible placebos, they argue, are used to help understand *why* treatments work, not whether they work.

I agree with Codray and Bootzin to this extent. For a therapy to be effective in treating disorder d, it is sufficient that it have a certain causal capacity: the capacity to help diminish or eliminate d. It is not necessary to have the capacity to outperform a placebo if the placebo is also effective in treating d. Nevertheless, there are at least two reasons for insisting on placebo controls even if effectiveness is the only issue. These reasons are generally not distinguished in the psycho-therapy literature: the first concerns an epistemological standard, whereas the second pertains to a clinical standard.

The epistemological standard is that discussed in the previous section: to confirm the effectiveness of a therapy, we need to rule out plausible competing explanations. Consider two different types of cases. Suppose, for example, that Freudian theory specifies the use of dream interpretation, the working through of conflicts, and the resolution of transference neurosis as the potent factors in psycho-analysis. Even if these factors operate solely by affecting the patient's expectations, rather than for the reasons Freud thought, the therapy may still be effective. However, suppose that none of these factors makes any difference to the outcome; suppose that the patient's expectation of cure results from his merely beginning the therapy or receiving the rationale of the therapy at the outset and that substituting any plausible therapy would yield the same outcome. In this second case, the therapy does not work through a certain mechanism; it does not work at all. So unless we have a way of ruling out the second sort of possibility, we are not entitled to infer that a positive outcome was caused by the therapy. The usual substitute for a placebo control, a waiting-list control, is generally insufficient to do this, to rule out the possibility that expectations *not* engendered by the therapy were the real causes of improvement. Other factors besides the client's expectations of improvement also need to be considered. These include the expectations of the therapist, the therapist's "demand" for improvement, the therapist's warmth and empathy, the client's very act of entering therapy, and the pretreatment interview. If a therapy group is compared only to a no-treatment or a minimum contact waiting-list control and one or more of the above factors can just as plausibly explain the improvement as can the treatment, then the inference that the therapy was effective is unwarranted. So it is not true that the only legitimate purpose of a placebo control is to answer a question about *why* a therapy works; it may also be required to show that a therapy works at all.

A second reason for including a placebo control concerns a clinical standard. We want to know not merely if a therapy works to some degree but also if it works better than a sugar pill or some other placebo that is inexpensive, simple to use, free from negative side effects, and quick. The standard way to see whether this clinical standard is met is to compare a treatment to such a placebo. (There may be some cases, such as treatment of severe depression, where we know in advance that a sugar pill or some similar placebo is unlikely to be effective.)

Why require that this clinical standard be met? Consider the consequences of generally failing to meet it. Suppose that Kazdin (1986, 50) is correct in contending that when control conditions generate high levels of credibility, treatment and placebo-control conditions rarely differ in outcome. If this is generally true (some forms of behavior therapy, cognitive therapy, and interpersonal psychotherapy may be exceptions) and if the placebo treatment is a sugar pill plus minimum therapeutic contact (or some brief, inexpensive substitute), this has serious implications for the field of psychotherapy. First, this result would be evidence that most of the therapeutic theories in the field are wrong and that most forms of psychotherapy are, in Grünbaum's terminology (this volume), "inadvertent placebos." Second, a serious problem would arise concerning the training of therapists. Why spend a lot of money and time learning how to use certain psychotherapies if basically what one needs to learn is how to make a treatment credible to the patient? Third, if most psychotherapies work only because of their credibility, this raises other serious questions. For example, what will happen to consumer satisfaction if the public finds out that they are paying for treatment that works, if at all, only because they believe it works? Will the public's confidence in psychotherapy begin to fade, which would wipe out the only potent ingredient in most psychotherapies? Will insurance companies pay for treatment that is only placebogenic?

Finally, Critelli and Neumann (1984, 58) endorse the use of psychotherapy even though they agree that, as far as we know, no current therapies have beneficial effects over and above those of a credible placebo. They ask, "Does the foregoing imply that current therapies may be no more effective or scientific than faith healing or the rituals of primitive societies?" (1984, 58). Their answer is affirmative, but they still give higher marks to psychotherapeutic procedures on the grounds that they are "the legitimate, indigenous healing practices of our society" (1984, 38). What does this mean, however, other than that psychotherapy is superior to voodoo or faith healing only in the sense that it is more credible to most segments of our society? I do not believe that this is the best that can be said about psychotherapy, but if it were, then its science would have *so far* produced little of value.

3   Meta-analysis

The issues discussed so far concern the proper standards to be used in judging a single study. However, to make judgments about psychotherapy in general, or even about particular types, it is often necessary to integrate and evaluate evidence from multiple studies. What are the rules for doing this? In the past 15 years, the answer that has been increasingly accepted in psychology is, We should use the rules of meta-analysis.

Meta-analysis has played an important role in the evaluation of psychotherapy effectiveness, but its use has potential consequences extending far beyond the borders of psychotherapy. For example Schmidt (1992, 1173) argues that meta-analysis requires major changes in the way psychologists view the general research process, and suggests that as a result of its use, even the fundamental nature of scientific discovery may change. In recent years, meta-analysis has also had an important impact on medical research. One leading medical researcher claims that it is "the wave of the future" and that its use is "going to revolutionize how the sciences, especially medicine, handle data" (quoted in Mann 1990, 378).

Some of the issues raised by meta-analysis also bear on important issues in the philosophy of science. For example, philosophers have often talked about interpreting "patterns of evidence," but there are no agreed on rules for doing this. Proponents of meta-analysis argue that their methods provide such rules. Meta-analysis also bears on philosophic issues about a total-evidence requirement, standards for weighting evidence from methodologically weak studies, assessing epistemological criteria for identifying a good study, and the comparative merits of qualitative and quantitative reviews of research. So far, however, philosophers have generally and, in my view, unjustifiably ignored the debates about meta-analysis.

The literature on this topic is now enormous. What follow are a few brief comments on some of the epistemological issues (for the technical statistical issues, see Hunter and Schmidt 1990, Wachter and Straf 1990, Rosenthal 1984).

In a broad sense, the term "meta-analysis" refers to any statistical method for averaging research results. In one of the best known uses of meta-analysis, Smith, Glass, and Miller (1980) transform different measures of psychotherapy outcome into a single measure called the "effect size" (ES). ES is calculated for each measure (if there are multiple measures for a single study) by subtracting the control group's average score on that measure from the treatment group's average score and dividing the result by the standard deviation for the control group. Thus,

$$ES = \frac{M(TG) - M(CG)}{S(CG)},$$

where $M(TG)$ is the mean score for the therapy group, $M(CG)$ is the mean score for the control group, and $S(CG)$ is the standard deviation for the control group.

Smith, Glass, and Miller calculated approximately 1,760 effect sizes for 475 controlled studies of psychotherapy and found that the average effect size was .85 (with a standard error of .03). As noted earlier, their results have been interpreted as showing that the average person receiving psychotherapy is better off at the end of it than 80 percent of those not undergoing psychotherapy (Glass and Kliegel 1983).

Many objections have been raised to the Smith, Glass, and Miller's argument (Eysenck 1983, Erwin 1984, Wilson 1985, Searles 1985, Bruno and Ellett 1988). One of the more serious objections concerns their weighting equally studies of good and poor methodological quality. Their justification for this democratic treatment is that both types of studies tended to yield the same types of results. I question this finding because I doubt that their criteria for distinguishing good and bad studies were sufficiently rigorous (Erwin 1984, 426–428), but even if they were, many of the studies included in Smith and Glass's (1977) original meta-analysis and incorporated in Smith, Glass, and Miller's (1980) full report were too weak to warrant a causal inference (see, for example, the criticisms of Rachman and Wilson [1980, 250–255]). For those types of psychotherapy examined only in these seriously deficient studies, no firm evidence of effectiveness is presented in Smith, Glass, and Miller 1980. Consequently, their first major, general conclusion, "Psychotherapy is beneficial, consistently so and in many different ways" (1980, 183), is not supported by their overall argument. The most that is shown is that certain *types* of psychotherapy are effective (and even for these, only for certain types of problems and clients). If the good studies they reviewed are primarily those of cognitive behavior therapy, the remaining studies may tell us little about the effectiveness of other types of psychotherapy. As noted earlier, when Prioleau, Murdock, and Brody (1983) performed a meta-analysis on the same data but excluded studies of cognitive behavior therapy, they found that for real patients, there was no evidence that the benefits of psychotherapy exceeded those of placebos.

In addition to the problems with Smith, Glass, and Miller's (1980) particular meta-analysis, there are problems (not necessarily insurmountable) that generally arise in doing a meta-analysis. Some concern the concept of an effect size. Suppose that a meta-analysis is performed on the results of 100 poorly controlled experiments on a certain type of psychotherapy. The effect size might be .90, and yet we might have no evidence that the therapy is effective in producing any beneficial outcome. In general, to say that an effect size is positive does not logically imply that there is any evidence that the outcomes were the results of the hypothesized causes. For this reason, talk of *effect* sizes can be misleading, especially where crucial epistemological requirements for a causal inference have been violated. I regard this objection as terminological, but there are also substantive problems with the calculation of effect sizes.

In the analysis of Smith, Glass, and Miller (1980), every measure for a study is counted as a separate effect size. This violates the requirement of statistical independence and has the consequence that studies with a greater number of outcome measures are given greater weight. Hunter and Schmidt (1990, 480) reply that this criticism is "statistically correct," but in a Glassian type of meta-analysis, the purpose of research integration is more descriptive than inferential. However, as Smith, Glass, and Miller (1980) make quite clear, they do use their meta-analytic results in making important causal inferences about the effects of psychotherapy. Had they not made such inferences, it is doubtful that their work would have had the tremendous impact it has had in the field of psychotherapy.

Another way of treating effect sizes is to calculate one for each study, which thus insures statistical independence (Hunter and Schmidt 1990, 482). One could select one outcome measure among many as "primary," but that would require the kind of substantitative methodology judgment that meta-analysts generally wish to avoid; more serious, in the field of psychotherapy, at least, it would run counter to the generally accepted requirement that multiple outcome measures are required to adequately assess therapeutic effectiveness. Consequently, the preferred way to arrive at one effect size per study is to average the effect sizes for a single study. This solution, however, generates other problems. Suppose that in a treatment of depression, treated subjects show only a marginal decrease in depression but a major change in the average effect size of various test scores reflecting only tiny beneficial changes. Averaging the results will seriously overestimate the beneficial effects. As Paul (1985) demonstrates, the opposite problem can also occur. In one of his studies, the average effect size for his two focal scales was .45, but in the meta-analysis of Landman and Dawes (1980), averaging *all* the outcomes for this same study resulted in a meager effect size of only .04. Apart from problems of underrepresentation or overrepresentation, some averaging of outcome measures, as Wilson (1985, 40) points out, make no clinical sense, as in a study of obesity where we obtain a mean effect size for body fat, body weight, body image, lipoproteins, systolic and diastolic blood pressure, depressed affect, and marital satisfaction. Other problems with the concept of an effect size are raised by Bruno and Ellett (1988).

Even if some of the general difficulties with meta-analysis have not yet been resolved, this does not necessarily argue in favor of non-meta-analytic methods of research integration. All known methods have at least some problems. Furthermore, proponents of meta-analysis argue that their methods have weighty advantages over rival methods. I turn now to some of the more important of these alleged comparative virtues of meta-analysis.

One of these is that the method is quantitative. If everything else were equal, this would make meta-analysis decidedly more attractive than standard so-called "narrative" methods of data analysis. I assume that this point is acceptable even to critics of meta-analysis.

A second alleged virtue of meta-analytic reviews is that they are more complete than narrative reviews. This may be insignificant in areas of science where only a few studies are available, but it is very important in a field such as psychotherapy, where there are hundreds of studies. However, two issues need to be separated. One is the failure of a reviewer to consider all relevant studies, and the second concerns the deliberate decision of a reviewer to dismiss certain studies because of methodological defects.

As to the first issue, there is nothing in the nature of meta-analysis that guarantees completeness or in narrative reviews that necessitates incompleteness. Smith, Glass, and Miller's (1980) meta-analytic review, for example, is seriously incomplete. In assessing the effects of behavior modification and cognitive behavior therapy, for example, substantial chunks of evidence from studies having a single-subject design were ignored. Other omissions are discussed in Rachman and Wilson 1980, 251–252. A narrative review, in contrast, could cover all of the studies reviewed by Smith, Glass, and Miller *plus* those that they failed to consider. So a meta-analytic review need not be more comprehensive than a narrative review.

As to the question of deliberately excluding very poor studies, some proponents of meta-analysis (Hunter and Schmidt 1990, 468) complain that this tactic unjustifiably wastes much information. It is crucial to distinguish, however, between information that is evidentially relevant and information that is not. If a study of psychotherapy lacks a control group (or the subject's base rate in a single-subject design) or provides no evidence that any of the outcome measures reflect any beneficial effect, then the study provides no evidence of effectiveness. Excluding such a study may be to "waste information," but none that has any evidential bearing on the issue of therapeutic effectiveness. Some proponents of meta-analysis are likely to respond that the rules for determining which information is evidentially relevant and which is not are subjective and arbitrary. I take up this issue next, but so far, on the assumption that studies can be impeached on objective and nonarbitrary grounds, I see no inherent advantage for meta-analysis on either of the two issues of comprehensiveness:

the simple failure to even consider some studies and the considered judgment that some ought to be excluded.

A third alleged advantage of meta-analysis is that it solves the problem of how to treat studies that differ considerably in quality and avoid the subjectivity of narrative reviews. In traditional, non-quantitative reviews, reviewers often disqualify studies that fall below a certain epistemological standard, but some proponents of meta-analysis, including Smith, Glass, and Miller (1980, 48), complain that such standards are often subjective and arbitrary. Thus Schmidt (1992, 1179) refers to traditional reviews as being based on "the narrative-subjective method," and Hunter and Schmidt write, "Glass's position—one that we agree with—is that judgments of overall methodological quality are often very subjective, and inter-evaluator agreement is often low. Therefore, the question should be decided empirically by meta-analyzing separately the studies judged methodologically strong and weak and comparing the results. If they differ, one should rely on the 'strong' studies; if they do not, then all studies should be used" (1990, 480–481).

In assessing Hunter and Schmidt's position, it is important to distinguish between an empirical claim about the behavior of reviewers of the empirical literature and a philosophical claim about epistemological standards. If their claim is an empirical one, namely that reviewers often use subjective standards in rejecting certain studies, nothing follows without additional premises about the proper treatment of allegedly weak research studies. If reviewers typically use the wrong standards, the proper remedy is to employ the correct ones. However, if Hunter and Schmidt are making a philosophical claim—that there are no right, objective standards or, more weakly, none that are warranted—this too is not a reason to accept their solution. If the standards for judging psychotherapy outcomes are inevitably subjective and arbitrary, there is no way of knowing whether any type of psychotherapy is effective. Switching to meta-analysis will do nothing to avoid this skeptical result. Indeed, the solution suggested by Smith, Glass, and Miller (1980) and by Hunter and Schmidt (1990) presupposes that we *can* objectively distinguish between good and bad studies; if that were impossible, we could not empirically determine if the trends of the good and bad studies differ.

Fortunately, there are at least some objective, defensible rules for impeaching poor studies of outcomes (for a brief discussion of some obvious ones, see Erwin 1984, 434–435). So traditional narrative reviews need not employ methods that are subjective or arbitrary. Furthermore, the solution recommended by Smith, Glass, and Miller (1980) and Hunter and Schmidt (1990) to the problem of integrating data from good and bad studies encounters its own problems. Assume that a meta-analyst correctly divides psychotherapy studies into "good" and "bad" categories, finds that their trends are the same, and consequently weights them equally. Suppose, however, that therapies of types t_1 and t_2 are examined only in studies lacking placebo controls, or in those having some other serious defect that prohibits a causal inference, and that the average effect sizes are comparable to those of good studies. In this case we are not entitled to infer from a conclusion about the overall average effect size that either t_1 or t_2 is effective *at all*, let alone that either therapy is as effective as the treatments examined in the superior studies.

Even if there are some objective, defensible rules for disqualifying certain studies, something that the meta-analyst must presuppose, they may nevertheless yield no decision in certain cases of data integration. Suppose, for example, that there is *some* evidence that the "therapy integrity" problem was resolved in a study (i.e., the therapy described in the study was actually employed) and that the outcome measures were adequate and that the placebo treatment was credible to the clients but *also* that there is some reason to doubt one or more of these things. To use Rosenthal's (1990, 126) terminology, we do not give the study a zero, but rather a three or four (out of ten). Exactly how do we weight the evidence from these studies in comparison with evidence from better studies? This raises complex epistemological issues for the traditional narrative reviewers, but they arise equally for the meta-analyst. There are various proposals for handling this problem, but none has won general assent. It may even be that the search for a general solution will prove futile; different rules may have to be devised for different areas of research and even different subareas.

This third putative advantage for meta-analysis, then, looks dubious. In cases where certain studies clearly provide no evidence to support a causal inference, a narrative reviewer can disqualify the studies on objective, defensible grounds. Where the evidence from some studies is weak but not entirely absent, the narrative reviewer may have no general solution to the problem of how to weight the evidence, but using meta-analysis does not by itself solve the problem.

Another important argument for using meta-analysis concerns statistical power. In some research areas, the available studies have low statistical power either because the effects of a treatment are small (but still possibly important) or the number of subjects is small. If general problems with meta-analysis (such as those raised by Searles [1985] and Bruno and Ellett [1988]) are resolved and certain favorable conditions are met (for example, the treatments are of the same type, and the outcomes are homogenous), then a meta-analytic treatment may be warranted. (I am not suggesting that it would be warranted *only* under these conditions.) If certain studies individually fail to reach statistical significance because in each one the number of subjects is small, then we may be justified in grouping them together and, in effect, treating them as a single large study.

In a review of studies of low statistical power, then, meta-analysis may have an advantage over traditional methods of research integration. I want to conclude, however, by noting a few reservations about this issue.

Schmidt (1992, 1173) defends the thesis that traditional data analysis and interpretation based on tests of statistical significance militate against the discovery of the underlying regularities and relationships that are the foundations for scientific progress, and that meta-analysis methods can solve these problems.

To support his claim, Schmidt constructs a hypothetical case where the effect of a drug on learning is a .50 standard deviation increase in the amount learned. Suppose that the drug has exactly this effect in a large number of studies each having 15 rats in the experimental group and 15 in the control group. To be significant at the .05 level (with a one-tailed test), the effect size must be at least .62. Consequently, Schmidt argues (1992, 1174), only 37 percent of the studies will obtain a significant effect size. Because the majority of the studies will show no causal relation between drug dosage and learning, many reviewers, Schmidt notes, would conclude that the drug had no effect (on learning). A second interpretation would be that it had no effect in 67 percent of the cases, but in 37 percent of the cases, it had an effect. Both interpretations, Schmidt notes (1992, 1175), are erroneous, but a meta-analytic treatment of the data, he argues, would reach the correct conclusion: that the effect of the drug is .50.

Schmidt's purpose, he claims (1992, 1176), is "to demonstrate that traditional data analysis and interpretation methods logically lead to erroneous conclusions and to demonstrate that meta-analysis can solve these problems." Here we need to distinguish between two different problems: one about reliability and one about justification. Schmidt, I believe, is talking only about the first problem.

In his hypothetical example, meta-analysis was more reliable than interpretations based on the lack of statistical significance. It was more reliable in the sense that only it yielded the correct conclusion, namely that the drug generally had an effect on learning. How do we know that this conclusion is correct? The answer is, Because Schmidt stipulated that in this made-up case the drug had precisely this effect. However, we can just as easily stipulate a case exactly the same except that the drug has no effect. In this event, meta-analysis gives the wrong conclusion and the traditional methods the right one. So far there is no advantage in reliability for either method. What about actual cases? Is meta-analysis *generally* more reliable, at least in dealing with studies of low statistical power? If in most such cases the postulated causal relationship exists but reviewers using traditional methods infer that it does not and meta-analytic methods would yield the opposite conclusion, then the latter methods are more reliable, but if in most such cases the alleged causal relationship does *not* exist, then, given the just mentioned conclusions for each method, meta-analysis is *less* reliable. So, to determine whether meta-analysis is generally more reliable in the sort of cases being discussed, we would need to know not only how each method would vote but also whether the postulated causal relationship exists. In the absence of evidence about such putative causal relationships, a conclusion that meta-analysis is generally more reliable in such cases is unwarranted.

In his defense, Schmidt does say that for most areas of research, as time goes by and researchers gain a better understanding of the processes they are studying, type 1 errors decrease in importance and type 2 errors become more important (1992, 1176). (A type 1 error consists of concluding that there is a causal relation, or some other type of relation, when there is none; a type 2 error is the opposite: concluding that there is no causal relation when there is one.) I doubt that anyone knows whether or not we *now* have reached this happy time when type 1 errors are less frequent than type 2 errors in most areas of psychological research. Even if it were true, it is questionable that this has happened in the area of psychotherapy research in particular. To demonstrate that it has, we would have to resolve the very epistemological problems that have generated so much controversy about the actual effects of psychotherapy.

A different claim that might be made about meta-analysis is that it solves a justification problem rather than one about reliability. That is, if a statistic in a given study fails to reach significance because of low statistical power, a reviewer may be unjustified in inferring the lack of a causal relationship. The proper inference is that the data from this particular study fail to support such a relationship, not that it does not exist. It would be misleading, however, to say that meta-analytic methods solve the justification problem. Even in the hypothetical case that Schmidt constructs, where the drug does affect learning, meta-analysis may yield the correct conclusion but utterly fail to warrant it. If each study of the rats is badly controlled, averaging the effects of each study may provide *no* good evidence of the hypothesized causal connection. To be justified in inferring a causal connection, we clearly need not merely to get the right answer but to develop a credible argument. This requires the resolution of certain epistemological problems, some of which are particularly difficult in the field of psychotherapy research. Meta-analysis does not resolve these problems, although it might aid in the resolution of some of them.

References

Bachrach, H., A. Galatzer-Levy, A. Skolnikoff, and S. Waldron. 1991. "On the Efficacy of Psychoanalysis." *Journal of the American Psychoanalytic Association* 39:871–916.

Binns, P. 1990. "Experimental Evidence and Psychotherapy." *British Journal for the Philosophy of Science* 41:531–551.

Brill, N., R. Koegler, L. Epstein, and E. Forgy. 1964. "Controlled Study of Psychiatric Outpatient Treatment." *Archives of General Psychiatry* 10:581–595.

Bruno, J., and F. Ellett. 1988. "A Core-Analysis of Meta-analysis." *Quality and Quantity* 22:111–126.

Campbell, D., and J. Stanley. 1963. *Experimental and Quasi-experimental Designs for Research.* Chicago: Chicago University Press.

Cordray, D., and R. Bootzin. 1983. "Placebo Control Conditions: Tests of Theory or Effectiveness?" *Behavioral and Brain Science* 6:286–287.

Critelli, J., and K. Neumann. 1984. "The Placebo." *American Psychologist* 39:32–39.

Erwin, E. 1978. *Behavior Therapy: Scientific, Philosophical, and Moral Foundations.* New York: Cambridge University Press.

Erwin, E. 1984. "Establishing Causal Connections: Meta-analysis and Psychotherapy." In *Causation and Causal Theories,* ed. P. French, T. Uehling, and H. Wetlstein, Midwest Studies in Philosophy, no. 9, 421–436.

Erwin, E. 1988. "Psychoanalysis: Clinical versus Experimental Evidence." In *Mind, Psychoanalysis, and Science,* ed. P. Clark and C. Wright. New York: Basil Blackwell.

Erwin, E., and H. Siegel. 1989. "Is Confirmation Differential?" *British Journal for the Philosophy of Science* 40:105–119.

Eysenck, H. J. 1952. "The Effects of Psychotherapy: An Evaluation." *Journal of Consulting Psychology* 16:319–324.

Eysenck, H. J. 1983. "The Effectiveness of Psychotherapy: The Specter at the Feast." *Behavioral and Brain Sciences* 6:290.

Fine, A., and M. Forbes. 1986. "Grünbaum on Freud: Three Grounds for Dissent." *Behavioral and Brain Sciences* 9:237–238.

Glass, G., and R. Kliegel. 1983. "An Apology for Research Integration in the Study of Psychotherapy." *Journal of Consulting and Clinical Psychology* 51:28–41.

Grünbaum, A. 1984. *The Foundations of Psychoanalysis: A Philosophical Critique.* Berkeley: University of California Press.

Hunter, J., and F. Schmidt. 1990. *Methods of Meta-analysis: Correcting Bias in Research Findings.* London: Sage Publications.

Kazdin, A. 1981. "Drawing Valid Inferences from Case Studies." *Journal of Consulting and Clinical Psychology* 49:183–192.

Kazdin, A. 1986. "Research Designs and Methodology." In *Handbook of Psychotherapy and Behavior Change*, ed. S. Garfield and A. Bergin. New York: John Wiley.

Landman, J., and R. Dawes. 1982. "Psychotherapy Outcome: Smith and Glass Conclusions Stand Up under Scrutiny." *American Psychologist* 37:504–516.

Mann, C. 1986. "Meta-analysis in the Breech." *Science* 249:476–480.

Meehl, P. 1955. "Psychotherapy." *Annual Review of Psychology* 6:357–379.

Michaels, R. 1986. "Freud." British Broadcasting Corporation Program.

O'Leary, K., and T. Borkovec. 1978. "Conceptual, Methodological, and Ethical Problems of Placebo Groups in Psychotherapy Research." *American Psychologist* 33:821–830.

Paul, G. 1966. *Insight vs. Desensitization in Psychotherapy*. Stanford: Stanford University Press.

Paul, G. 1985. "Can Pregnancy Be a Placebo Effect? Terminology, Designs, and Conclusions in the Study of Psychosocial and Pharmacological Treatments of Behavioral Disorders." In *Placebo: Theory, Research, and Mechanisms*, ed. L. White, B. Tursky, and G. Schwartz. New York: Guilford Press.

Prioleau, L., M. Murdock, and N. Brody. 1983. "An Analysis of Psychotherapy versus Placebo Studies." *Behavioral and Brain Sciences* 6:275–310.

Rachman, S., and G. T. Wilson. 1980. *The Effects of Psychological Therapy*. New York: Pergamon Press.

Rosenthal, R. 1984. *Meta-analysis Procedures for Social Research*. Beverly Hills, Calif.: Sage.

Rosenthal, R. 1990. "An Evaluation of Procedures and Results." In *The Future of Meta-analysis*, ed. K. Wachter and M. Straf. New York: Russell Sage Foundation.

Schmidt, F. 1992. "What Do Data Really Mean? Research Findings, Meta-analysis, and Cumulative Knowledge in Psychology." *American Psychologist* 47:1173–1181.

Searles, J. 1985. "A Methodological and Empirical Critique of Psychotherapy Outcome: Meta-analysis." *Behavioral Research and Therapy* 23:453–463.

Smith, M., and G. Glass. 1977. "Meta-analysis of Psychotherapy Outcome Studies." *American Psychologist* 32:752–760.

Smith, M., G. Glass, and T. Miller. 1980. *The Benefits of Psychotherapy*. Baltimore: Johns Hopkins University Press.

Taylor, C. 1985. "Peaceful Coexistence in Psychology." In his *Human Agency and Language*. New York: Cambridge University Press.

Wachter, K., and M. Straf. 1990. *The Future of Meta-analysis*. New York: Russell Sage Foundation.

Wilson, G. T. 1985. "Limitations of Meta-analysis in the Evaluation of the Effects of Psychological Therapy." *Clinical Psychology Review* 5:35–47.

The Placebo Concept in Medicine and Psychiatry

Adolf Grünbaum

The standard technical vocabulary used to define placebo therapies and experimental placebo controls in medicine and psychiatry is both confusing and obscure. To achieve conceptual clarity in the theory of placebogenic phenomena, this paper offers a rigorous articulation of the placebo notion, a lucid new terminology that obviates the defects intrinsic to the traditional locutions employed in the placebo literature, and a substantial revamping of A. K. Shapiro's influential prior definition of "placebo."

1 Introduction

Just what is the problem of identifying an intervention or treatment t of one sort or another as a placebo for a target disorder D? One set of circumstances, among others, in which the need for such an identification may arise is the following: After the administration of t to some victims of D, some of them recover from their affliction to a significant extent. Now suppose that there is cogent evidence that this improvement can indeed be causally attributed at all to some factors or other among the spectrum of constituents comprising the dispensation of t to a patient. Then it can become important to know whether the therapeutic gain that ensued from t in the alleviation of D was due to *those particular factors* in its dispensation that the advo-

This paper has been previously published in the same or similar form in *Non-specific Aspects of Treatment*, edited by Michael Shepherd and N. Sartorius (Toronto: published on behalf of the World Health Organization by H. Huber, 1989), in *Psychological Medicine 16* (1986): 19–38, and in *Placebo: Theory, Research, and Mechanisms*, edited by L. White, B. Tursky, and G. E. Schwartz (New York: Guilford Press, 1985), pp. 9–36. Copyright by Adolf Grünbaum.

cates of *t* have theoretically designated as deserving the credit for the positive treatment outcome. And one aim of this paper is to articulate in detail the bearing of the answer to this question on whether *t* qualifies generically as a placebo or not. For, as will emerge, the medical and psychiatric literature on placebos and their effects is conceptually bewildering, to the point of being a veritable Tower of Babel.

The proverbial sugar pill is hardly the sole placebo capable of producing therapeutic benefits for ailments other than hypoglycemia and other glucose deficits. Indeed, the long-term history of medical treatment has been characterized as largely the history of the placebo effect (A. K. Shapiro and Morris 1978). After all, it is not only the patients who can be unaware that the treatments they are receiving are just placebos for their disorders; the physicians as well may mistakenly believe that they are administering nonplacebos for their patients' ailments, when they are actually dispensing placebos, while further enhancing the patients' credulity by communicating their own therapeutic faith. For example, as we shall see, surgery for angina pectoris performed in the United States during the 1950s turned out to be a mere placebo. Unbeknown to the physicians who practiced before the present century, most of the medications they dispensed were at best pharmacologically ineffective, if not outright physiologically harmful or even dangerous. Thus, during all that time, doctors were largely engaged in the unwitting dispensation of placebos on a massive scale. Even after the development of contemporary scientific medicine some 80 years ago, "the placebo effect flourished as the norm of medical treatment" (A. K. Shapiro and Morris 1978, 371).

The psychiatrist Jerome Frank (1973) has issued the sobering conjecture that those of the roughly 200 psychotherapies whose gains exceed those from spontaneous remission do *not* owe such remedial efficacy to the *distinctive* treatment factors credited by their respective therapeutic advocates, but succeed for other reasons. Nonetheless, Frank admonishes us not to disparage such placebogenic gains in therapy, at least as long as we have nothing more effective. And even in internal medicine and surgery, a spate of recent articles has inveighed against downgrading placebogenic benefits, the grounds being that we should be grateful even for small mercies. Yet the plea not to forsake the benefits wrought by placebos has been challenged on ethical grounds: the injunction to secure the patient's informed consent is a demand whose fulfilment may well render the placebo ineffective, though perhaps not always (Park and Covi 1965).

The physician Arthur K. Shapiro is deservedly one of the most influential writers in this field of inquiry. He has been concerned with the history of the placebo effect (1960) and with the semantics of the word "placebo" (1968), no less than with current empirical research on placebogenic phenomena in medical and psychological treatments (A. K. Shapiro and Morris 1978). Thus, in his portion of the last-cited paper, he refined (1978, 371) his earlier 1971 definition of "placebo" in an endeavor to codify the current uses of the term throughout medicine and psychiatry. The technical vocabulary employed in A. K. Shapiro's earlier and most recent definitions is standard terminology in the discussion of placebo therapies and of experimental placebo controls, be it in pharmacology, surgery, or psychiatry. Yet just this standard technical vocabulary, I submit, generates confusion by being misleading or obfuscating, and indeed cries out for conceptual clarification. Thus, it is my overall objective to revamp Shapiro's definitions substantially so as to provide a clear and rigorous account of the placebo notion appropriate to current medicine and psychiatry.

2   Critique, Explication, and Reformulation of A. K. Shapiro's Definition

Critique

While some placebos are known to be such by the dispensing physician—though presumably not by the patient—other placebo therapies are mistakenly believed to be nonplacebos by the physician as well. Mindful of this dual state of affairs, A. K. Shapiro's definition of a placebo therapy makes it clear that, at any given stage of scientific knowledge, a treatment modality actually belonging to the genus placebo can be of the latter kind rather than of the traditionally recognized first sort. To capture both of these two species of placebo therapy, he casts his definition into the following general form, in which the expression "$=_{\text{def.}}$" stands for the phrase "is definitionally equivalent to":

Therapy *t* is a placebo therapy
= $_{def.}$ *t* is of a kind *A* OR *t* is of kind *B*.

Any definition of this "either-or" form is called a "disjunctive" definition, and *each* of the two independent clauses connected by the word
"or" is called a "disjunct." For example, suppose we define a "parent"
by saying:

Person *X* is a parent
= $_{def.}$ *X* is a father OR *X* is a mother.

This is clearly a *disjunctive* definition. And it is convenient to refer to
each of the separate clauses "*X* is a father" and "*X* is a mother" as a
"disjunct." Thus, the sentence "*X* is a father" can obviously be regarded as the first of the two disjuncts, while the sentence "*X* is a
mother" is the second disjunct. Hence, for brevity, I thus refer respectively to the corresponding two parts of Shapiro's actual disjunctive definition (A. K. Shapiro and Morris, 1978):

A *placebo* is defined as any therapy or component of therapy that is deliberately used for its nonspecific, psychological, or psychophysiological effect,
or that is used for its presumed specific effect, but is without specific activity
for the condition being treated. (P. 371)

Shapiro goes on to point out at once that the term "placebo" is used
not only to characterize a treatment modality or therapy, but also a
certain kind of experimental control:

A *placebo,* when used as a control in experimental studies, is defined as a
substance or procedure that is without specific activity for the condition
being evaluated [*sic*]. (P. 371)

And then he tells us furthermore that

A *placebo effect* is defined as the psychological or psychophysiological effect
produced by placebos. (P. 371)

All of the conceptual puzzlement warranted by these three statements arises in the initial disjunctive definition of a "placebo therapy." For it should be noted that this definition employs the
tantalizing words "non-specific effect," "specific effect," and "specific
activity" in unstated *technical* senses. Once these terms are elucidated,
the further definitions of a "placebo control" and of a "placebo ef-

fect" become conceptually unproblematic. Hence let us now concentrate on the disjunctive definition of a "placebo therapy," and see what help, if any, Shapiro gives us with the technical terms in which he has expressed it. Contrary to the belief of some others, I make bold to contend that his explicit comments on their intended construal still leaves them in an unsatisfactory logical state for the purposes at hand.

In their joint 1978 paper, A. K. Shapiro and Morris elaborate quite vaguely on the key concept of "specific activity" as follows:

Specific activity is the therapeutic influence attributable solely to the contents or processes of the therapies rendered. The criterion for specific activity (and therefore the placebo effect) should be based on scientifically controlled studies. (P. 372)

They provide this characterization as part of a longer but very rough delineation of the complementary notions denoted by the terms "specific" and "nonspecific," locutions that are as pervasive as they are misleading or confusing in the literature on placebos. Thus, they make the following comment on the definition of "placebo" given above, which I amplify within brackets:

Implicit in this definition is the assumption that active treatments [i.e., non-placebos] may contain placebo components. Even with specific therapies [i.e., nonplacebos] results are apt to be due to the combination of both placebo and nonplacebo effects. Treatments that are devoid of active, specific components are known as pure placebos, whereas therapies that contain nonplacebo components are called impure placebos. . . . Treatments that have specific components but exert their effects primarily through non-specific mechanisms are considered placebo therapies. . . .

The key concept in defining placebo is that of "specific activity." In non-psychological therapies, specific activity is often equated with nonpsychological mechanisms of action. When the specific activity of a treatment is psychological [i.e., in psychotherapies that derive therapeutic efficacy from those particular factors in the treatment that the pertinent theory singles out specifically as being remedial] this method of separating specific from nonspecific activity is no longer applicable. Therefore, a more general definition of specific activity is necessary. Specific activity is the therapeutic influence attributable solely to the contents or processes of the therapies rendered [i.e., the therapeutic influence, if any, that derives solely from those component factors of the therapy that are specifically singled out by its advocates as deserving credit for its presumed efficacy]. The criterion for specific activity (and therefore the placebo effect) should be based on scientifically controlled studies. . . . In behavior therapy, some investigators have utilized "active placebo" control groups whereby some aspects of the therapy affect behavior but those aspects differ from the theoretically relevant ingredients of concern to the investigator. (Pp. 371–372)

This passage urgently calls for clarification beyond what I have supplied within brackets. In particular, the terms "specific activity" and "nonspecific effect," though standard, are anything but clear. Yet, as the authors emphasize further on, it is by virtue of a treatment's *lack* of so called "specific activity" for a given target disorder that this treatment *objectively* qualifies as a placebo, regardless of whether the dispensing physician believes the treatment to have actual placebo status or not. They import this emphasis on the irrelevance of belief to generic placebo *status* into their definition. There, in its first paragraph, a disjunction makes explicit provision for the presence of such belief on the part of the dispenser, as well as for its absence. In the first disjunct, it is a placebo that the physician *believes* himself or herself to be giving the patient, and the doctor is right in so believing. In the second disjunct, the physician believes himself or herself to be administering a *non*placebo, but he or she is definitely mistaken in so believing.

In either case, a placebo is actually being dispensed, be it wittingly or unwittingly. For brevity, I distinguish between the two situations to which these disjuncts pertain by saying that the treatment is an "intentional placebo" in the former case, while being an "inadvertent placebo" in the latter. Note that if a treatment *t* is actually not a placebo generically while its dispenser or even the whole professional community of practitioners believes *t* to be one, then *t* is precluded from qualifying as a "placebo" by the definition. To earn the label "intentional placebo," a treatment not only must be *believed* to be a placebo by its dispenser, but must also actually *be* one generically. Thus, therapists have administered a nonplacebo in the erroneous belief that it is a placebo. For example, at one time, some psychoanalysts used phenothiazines to treat schizophrenics in the belief that these drugs were mere (anger-reducing, tranquilizing) placebos; they presumed them to be ineffective for the psychic dissociation and the pathognomonic symptoms of schizophrenia. But controlled studies showed that these medications possessed a kind of

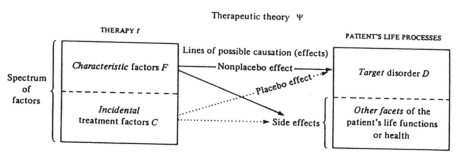

Figure 1

Illustration of therapeutic theory, Ψ, used in clarifying the definition of "placebo."

therapeutic efficacy for the disorder that was not placebogenic (Davis and Cole 1975a, 1975b).

Incidentally, besides not being placebos for schizophrenia, the phenothiazines turned out to be capable of inducing the negative side effects of parkinsonism, at least transiently (Blakiston's *Gould Medical Dictionary*, 1972, 1130). But the motor impairment manifested in parkinsonism is attributed to a deficiency of brain dopamine. Thus the unfavorable parkinsonian side effect of the phenothiazine drugs turned out to have *heuristic* value because it suggested that these drugs block the dopamine receptors in the brain. And since the drugs were also effective nonplacebos for schizophrenia, the parkinsonian side effect raised the possibility that an excess of dopamine might be implicated in the aetiology of schizophrenia. In this way, a *biochemical* malfunction of the brain was envisioned quite specifically as causally relevant to this psychosis (Kolata 1979).

Let me now specify the terminology and notation that I employ in my rectifying explication of "placebo," using the diagram shown in figure 1. Overall, there is some stated or tacit therapeutic theory, which I call "Ψ". Now Ψ designs or recommends a particular treatment or therapy *t* for a particular illness or target disorder *D*. In the left-hand box of figure 1, I generically depict a treatment modality or therapy *t*. Note that it contains a spectrum of ingredients or treatment factors. For example, the theory Ψ may insist that if it is to recommend surgery for the treatment of gallstones, then the surgical process must obviously include the removal of the gallstones, rather than a mere sham abdominal incision. I want a name for those treatment factors that a given theory Ψ thus *picks out* as the defining characteristics of a given type of therapy t. And I call these factors the "characteristic factors F" of t. But Ψ recognizes that besides the characteristic factors F, the given therapy normally also contains other factors which it regards as just incidental. For example, a theory that deems the removal of gallstones to be therapeutic for certain kinds of pains and indigestion will assume that this abdominal surgery includes the administration of anesthesia to the patient. To take a quite different example, when Freud recommended psychoanalytical treatment, he insisted on the payment of a hefty fee, believing it to be perhaps a catalyst for the patient's receptivity to the therapeutic task. Furthermore, a therapeutic theory may well allow that a given therapy includes not only known incidental factors, but also others that it has failed to recognize. And the letter C in the diagram, which labels "incidental treatment factors," is intended to apply to both known and unknown factors of this type.

Turning to the right-hand box in figure 1, we note that the patient's life functions and activities are generically subdivided into two parts: the target disorder D at which the therapy t is aimed, and then the rest of his or her functions. But there may well be some vagueness in the circumscription of D. Both its pathognomonic symptoms and the presumed aetiological process responsible for them will surely be included in the syndrome D. Yet some nosologists might include, while others exclude, certain accessory manifestations of D that are quite secondary, because they are also present in a number of other, nosologically distinct syndromes. Somewhat cognate conceptual problems of taxonomic circumscription arose in chemistry upon the discovery of isomerism, and even in the case of chemical isotopy.

Finally, in the middle of figure 1, arrows represent some of the interesting possible causal influences or effects that may result from each of the two sets of treatment factors. Thus, one or more of the characteristic factors F may be remedial for the target disorder D, or the F factors may have no effect on D, or the F factors conceivably could make D even worse. By the same token, these factors F may have these three kinds of influence on other facets of the patient's health. And any of these latter effects—whether good or bad—will be called "side effects." Now *if (and only if) one or more of the characteristic factors do have a positive therapeutic effect on the target disease D, then the therapy as a whole qualifies generically as a nonplacebo for D.* This is the situation that is depicted in the diagram by the words "nonplacebo effect" in the horizontal solid arrow from *F* to *D*.

It is vital to realize that, in figure 1, the causal arrows are intended to depict *possible* (imaginable) effects, such that the given treatment factors may have various sorts of positive *or* adverse effects on the target disorder, or on other facets of the patient's health. Thus, the diagram can be used to depict a nonplacebo therapy as well as a placebo therapy. In the former case, there is an actual beneficial causal influence by the characteristic factors on *D*, whereas in the latter case such an influence does not—as a matter of actual fact—exist, though it is imaginable (logically possible).

Similarly, the incidental treatment factors *C* may or may not have positive or negative effects on *D*. Furthermore, these factors *C* may have desirable or undesirable effects *outside* of *D*, which we again call side effects. If the incidental factors do have an effect on *D*, we can refer to that effect as a "placebo effect," even if the therapy qualifies overall as a generic nonplacebo by containing therapeutically effective characteristic factors. For example, suppose that the characteristic factors in a certain chemotherapy are effective against a given kind of cancer, at least for a while, so that this chemotherapy is a nonplacebo for this affliction. Then this therapeutic effectiveness may well be *enhanced*, if the dispensing physician communicates his or her confidence in this therapy to the patient. And if there is such enhancement, the treatment factors *C* do indeed produce a positive placebo effect on *D*, a situation depicted in the diagram by the broken diagonal arrow. Thus we can say that *whether a given positive effect on D is or is not a placebo effect depends on whether it is produced by the incidental treatment factors or the characteristic ones.* (For *other* placebo effects, see p. 310.)

Let me now use the preceding informal preliminary account to give a more systematic and precise characterization of the genus placebo as well as of two of its species, thereby also revamping A. K. Shapiro's definitions.

A treatment process normally has a spectrum of constituent factors as well as a spectrum of effects when administered for the alleviation of a given target disorder D. Effects on the patient's health not pertaining to D are denominated "side effects." Though the term "side effects" often refers to *undesirable* effects outside D, there is neither good reason nor general agreement to restrict it in this way. As I soon illustrate, the therapeutic theory Ψ that advocates the use of a particular treatment modality t to remedy D demands the inclusion of certain characteristic constituents F in any treatment process that Ψ authenticates as an application of t. Any such process, besides qualifying as an instance of t according to Ψ, will typically have constituents C other than the characteristic ones F singled out by Ψ. And when asserting that the factors F are remedial for D, Ψ *may* also take cognizance of one or more of the noncharacteristic constituents C, which I denominate as "incidental." Thus, Ψ may perhaps attribute certain side effects to either F or C. Indeed, it may even maintain that one or another of the incidental factors affects D—say, by enhancing the remedial effects that it claims for F. In short, if a doctor is an adherent of Ψ, it may well furnish him or her with a therapeutic rationale for administering t to a patient afflicted by D, *or* for refraining from doing so.

For instance, consider pharmacological treatment, such as the dispensation of digitoxin for congestive heart dysfunction or of nitroglycerin for angina pectoris. Then it is perfectly clear that the water with which such tablets are swallowed, and the patient's awareness of the reputation of the prescribing cardiologist, for example, are incidental treatment factors, while the designated chemical ingredients are characteristic ones. But Freud also specified these two different sorts of treatment factors in the nonpharmacological case of psychoanalytical treatment, while recognizing that some of the incidental factors may serve initially as catalysts or icebreakers for the operation of the characteristic ones. Thus, he identified the characteristic constituents as the educative and affect-discharging lifting of the patient's presumed repressions, effected by means of overcoming ("working through") the analysand's resistance to their conscious recognition in the context of "resolving" his or her "transference" behavior towards the doctor. And Freud depicted the patient's faith in the analyst, and the derivation of emotional support from that authority figure, as mere catalysts or icebreakers in the initial stage of treatment—factors that are incidental, because they are avowedly quite incapable of extirpating the pathogenic causes, as distinct from producing merely cosmetic and temporary relief.

Hence Freud stressed tirelessly that the patient's correct, affect-discharging insight into the aetiology of his or her affliction is the one quintessential ingredient that distinguishes the remedial dynamics of his treatment modality from any kind of treatment by suggestion. Treatments by suggestion, he charged, leave the pathogenic repressions intact, and yield only an ephemeral cosmetic prohibition of the symptoms (see Grünbaum 1984). In the same vein, Freud came to maintain early in his career that the characteristic factors of Erb's electrotherapy for nervous disorders were therapeutically unavailing, and that any gains from treatment with that electric apparatus were achieved by its incidental factors.

Explications and Reformulations

The schematic diagram in figure 1 can serve as a kind of glossary for the notations Ψ, t, F, and C that I have introduced. Using this notation, I shall offer several explications, which supersede those I have offered earlier (Grünbaum 1981). In the first of these explications, which pertains to the "intentional" species of placebo, the fourth condition (d) is somewhat tentative:

1

A treatment process t characterized by a given therapeutic theory Ψ as having constituents F, but also possessing other, perhaps unspecified incidental constituents C, will be said to be an "intentional placebo" with respect to a target disorder D, suffered by a victim V and treated by a dispensing practitioner P, just when the following conditions are jointly satisfied: (a) none of the characteristic treatment factors F are remedial for D; (b) P believes that the factors F indeed all *fail* to be remedial for D; (c) but P also believes that—at least for a certain type of victim V of D—t is nonetheless therapeutic for D by virtue of containing some perhaps even unknown incidental factors C different from F; and (d) yet—more often than not—P abets or at least acquiesces in V's belief that t has remedial efficacy for D by virtue of some constituents that belong to the set of characteristic factors F in t, provided that V is aware of these factors.

Note that the first of these four conditions explicates what it is for a treatment type t to have the objective generic property of being a placebo with respect to a given target disorder D. The objective property in question is just that the characteristic constituents F of t are actually not remedial for D. On the other hand, the remaining three of the four conditions describe the property of belonging to the species of intentional placebo, over and above being a placebo generically. And, clearly, these three further conditions pertain to the beliefs and intentions of the practitioners who dispense t and of the patients who receive it. In particular, they render whether the therapist is *intentionally* administering a generic placebo to the patient, rather than unaware of the placebo status of the treatment. But notice that the fourth condition would require modification, if there were enough cases, as has been suggested, in which a patient may benefit therapeutically even after being *told* that he or she is receiving a generic placebo. On the other hand, the fourth condition apparently still suffices to cover those cases in which surgeons perform appendectomies or tonsillectomies solely at the behest of their patients, who, in turn, may be encouraged by their families. The need to accommodate such interventions has been stressed by Piechowiak (1982, 1983).

The caveat regarding the fourth condition (d) is occasioned by a report (Park and Covi, 1965) on an exploratory and "paradoxical" study of 15 adult neurotic out-patients, who presented with anxiety symptoms. The treating therapists did provide support and reassurance, yet "the responsibility for improvement was thrown back to the patient by means of the paradoxical statement that he needed treatment but that he could improve with a [placebo] capsule containing no drug" (p. 344). Of the 14 patients who remained willing to receive the capsules for a week, six *disbelieved* the purported pharmacological inertness of the capsules, and three of them even experienced "side-reactions," which they attributed to the pills (p. 342). But the three patients who did firmly believe in the doctor's candid disclosure of inertness improved after 1 week, no less than the "sceptics," who thought they were receiving an effective nonplacebo after all. Hence Park and Covi concluded that "unawareness of the inert nature of the placebo is not an indispensable condition for improvement on placebo" (p. 342). Yet, as these authors acknowledged at once, in so small a sample of patients, improvement may have occurred "in spite of" the disclosure as a matter of course, under *any* sort of treatment or even as a matter of spontaneous remission. And since it is quite unclear whether the moral drawn by Park and Covi is at all generalizable beyond their sample, I have let the fourth condition stand.

Piechowiak (1983) also calls attention to uses of diagnostic procedures (e.g., endoscopy, stomach X rays) when deemed unnecessary by the physician, but demanded by the anxious patient suffering from, say, cancerphobia, who may even believe them to be therapeutic. In the latter sort of instance, the gastroenterologist may justify an invasive procedure to himself or herself and the patient, because when the expected negative finding materializes, it may alleviate the patient's anxiety as well as the vexatious somatic effects of that anxiety. In some cases (e.g., Wassermann test for syphilis), the patient may be under no illusions as to the dynamics by which this relief was wrought, any more than the doctor. But Piechowiak is concerned to point out that in other cases (e.g., angiography), the patient may well conceptualize the diagnostic intervention as *itself* therapeutic. And hence this author suggests the assimilation of these latter cases to intentional placebos. In this way, he suggests, account can be taken of the cognizance taken by doctors of the therapeutic beliefs of their patients—beliefs that are psychological realities, even if they are scientifically untutored.

As we have seen, a particular treatment modality *t* derives its identity from the full set of its characteristic treatment factors, as singled out by the therapeutic theory that advocates the use of *t* in stated circumstances. Hence therapies will be distinct, provided that they differ in at least one characteristic factor. By the same token, therapies whose distinct identities are specified in each case by two or more characteristic factors can have at least one such factor in common without detriment to their distinctness, just as they can thus share one or more incidental factors. Indeed, as I illustrate later, a shared factor that counts as characteristic of one therapy may qualify as merely incidental to another. And clearly these statements concerning factors common to distinct therapies hold for somatic medicine and psychotherapy alike.

Thus, in *either* of these two classes of healing interventions, a therapy that qualifies as a nonplacebo for a certain target D derives precisely this therapeutic status from the remedial efficacy of some or all of its characteristic factors. Yet it may share these efficacious ingredients with other, distinct therapies that differ from it in at least one characteristic factor. In fact, one or all of the common factors may count as only incidental to some of the other therapies. And it is to be borne in mind that a therapy having at least one remedial characteristic ingredient is generically a nonplacebo, even if the remaining characteristic factors are otiose. Hence a therapy t can be a nonplacebo with respect to a particular D, even if all of its efficacious characteristic treatment ingredients are common to both t and distinct other therapies!

Unfortunately, Critelli and Neumann (1984) run foul of this important state of affairs by concluding incorrectly that "the common-factors criterion . . . appears to be the most viable current definition of the placebo for the study of psychotherapy" (p. 35). They see themselves as improving on A. K. Shapiro's explication of the placebo concept, at least for psychotherapy. Yet they actually impoverish it by advocating the so-called "common-factors definition" (for psychotherapy), which they do not even *state*, and by altogether failing to render the two species of placebo adumbrated in the 1978 definition given by Shapiro and Morris. Besides, Critelli and Neumann contend that Shapiro's explication of the notion of a generic placebo suffers from his abortive attempt to encompass somatic medicine and psychotherapy simultaneously. But once I have completed my thorough recasting of Shapiro's pioneering definition below, it will be clear that—contrary to Critelli and Neumann—his endeavor to cover medicine and psychotherapy with one definitional stroke is *not* one of the defects of his explication.

Turning now to placebo *controls*, we must bear in mind that to assess the remedial merits of a given therapy t^* for some D, it is imperative to disentangle from each other two sorts of possible positive effects as follows: (1) those desired effects on D, if any, actually wrought by the characteristic factors of t^*; and (2) improvements

produced by the expectations aroused in both the doctor and the patient by their belief in the therapeutic efficacy of t^*. To achieve just such a disentanglement, the baseline measure (2) of expectancy effect can be furnished by using a generic placebo t in a control group of persons suffering from D. For ethical reasons, informed consent has presumably been secured from a group of such patients to be "blindly" allocated to either the control group or the experimental group.

Ideally, this investigation should be a triply blind one. To say that the study is triply blind is to say the following: (a) the patients do not know to which group they have been assigned; (b) the dispensers do not know whether they are administering t^* or t; and (c) the outcome assessors do not know which patients were the controls. But there are treatment modalities—such as surgery and psychotherapy—in which the *second* of these three sorts of blindness obviously cannot be achieved.

By subtracting the therapeutic gains with respect to D in the control group from those in the experimental group, investigators can obtain the sought-after measure (1) of the incremental remedial potency of the characteristic factors in t^*. And, for brevity, one can then say that with respect to D the generic placebo t functions as a "placebo control" in the experimental evaluation of the therapeutic value of t^* as such. More briefly, the placebo served in a controlled clinical trial of t^*.

As will be recalled, the relevant definition of that term given by A. K. Shapiro and Morris (1978, 371) reads as follows: "A placebo, when used as a control in experimental studies, is defined as a substance or procedure that is without specific activity for the condition being evaluated." But just this characterization of a "placebo control," as used in experimental studies in medicine or psychotherapy, is in dire need of emendation. As they would have it, "the condition" D is "being evaluated" in an experimental study employing a placebo control. But surely what is being evaluated instead is the conjectured therapeuticity of a designated treatment t^* (substance, procedure) for D. And I suggest that their definition of a placebo control be recast as follows. A treatment type t functions as a "placebo control" in a given context of experimental inquiry, which is designed to evaluate the characteristic therapeutic efficacy of another modality t^* for a target disorder D, just when the following requirements are jointly satisfied: (1) t is a *generic placebo* for D, as defined under the first condition (a) in the definition above of "intentional placebo"; (2) the experimental investigator conducting the stated controlled trial of t^* believes that t is not only a generic placebo for D, but also is generally quite harmless to those victims of D who have been chosen for the control group. And, as I have noted, the investigator's reason for using t as a placebo control when evaluating the characteristic therapeutic value of t^* for D is as follows: especially if t^* is expensive or fraught with negative side effects, clinicians wish to know to what extent, if any, the beneficial effects on D due to its characteristic treatment factors *exceed* those produced by its incidental ones.

When schematized in this way, some of the complexities inherent in the notion of a placebo control are not apparent. To their credit, Critelli and Neumann (1984) have perceptively called attention to some of the essential refinements in psychotherapy research:

It is imperative that test procedures be compared to realistic placebo controls. Too often in the past, false claims of incremental effectiveness have resulted from the experimental use of placebos that even the most naive would not mistake for genuine therapy. There appears to be a tendency for experimental placebos to be in some sense weaker, less credible, or applied in a less enthusiastic manner than treatments that have been offered as actual therapies. At a minimum, placebo controls should be equivalent to test procedures on all major recognized common factors. These might include induced expectancy of improvement; credibility of rationale; credibility of procedures; demand for improvement; and therapist attention, enthusiasm, effort, perceived belief in treatment procedures, and commitment to client improvement. (P. 38)

Having issued this salutary caveat, these authors claim that "current [psycho]therapies have yet to meet the challenge of demonstrating incremental effects" (p. 38). Yet one of the reasons they go on to give for posing this challenge relies on their belief that treatment factors common to two or more therapies *must* be—in my parlance—incidental rather than characteristic ingredients. As I have pointed out, however, formulations invoking this belief tend to darken counsel. Here too, placebo controls cannot be *doubly* blind.

Suedfeld (1984) likewise addresses methodological (and also ethical) problems arising in the employment of placebo controls to evaluate psychotherapy. As he sees it, "the necessity for equating the expectancy of the active [nonplacebo] and placebo treatment groups implies the acceptance of the null hypothesis, a position that is better avoided" (p. 161). To implement this avoidance, he advocates the use of a "subtractive expectancy placebo," which he describes as follows:

It consists of administering an active, specific therapeutic procedure but introducing it with the orientation that it is inert with respect to the problem being treated. In other words, the client is led to expect less of an effect than the treatment is known to produce. The Subtractive Expectancy Procedure avoids the need to invent or find an inert technique, attempts to create initial differences in expectancy which can be substantiated by the rejection of the null hypothesis, and also makes it feasible to assess the specific effect of an active treatment in a design with one treated and one untreated (control) group. (P. 161)

Here I am not concerned with the pros and cons of the subtractive expectancy placebo procedure advocated by Suedfeld, qua alternative to the null hypothesis on which my definition above of a "placebo control" is implicitly predicated. Whatever that balance of investigative cogency, there can be little doubt that some of the ideas in Suedfeld's paper are illuminating or at least suggestive. Besides, I appreciate his several citations of my initial paper "The Placebo Concept" (Grünbaum 1981). There I made concrete proposals for the replacement of the standard technical vocabulary used in the placebo literature, precisely because of the Tower of Babel confusion that is engendered by it.

Alas, in criticism of Suedfeld, I must point out that his exposition is genuinely marred by just the penalties of ambiguity, obscurity, and confusion exacted by the received placebo vocabulary, because he unfortunately chooses to retain that infelicitous terminology for the formulation of his ideas. As we shall see in due course, the terms "active," "specific," and "nonspecific" are especially insidious locutions in this context. Yet these ill-fated terms, and their cognates or derivatives, abound in Suedfeld's presentation. In any case, so much for the notion of a placebo control.

Recently there have been interesting conjectures as to the identity of the incidental constituents C that confer somatic remedial potency on medications qualifying as intentional placebos for some Ds with respect to certain therapeutic theories. It has been postulated (J. Brody 1979) that, when present, such therapeutic efficacy derives from the placebo's psychogenic activation of the secretion of substances as follows: (1) pain-killing endorphins, which are endogenous opiate-like substances; (2) interferon, which counters viral infections; and (3) steroids, which reduce inflammations. Indeed, the physiological mechanisms involved are believed to be operative as well in the so-called miracle cures by faith healers, holy waters, and so-called quacks. As an example, there is evidence from a study of dental postoperative pain (Levine et al. 1978) that endorphin release does mediate placebo-induced analgesia. And this suggests analgesic research focusing on variables that affect endorphin activity (Levine et al. 1979).

So far I have explicated only one of the two species of placebo *therapy* adumbrated in the disjunctive definition given by A. K. Shapiro and Morris (1978). Hence let me now explicate their second disjunct, which pertains to the second species of placebo.

2

A treatment process t characterized by a given therapeutic theory Ψ as having constituents F will be said to be an "inadvertent placebo" with respect to a target disorder D, suffered by a victim V and treated by a dispensing practitioner P, just when each of the following three conditions is satisfied: (a) none of the characteristic treatment factors F are remedial for D; (b) but—at least for a certain type of victim V of D—P credits these very factors F with being therapeutic for D, and indeed he or she deems at least some of them to be causally *essential* to the remedial efficacy of t; also (c) more often than not, V believes that t derives remedial efficacy for D from constituents belonging to t's characteristic factors, provided that V is aware of these factors.

It is to be clearly understood that, as before, the first condition (a) codifies the *generic* property of being a placebo. The second condition (b) of this second explication renders the following: P denies that t's efficacy, if any, might derive mainly from its incidental constituents. Here the third condition (c) is subject to the same caveat (Park and Covi 1965) that I have issued for the fourth condition (d) in my first explication above.

The Placebo Concept in Medicine and Psychiatry

Clarifying Comments

Let me now add four sets of clarifying comments on my explications, because of questions put to me by Edward Erwin (personal communication, 1981), a philosopher of psychology.

1

Clearly, it was the intentional species of placebo that was denoted by the term "placebo" in its original pharmacological use. And its use in A. K. Shapiro's definition to denote as well what I have called the inadvertent species constitutes a *generalization* of the genus placebo, prompted by the sobering lesson of the history of medicine that most treatments were inadvertent rather than intentional placebos, and often harmful to boot! But the tacit intuitions of many people as to what a placebo is are strongly geared to its original status in pharmacology. No wonder that these intuitions call for identifying the intentional species of placebo with the entire genus. Consequently, some people will be ruffled by the fact that, in my explication of the *generalized* use of the term, the generic property of being a placebo is, of course, considerably less restrictive than the property of being an intentional placebo. For, as is clear from the codification of the generic placebo property in the first condition (a) of both of my explications, any treatment t qualifies generically as a placebo for a given target disorder D merely on the strength of the failure of *all* of its characteristic factors F to be remedial for D.

But once the source of the counterintuitiveness is recognized, it should be dispelled and should occasion no objection to my explication of the generic property. Furthermore, in the generalized generic sense of "placebo," a treatment t does belong to the genus placebo even if its characteristic factors exacerbate D, since exacerbation is a particularly strong way of failing to be remedial for D. Surely, it is the failure of the *characteristic* treatment factors to be *remedial* for D that is at the heart of the notion of a placebo therapy, *not* their failure to have an *effect* on D, either bad or good. And the failure of a practitioner who dispenses a harmful inadvertent placebo t to be cognizant of its ill effect hardly detracts from t's objective status as a generic placebo. Nor does the malaise of those who would invoke the favorable *etymological* significance of the term "placebo" in order to forbid a generalized generic concept that fails to exclude the envisaged untoward case. Either species of placebos can *undesignedly* exacerbate *D*! History teaches that many well-intended treatments were *worse than useless.*

Finally, note that if one were to define a generic placebo therapy *t alternatively* as one whose characteristic factors are *without effect* on *D*, it would have the consequence that a *non*placebo *t* would either exacerbate *D* or be remedial for it, or would have a merely neutral effect on it. But in my definitional scheme, one or more of the characteristic factors of a *non*placebo must be positively therapeutic.

2

There are treatments only *some* of whose characteristic factors *F* are therapeutic for a given *D*, while the therapeutic theory Ψ that advocates their dispensation claims that *all* of the factors *F* are thus remedial. For example, it has recently been claimed (Kazdin and Wilson, 1978) that in the systematic desensitization brand of behavior therapy, which is an effective treatment for certain phobias, only one of its three *F* factors is thus therapeutic, while the other two appear unavailing. What, it might be asked, is the classificatory verdict of my explication as to whether a therapy whose characteristic factors comprise both efficacious and otiose members qualifies generically as a nonplacebo?

To answer this question, note that within the class of treatments for any given *D*, any member *t* will belong to the genus placebo exactly when *none* of its characteristic factors are remedial for *D*. Therefore any therapy whose characteristic factors include *at least one* that is therapeutic for *D* will pass muster as a nonplacebo. Evidently it is not necessary for being a nonplacebo that all of the *F* factors be remedial. It follows that, in the absence of further information, the designation of a given therapy—such as desensitization in the example above—as a nonplacebo does not tell us whether only some of its characteristic factors are remedial or whether all of them are. But this fact hardly militates against either my explication or the usefulness of the concept of nonplacebo as rendered by it.

Upon recalling A. K. Shapiro and Morris's cited characterizations of "pure" and "impure" placebos (1978, 372), we see that my construal of the generic placebo notion explicates what they call a "pure placebo." Their "impure placebos" are, as they put it vaguely, "treatments that have specific components but exert their effects primarily through nonspecific mechanisms" (p. 372). This sort of treatment does count as a nonplacebo, according to my formulation. But my parlance can readily characterize their so-called impure placebos by saying the following. Although the characteristic ingredients of these therapies do make some therapeutic contribution, this remedial effect is exceeded by the therapeutic benefit deriving from the *incidental* treatment factors. This quantitative vagueness is, of course, not my problem but theirs.

3

It must not be overlooked that my explication of "placebo" is relativized not only to a given target disorder D, but also to those characteristic factors that are singled out from a particular treatment process by a specified therapeutic theory Ψ. It is therefore not my explication but a given theory Ψ that determines which treatment factors are to be classified as the characteristic factors in any one case. And by the same token, as I illustrate presently, the given therapeutic theory Ψ (in medicine or psychiatry) rather than my explication determines whether any factors in the physician-patient relationship are to count as only "incidental." Clearly, for example, a particular psychiatric theory might well designate some such factors as being characteristic. And just this sort of fact prompted A. K. Shapiro and Morris to disavow the common restriction of "specific activity" to "nonpsychological mechanisms of action," and to offer their "more general definition of specific activity" cited above.

An example given to me in a discussion at Maudsley Hospital in London called my attention to allowing for the possible *time-dependence* of the effects of *incidental* treatment factors. In pharmacological research on rats, it was noticed that the effects of injected substances were enhanced after a while, via Pavlovian conditioning, by the continued presence of blue light. That light can be deemed an incidental treatment factor throughout, I claim, although its effects will vary as time goes on. Hence I reject the suggestion that once the blue light has begun to potentiate the effects of the injected substances, the light must be reclassified to become a characteristic treatment factor, after starting out as a merely incidental one.

The divergence between Jerome Frank's (1973) theory of healing as persuasion on the one hand, and such psychotherapeutic theories as Freud's or Hans Eysenck's on the other, will now serve to illustrate three important points as follows. (a) As is evident from my explication, it is the given therapeutic theory Ψ rather than my explication of "placebo" that decides *which* treatment factors are to be respectively classified as "characteristic" and as "incidental." (b) Precisely because my analysis of the placebo concept does make explicit provision for the dependence of the memberships of these classes on the particular theory Ψ at hand, it allows for the fact that rival therapeutic theories can *disagree* in regard to their classification of particular treatment factors as "characteristic," no less than in their attribution of significant therapeutic efficacy to such factors. (c) Hence, the relativization of the classification of treatment factors to a given theory Ψ that is built into my explication prevents seeming inconsistencies and confusions, generated when investigators want to assess the generic placebo status of a therapy t across rival therapeutic theories, and without regard to whether these theories use different characteristic factors to identity t.

In the language and notions of my explications, Jerome Frank's (1973, xv–xx) view of the therapeutic status of the leading rival psychotherapies can now be outlined. For *each* of these treatment modalities t and its underlying theory Ψ, he hypothesizes that t is as follows:

1. A generic placebo with respect to the characteristic treatment factors singled out by *its own* particular Ψ.

2. An inadvertent placebo with respect to the beliefs of those dispensers of t who espouse Ψ.

3. Therapeutically effective to the extent that the patient's hope is aroused by the doctor's healing symbols, which mobilize the patient's sense of mastery of his or her demoralization.

As is clear from the third item, Frank credits a treatment ingredient *common* to the rival psychotherapies with such therapeutic efficacy as they do possess. But his categorization of each of these therapies as a generic placebo rather than as a nonplacebo is now seen to derive just from the fact that he is tacitly classifying as "incidental," rather than as "characteristic," all those treatment factors that he deems to be therapeutic. In adopting this latter classification, he is speaking the classificatory language employed by the theories underlying the various therapies, although he denies their claim that the treatment ingredients they label "characteristic" are actually effective.

Yet in a language suited to Frank's own therapeutic tenets, it would, of course, be entirely natural to label as "characteristic" just those treatment factors that his own theory T deems remedial, even though these same ingredients count as merely incidental within each of the psychotherapeutic theories rejected by him. And if Frank were to couch his own T in that new classificatory language, then he would no longer label the leading psychotherapies as generic placebos, although he would be holding the same therapeutic beliefs as before. It should now be clear that by explicitly relativizing to a given Ψ the classification of particular treatment factors as "characteristic" or "incidental," no less than by relativizing their respective therapeutic efficacy to a particular D my explication obviates the following sort of question, which is being asked across unspecified, tacitly presupposed therapeutic theories: If the effectiveness of a placebo modality depends on its symbolization of the physician's healing power, should this ingredient not be considered a *characteristic* treatment factor?

4

In a paper devoted mainly to the ethical complexities of using placebo control groups in psychotherapy research, O'Leary and Borkovec (1978) write: "Because of problems in devising a theoretically and practically inert placebo, we recommend that the term *placebo* be abandoned in psychotherapy research" (p. 823). And they propose to "circumvent the ethical concerns inherent in placebo methodology" (p. 825) by devising alternative methods of research control. In this way, they hope to assure as well that "the confusion associated with the term *placebo* would be avoided" (p. 823).

But I hope it will become clear from my comparison of my explication above with the usual parlance in the literature that these confusions indeed can be avoided without abandoning the placebo concept in any sort of therapeutic research. Nor do I see why the theoretical identification of a particular incidental treatment factor that is effective for *D* rather than "inert" ever has to be detrimental to therapeutic research.

Logical Defects of Received Vocabulary

On the basis of my explications, I can now make two sets of comments on the logical defects of the key locutions commonly employed as technical terms throughout the medical and psychiatric literature on placebos.

1

We are told that any effect that a placebo has on the target disorder *D* is "nonspecific." But a placebo can have an effect on *D* that is no less sharply defined and precisely known than the effect of a nonplacebo. To take a simple example, consider two patients *A* and *B* suffering from ordinary tension headaches of comparable severity. Suppose that *A* unwittingly swallows the proverbial sugar pill and gets no relief from it, because it is indeed pharmacologically "inert" or useless for such a headache qua mere sugar pill. *A* stoically endures his or her discomfort. Assume further that *B* consults his or her physician, who is very cautious. Mindful of the potential side effects of tranquilizers and analgesics, the doctor decides to employ a little benign deceit and gives *B* a few lactose pills, without disabusing *B* of his or her evident belief that he or she is receiving a physician's sample of analgesics. Posit that shortly after *B* takes the first of these sugar pills, the headache disappears altogether. Assume further that *B*'s headache would not have disappeared just then from mere internal causes. Both of these conditions might well apply in a given case. Thus *B* assumedly received the same headache relief from the mere sugar pill as he or she would have received if a pharmacologically *non*inert drug had been slipped into his food without his knowledge.

Clearly, in some such situations, the therapeutic effect of the sugar pill placebo on the headache can have attributes fully as sharply defined or "specific" as the effect that would have been produced by a so-called "active" drug like aspirin (Frank 1973). Moreover, this placebogenic effect can be just as precisely described or known as the nonplacebogenic effect of aspirin. In either case, the effect is complete headache relief, even though the sugar pill as such is, of course, pharmacologically inert for headaches whereas aspirin as such is pharmacologically efficacious. It is therefore at best very misleading to describe as "nonspecific" the *effect* that the placebo produces on the target disorder, while describing the at least qualitatively like effect of the nonplacebo as "specific." Yet just such a use of the terms "nonspecific" and "specific" as modifiers of the term "effect" is made in A. K. Shapiro's above-cited definition of "placebo," in a leading treatise on pharmacological therapeutics (Goodman and Gilman 1975), in a German work on psychoanalysis (Möller 1978), in a German survey article on placebos (Piechowiak 1983), and in a fairly recent article on treatments to reduce high blood pressure (A. P. Shapiro et al. 1977). Equally infelicitously, Schwartz (1978, 83) speaks of a "nonspecific placebo response." Why describe a treatment effect as "nonspecific" in order to convey that the incidental treatment factors, rather than the characteristic elements, were the ones that produced it? Relatedly, Klein (1980) points out that when a placebo counteracts demoralization in a depressed person, it is wrong-headed to describe this therapeutic outcome as a "nonspecific" effect. After all, the demoralization and the effect on it are quite specific in the ordinary sense.

Worse, as it stands, the locution "specific effect" is quite ambiguous as between the following two very different senses: (a) the therapeutic effect on D is wrought by the characteristic ("specific") factors F of the therapy t; or (b) the remedial effectiveness of t is specific to a quite small number of disorders, to the exclusion of a far more multitudinous set of nosologically different afflictions and of their respective pathognomonic symptoms. Most writers on placebos, though not all, intend the first construal when speaking of "specific effect." But others use the term "specific" in the second of these senses. Thus, as we shall see in greater detail further on, according to whether the effects of a given therapy are or are not believed to be "specific" in the *second* sense above, H. Brody (1977, 40–43) classifies that *therapy* as a "specific therapy" or as a "general therapy." And he wishes to allow for the fact that the placebogenic remedial efficacy of the proverbial sugar pill is presumed to range over a larger number of target ailments than the nonplacebogenic efficacy of widely used medications (e.g., penicillin). In an endeavor to make such an allowance, he uses the belief in the ability of a therapy to engender "specific effects" in the second sense above as the touchstone of its being a nonplacebo. In addition, Shepherd (1961) has pointed out yet another ambiguity in the loose use of "specific" and "nonspecific" to designate treatment factors in psychopharmacology. And Wilkins (1985, 120) speaks of "nonspecific events" not only to refer to treatment-factors *common* to rival therapies, but also to denote life events outside the treatment process altogether. How much better it would be, therefore, if students of placebo phenomena banished the seriously ambiguous use of "specific" as a technical term altogether. Yet established usage prompted the editors of one volume on placebos to choose the title *Non-specific Aspects of Treatment* for it.

As if this degree of technical confusion were not enough, the misleading use of "specific" in the sense of "nonplacebo" is sometimes encountered alongside the use of "specific" in the usual literal sense of "precise" or "well defined." Thus, when Miller (1980) writes that "placebo effects can be quite specific" (p. 476), the illustrations he goes on to give show that here "specific" has the force of "quantitatively precise." But in the very next paragraph, he uses the term "specific" as a synonym for "nonplacebo" when reporting that "it is only in the past 80 years that physicians have been able to use an appreciable number of treatments with specific therapeutic effects" (p. 476).

Indeed, the placebo research worker Beecher (1972), who is renowned for investigating the role of placebos in the reduction of pain, entitled one of his essays "The placebo effect as a non-specific force surrounding disease and the treatment of disease". But even metaphorically and elliptically, it seems inappropriate to speak of the placebo *effect* as being a nonspecific *force*, as Beecher (1972) does repeatedly.

On the basis of the explications I have given, it is appropriate to speak of an *effect* as a "placebo effect" under two sorts of conditions: (a) even when the treatment *t* is a *non*placebo, effects on *D*—be they good, bad, or neutral—that are produced by *t*'s *incidental* factors count as placebo effects, precisely because these factors wrought them; and (b) when *t* is a generic placebo whose characteristic factors have harmful or neutral effects on *D*, these effects as well count as placebo effects (see pp. 303–304). Hence, if *t* is a placebo, then *all* of its effects qualify as placebo effects.

2

A. K. Shapiro and Morris (1978) tell us in their definition that a placebo "is without specific activity for the condition being treated." And, as we recall, they contrast "active treatments" with placebos by saying that "active treatments may contain placebo components" (p. 371). Yet they also tell us that "in behavior therapy, some investigators have utilized 'active placebo' control groups" in which "some aspects of the therapy affect behavior but those aspects differ from the theoretically relevant ingredients of concern to the investigator" (p. 372). Furthermore, in the common parlance employed by two other investigators, even placebos that are acknowledged to be "potently therapeutic" or "effective" (for angina pectoris) are incongruously dubbed "inactive" just because they are placebos (Benson and McCallie 1979). And Beecher (1972) emphasizes that some placebos "are capable of *powerful action*" (p. 178; italics in original), while contrasting them with treatments that he and others call "active" to convey that they are indeed nonplacebos.

By contrast to Beecher's use of "active," Bok (1974) tells us that any medical procedure, "whether it is active or inactive, can serve as a placebo whenever it has no specific effect on the condition for which is is prescribed" (p. 17). Thus, in Bok's parlance, placebos may be said to be "active" (p. 17) and "placebos can be effective" (p. 18), but they must be devoid of so-called "specific effect." Yet just what is it for a placebo to be "active"? Clearly, a placebo therapy as a whole *might* be productive of (remedial or deleterious) effects on the target disorder while being devoid of significant (negative or positive) side effects, or it may have only side effects. On the other hand, it might have both kinds of effects. And it matters therapeutically, of course, which of these effects—if either—is produced by any particular placebo. Hence clarity will be notably served by explicitly indicating the *respect* in which a given placebo intervention is being said to be "active." Yet such explicitness is lacking when Bok tells us, for example, that there is a clear-cut "potential for damage by an active drug given as a placebo" (p. 20). Thus it is only a conjecture just what she intends the term "active" to convey in the latter context. Is it that there are pharmacologically induced side effects in addition to placebogenic effects on the target disorder D? By the same token, her usage of "inactive" is unclear when she reports that "even inactive placebos can have toxic effects" (p. 20), even though she goes on to give what she takes to be an illustration. Bok's concern with placebos focuses, however, on ethically questionable dispensations of intentional placebos. But if a treatment is truly remedial, why should it matter to the patient that the treatment is *technically* a placebo relative to the therapist's theory?

Evidently there are divergences among writers on placebos in regard to the usage of the term "active." But they tell us in one voice, as Bok does, that a placebo procedure "has no specific effect on the condition for which it is prescribed" (p. 17). To this conceptually dissonant discourse, I say: in the case of a placebo it is, of course, recognized that incidental treatment factors *may* be potently remedial for D, although the characteristic ones by definition are not. And if some of the incidental constituents are thus therapeutic, then the actual specificity of their activity—in the ordinary sense of "specificity"—clearly does *not* depend on whether the pertinent therapeutic theory Ψ is able either to specify their particular identity or to afford understanding of their detailed mode of action. Hence if some of the incidental constituents of t are remedial but presently elude the grasp of Ψ, the current inability of Ψ to pick them out from the treatment process hardly lessens the objective specificity of their identity, mode of action, or efficacy. A theory's current inability to spell out certain causal factors and to articulate their mode of action because of ignorance is surely not tantamount to their being themselves objectively "nonspecific" as to their identity, over and above being unknown! At worst, the details of the operation of the incidental factors are left unspecified.

Hence, despite the assumed present inability of the pertinent theory Ψ to spell out which particular incidental constituents render the given placebo remedial for D, it is at best needlessly obscure to say that these constituents are "without specific activity" for D and are "nonspecific." A fortiori, it is infelicitous to declare of any and every placebo treatment modality as a whole that, qua being a placebo, it must be devoid of "specific activity." It would seem that, when speaking generically of a placebo, the risk of confusion as well as outright unsound claims can be obviated by steadfast avoidance of the term "nonspecific activity." Instead, as I have argued earlier, the objective genus property of being a placebo should be codified as follows. With respect to the target disorder D, the treatment modality t belongs to the genus placebo just when its characteristic constituents *fail* to be remedial for D. Furthermore, clarity is served by using the term "incidental" rather than "nonspecific" when speaking of those treatment constituents that differ from the characteristic ones. In short, the generic distinction between placebos and nonplacebos has nothing whatever to do with the contrast between nonspecificity and specificity, but only with whether the characteristic treatment factors do play a therapeutic role for D or not. So much for my proposed rectifications of the misleading conceptualizations conveyed by the standard locutions whose confusion I have laid bare.

3 Clarifying Ramifications of My Explications

As is clear from my formulation, the genus property of being a placebo is altogether independent of the belief of the dispensing practitioner as to whether the treatment in question is a placebo. But, equally clearly, the species property of being an inadvertent placebo is explicitly relativized to this belief, no less than the species property of being an intentional one. Thus, a placebo treatment t that qualifies as inadvertent with respect to one school of therapeutic thought may be explicitly avowed to have intentional placebo status in the judgment of another school. By the same token, advocates of t who do not even entertain the possibility of its being a placebo will be preoccupied with its characteristic constituents, to the likely disregard of incidental factors in t that may turn out to be remedially potent for D. Consequently, if patients who received treatment t register gains, such advocates will erroneously discount any remedial efficacy actually possessed by these incidental factors. Moreover, these theoreticians will give undeserved credit to the characteristic factors for any successful results that issue from t. As recounted in Beecher's classic (1961) paper "Surgery as Placebo," which is summarized by Benson and McCallie (1979), the history of surgical treatment for angina pectoris in the United States during the mid 1950s furnished a clear case in point.

Proponents of ligating the internal mammary artery claimed that this procedure facilitated increased coronary blood flow through collateral vessels near the point of ligation, thereby easing the ischemia of the heart muscle to which angina pectoris is due. And these enthusiasts then credited that ligation with the benefits exhibited by their surgical patients. But well-controlled, though ethically questionable, studies by sceptical surgeons in the late 1950s showed the following. When a mere sham bilateral skin incision was made on a comparison group of angina patients, then ligation of the internal mammary artery in randomly selected other angina patients yielded only equal or even less relief from angina than the sham surgery. Furthermore, the quality of the results achieved by the intentional placebo surgery was dramatic and sustained. Apart from subjective improvement, the deceived recipients of the sham surgery had increased exercise tolerance, registered less nitroglycerin usage, and improved electrocardiographically. Moreover, a similar lesson emerges from the use of a related surgical procedure due to Vineberg, in which the internal mammary artery was implanted into a tunnel burrowed into the myocardium. The results from this Vineberg operation (Benson and McCallie 1979) suggest that placebogenic relief occurred even in a sizable majority of angina patients who had angiographically verified coronary artery disease. This history has a sobering moral. It bears further monitoring to what extent the positive results from coronary artery bypass surgery are placebogenic (Detre et al. 1984).

Now consider those who allow that such beneficial efficacy as a therapy *t* has could well be placebogenic. This group may thereby be led to draw the true conclusion that the characteristic factors do not merit any therapeutic credit. On the other hand, the therapeutic efficacy of a nonplacebo is enhanced if its incidental factors *also* have a remedial effect of their own. Thus, it has been found (Gallimore and Turner, 1977) that the attitudes of physicians toward chemotherapy commonly contribute significantly to the effectiveness of nonplacebo drugs. Again, Wheatley (1967) reported that in the treatment of anxiety by one particular nonplacebo drug, enthusiastic physicians obtained better results than unenthusiastic ones, although enthusiasm did not enhance the positive effect of tricyclic antidepressants on depression. Indeed, there may be synergism between the characteristic and incidental treatment factors, such that they potentiate each other therapeutically with respect to the *same* target disorder.

On the other hand, one and the same treatment may be a placebo with respect to the target disorder and yet may function as a nonplacebo for a secondary ailment. For example, when a viral cold is complicated by the presence of a secondary bacterial infection, a suitable antibiotic may serve as an intentional placebo for the viral cold while also acting as a nonplacebo for the bacterial infection. This case spells an important moral. It serves to discredit the prevalent stubborn refusal to relativize the placebo status of a medication or intervention to a stated target disorder, a relativization I have explicitly built into my definitions. For example, in the misguided effort to escape such relativization, Piechowiak (1983, 40) is driven to classify antibiotics as "false placebos." As he sees it, they are placebos because they are not pharmacologically effective for the typical sort of upper respiratory viral infection; but what makes them "false" placebos, in his view, is that they *are* pharmacologically potent (genuine medications, or in the original German, *"echte Pharmaka"*) for other diseases (e.g., bacterial pneumonia).

But, according to this reasoning, "false" placebos are quite common. A telling illustration is provided by the following story reported by Jennifer Worrall, a British physician (personal communication, 1983). One of her patients, a middle-aged woman, complained of a superficial varicose leg ulcer. Worrall relates:

[The patient] was very demanding and difficult to please and claimed to suffer continuous agony from her ulcer (although there were none of the objective signs of pain, such as sleep disturbance, increased heart rate and blood pressure, pallor and sweating). All of the many mild-to-moderate analgesics were "useless" [according to the patient] and I did not feel opiates were justified, so I asked the advice of my immediate superior. The superior [here referred to as "W."] saw the patient, discussed her pain and, with a grave face, said he wanted her to try a "completely different sort of treatment," She agreed. He disappeared into the office, to reappear a few minutes later, walking slowly down the ward and holding in front of him a pair of tweezers which grasped a large, white tablet, the size of [a] half-dollar. As he came nearer, it became clear (to me, at least) that the tablet was none other than effervescent vitamin C. He dropped the tablet into a glass of water which, of course, bubbled and fizzed, and told the patient to sip the water carefully when the fizzing had subsided. It worked—the new medicine completely abolished her pain! W. has used this method several times, apparently, and it always worked. He felt that the single most important aspect was holding the tablet with *tweezers,* thereby giving the impression that it was somehow too powerful to be touched with bare hands!

Some may find this episode amusing. Yet it has a devastating moral for the not uncommon claim that without regard to the *specified* target disorder, a pharmacological agent can qualify as a generic and even as an intentional placebo. Assume that, for the varicose leg ulcer that afflicted the given patient, vitamin C is a generic placebo even in high doses; this assumption allows that, in such large doses, it may have negative side effects. And furthermore, relying on W.'s findings, grant that for at least some patients suffering from a superficial leg ulcer, the administration of vitamin C as an intentional placebo in W.'s ceremonious manner ("with tweezers"!) is therapeutic for such an ulcer. Then surely such a placebo status for leg ulcer hardly detracts from the fact that, at least in sufficient doses, vitamin C is a potent nonplacebo for scurvy. And if Linus Pauling is to be believed, sufficiently high doses of this vitamin can even afford prophylaxis for certain cancers. In short, only conceptual mischief results from the supposition that the property of being a (generic) placebo is one that a treatment—be it pharmacological or psychiatric—can have per se, rather than only with respect to a stated target disorder.

Ironically, none other than the much-maligned proverbial sugar pill furnishes a reductio ad absurdum of the notion that a medication can be generically a placebo simpliciter, without relativization to a target disorder. For even a lay person knows that the glucose in the sugar pill is anything but a generic placebo if given to a victim of diabetes who is in a state of insulin shock, or to someone suffering from hypoglycemia. But if an antibiotic were a "false placebo" on the strength of the properties adduced by Piechowiak (1983), then—by parity with his reasoning—so also is the notorious sugar pill, the alleged paradigm of a "true" nonrelativized placebo. Even the diehards among the believers in intrinsic, nonrelativized placebos will presumably regard this consequence of their view as too high a price to pay. Nor would they ever think someone's Uncle Charlie to be a "false" uncle merely because Charlie is not also somebody else's uncle!

Suppose that, for specified types of diseases, a certain class of afflicted victims does derive placebogenic remedial gain from the use of a particular set of therapeutic interventions. Then it may become important, for one reason or another, to ascertain—*within* the classes of incidental treatment factors picked out by the pertinent set of therapeutic theories—which particular kinds of factors are thus remedial. And this quest for identification can proceed across various sorts of treatment modalities (e.g., chemotherapy, radiation therapy, surgery), or may be focused more narrowly on factors within such modalities (e.g., surgery). Research during the past three decades has envisioned (1) that such placebogenic treatment gain may require a so-called "placebo reactor" type of victim of disease, characterized by a specifiable (but as yet unspecified) personality trait or cluster of such traits; or (2) that the therapeutic success of placebos may depend on certain kinds of characteristics or attitudes possessed by the treating physician. It should be noted that my explications of both the intentional and inadvertent species of placebo have made provision for these two possibilities. Both explications are relativized to disease victims of a specifiable sort, as well as to therapists (practitioners) of certain kinds. As it turns out, for some two dozen or so of proposed patient-trait correlates of placebo responsiveness, the first hypothesis named above—that of placebo reactivity—has been largely unsuccessful empirically, except for the following: generalized chronic anxiety has been frequently and reliably found to correlate with placebo responsivitiy, notably in the treatment of pain (Gallimore and Turner 1977). Yet in a 25-year series of studies of placebo responsiveness in psychotherapy, Frank (1974) found reason to discount the role of enduring personality factors in the patient (see also Liberman 1964). As for the second hypothesis, which pertains to the therapeutic relevance of the physician's communicated attitudes, I have already commented on the demonstrated role of physician's variables among incidental treatment factors in enhancing the therapeutic efficacy of nonplacebo drugs.

Having explicated the placebo concept by reference to A. K. Shapiro and Morris's proposed definition, I ought to comment on the divergences between theirs and the one offered by H. Brody (1977), which I have mentioned on page 309.

Shapiro and Morris's definition appeared in 1978 in the *second* edition of the Garfield and Bergin *Handbook of Psychotherapy and Behavior Change*. But in the first edition of this *Handbook*, which appeared in 1971, Shapiro alone had published an only slightly different definition. This 1971 definition is not discussed by Brody (1977). But Brody claims rough consistency between Shapiro's (1968) definition of "placebo effect" and his own account of that notion. Hence I am concerned to point out that there are several important divergences between the construals of "placebo" given by Shapiro and Morris on the one hand, and Brody on the other. And these differences are such, I claim, that Shapiro and Morris render the generic placebo concept implicit in the medical and psychiatric literature far more adequately than Brody, notwithstanding the important respects in which I have found Shapiro and Morris's definition wanting.

The reader is now asked to recall my earlier remarks as to the consideration that seems to have prompted Brody's introduction of his notion of a "specific therapy": the putative fact that the placebogenic remedial efficacy of the proverbial sugar pill is presumed to range over a larger number of target ailments than the nonplacebogenic efficacy of widely used medications (e.g., of penicillin). Then the essence of his account becomes quite clear from his proposed definitions of the following terms: "therapy;" "specific therapy," which Brody avowedly contrasts with "general therapy" (977, 410); and finally, "placebo." Let me first cite these definitions and Brody's comment on them. (For the sake of consistency, I am substituting the abbreviations used up to this point in this article for Brody's here.)

1) [*t*] is a therapy for condition [*D*] if and only if it is believed that administration of [*t*] to a person with [*D*] increases the empirical probability that [*D*] will be cured, relieved, or ameliorated, as compared to the probability that this will occur without [*t*]. (Brody, 1977, p. 38)
2) [*t*] is a specific therapy for condition [*D*] if and only if:
   (1) [*t*] is a therapy for [*D*].
   (2) There is a class *A* of conditions such that [*D*] is a subclass of *A*, and for all members of *A*, [*t*] is a therapy.
   (3) There is a class *B* of conditions such that for all members of *B*, [*t*] is not a therapy; and class *B* is much larger than class *A*.

For example, consider how the definition applies to penicillin used for pneumococcal pneumonia. Penicillin is a therapy for this disease, since it increases the empirical probability of recovery. Pneumococcal pneumonia is one of a class of diseases (infectious diseases caused by penicillin-sensitive organisms) for all of which penicillin is a therapy; but there is a much larger class of diseases (noninfectious diseases and infectious diseases caused by penicillin-resistant organisms) for which penicillin is not a therapy. (Brody 1977, 40–41)

It will be noted that Brody presumably intends the third requirement in the second definition to implement his stated objective of contrasting "specific therapy" with "general therapy"—an aim that, as we have seen, does *not* govern Shapiro and Morris's construal of "specific." For Brody's third requirement here makes the following demand. The membership of the class B of disorders for which *t* is believed to be *ineffective* has to be numerically greater than the membership of the class A of target disorders for which *t* is deemed to be remedial. But clearly, Shapiro and Morris's cited account of what it is for *t* to possess "specific activity" for *D* does *not* entail logically Brody's third restriction on the relative number of disorders for which *t* is (believed to be) therapeutic! For example, just think of how Shapiro and Morris would analyse the claim that aspirin is not a placebo for arthritis or tension headaches and that it affords nonplacebogenic prophylaxis for blood clotting and embolisms. Nor would Brody's third restriction seem to be often implicit in the medical and psychiatric usage of "specific therapy."

Yet Brody does deserve credit for pointing out, in effect, that the placebogenic efficacy of intentional placebos is believed to range over a larger number of target ailments, as a matter of empirical fact, than the nonplacebogenic efficacy of such medications as penicillin. This is *much less significant*, though, than he thinks: after all, the old sugar pill and penicillin alike have *placebogenic* efficacy, such that the sugar pill does not excel in regard to the number of target disorders!

The third of Brody's definitions reads:

A placebo is:

(1) a form of medical therapy, or an intervention designed to simulate medical therapy, that at the time of use is *believed* not to be a specific therapy

for the condition for which it is offered and that is used for its psychological effect or to eliminate observer bias in an experimental setting.
(2)   (by extension from (1)) a form of medical therapy now believed to be inefficacious, though believed efficacious at the time of use.

Clause 2 is added to make sense of a sentence such as, "Most of the medications used by physicians one hundred years ago were actually placebos." (Brody 1977, 43; italics added)

A further major divergence between Brody's and Shapiro and Morris's definitions of "placebo" derives from the multiple dependence of Brody's generic placebo concept on therapeutic *beliefs*, in contrast to Shapiro and Morris's explicit repudiation of any such dependence of the generic notion of placebo. As shown by Brody's definition of "therapy" above, what renders a treatment a "therapy" in his construal is that "it is believed" to be remedial (by its advocates or recipients). Consequently, this dependence on therapeutic belief enters into Brody's definition of "specific therapy" via each of the three requirements that he lays down in his definition of that term above. On the other hand, no such belief-dependence is present in Shapiro and Morris's counterpart notion of "specific activity." As if this were not enough, Brody's definition of "placebo" invokes yet another layer of belief by requiring that "at the time of use," a placebo treatment be "believed not to be a specific therapy" for the target disorder, presumably by the doctor but not by the patient.

It is patent, therefore, that Shapiro and Morris's construal of the *generic* placebo notion, which we have seen to be objective rather than dependent on therapeutic beliefs, makes incomparably better sense than Brody's of such claims as "most of the medications used by physicians a century ago were actually placebos," a claim that Brody avowedly hopes to accommodate via the second requirement of his definition of "placebo." For on Shapiro and Morris's construal, physicians can in fact be *objectively* mistaken in deeming a treatment modality to be a nonplacebo. But on Brody's definition, it is merely a matter of a change in their therapeutic beliefs. For this reason alone, I have made Shapiro and Morris's definition rather than Brody's the focus of my explication.

Note that each of the two species of placebo therapy I have considered is defined by a *conjunction* of two sorts of statement: (1) an assertion of *objective fact* as to the therapeutic failure of t's characteristic constituents with respect to *D;* and (2) claims concerning the *beliefs* held by the therapist and/or the patient in regard to *t.* Clearly, the belief-content of (2) does not lessen the objectivity of (1). Yet, in a reply to me, Brody (1985, 45) runs afoul of this point. For he thinks incorrectly that the belief-content of (2) negates the greater objectivity I have claimed for my definitions vis-à-vis his own *entirely belief-ridden* renditions of the pertinent concepts.

I hope it is now apparent that the customary notions and terminology of placebo research foster conceptual confusion, and that the adoption of the conceptualizations and vocabulary I have proposed would obviate the perpetuation of such confusion.

Acknowledgments

I thank Dr. Thomas Detre and Dr. Arthur K. Shapiro for useful expository comments on the first draft of this paper. And I am indebted to the Fritz Thyssen Stiftung, Cologne, West Germany, for the support of research. Furthermore, I am grateful to Dr. Jennifer Worrall, as well as to Dr. John Worrall, who offered some perceptive suggestions for clarifying some of the formulations in one of my early publications on this subject (Grünbaum 1981). Sections from this earlier paper are used by permission of Pergamon Press, Ltd.

References

Beecher, H. K. 1961. "Surgery as Placebo." *Journal of the American Medical Association* 176:1102–1107.

Beecher, H. K. 1972. "The Placebo Effect as a Non-specific Force Surrounding Disease and the Treatment of Disease." In *Pain: Basic Principles, Pharmacology, Therapy*, ed. R. Janzen, J. P. Payne, and R. A. T. Burt, pp. 176–178. Stuttgart: Thieme.

Benson, H., and D. P. McCallie. 1979. "Angina Pectoris and the Placebo Effect." *New England Journal of Medicine* 300:1424–1429.

Bok, S. 1974. "The Ethics of Giving Placebos." *Scientific American* 231 (November): 17–23.

Brody, H. 1977. *Placebos and the Philosophy of Medicine.* Chicago: University of Chicago Press.

Brody, H. 1985. "Placebo Effect: An Examination of Grünbaum's Definition." In *Placebo: Theory, Research, and Mechanisms*, ed. L. White, B. Tursky, and G. E. Schwartz, pp. 37–58. New York: Guilford Press.

Brody, J. 1979. "Placebos Work, but Survey Shows Widespread Misuse." *New York Times*, April 3, p. C.1.

Critelli, J. W., and K. F. Neumann. 1984. "The Placebo." *American Psychologist* 39:32–39.

Davis, J. M., and J. O. Cole. 1975a. "Antipsychotic Drugs." In *American Handbook of Psychiatry*, vol. 5, 2nd ed., ed. S. Arieti, pp. 444–447. New York: Basic Books.

Davis, J. M., and J. O. Cole. 1975b. "Antipsychotic Drugs." In *Comprehensive Textbook of Psychiatry*, vol. 2, 2nd ed., ed. A. M. Freedman, H. T. Kaplan, and B. J. Sadock, pp. 1922–1930. Baltimore: Williams and Wilkins.

Detre, K. M., P. Peduzzi, T. Takaro, N. Hultgren, M. L. Murphy, and G. Kroncke. 1984. "Eleven-Year Survival in the Veterans Administration Randomized Trial of Coronary Bypass Surgery for Stable Angina." *New England Journal of Medicine* 311:1333–1339.

Frank, J. D. 1973. *Persuasion and Healing*, rev. ed. Baltimore: Johns Hopkins University Press.

Frank, J. D. 1974. "Therapeutic Components of Psychotherapy." *Journal of Nervous and Mental Disease* 159:325–342.

Gallimore, R. G., and J. L. Turner. 1977. "Contemporary Studies of Placebo Phenomena." In *Psychopharmacology in the Practice of Medicine*, ed. M. E. Jarvik, pp. 51–52. New York: Appleton-Century-Crofts.

Goodman, L. S., and A. Gilman, eds. 1975. *The Pharmacological Basis of Therapeutics*, 5th ed. London: Macmillan.

Gould, G. M. 1972. *Blakiston's Gould Medical Dictionary*, 3rd ed. New York: McGraw-Hill.

Grünbaum, A. 1981. "The Placebo Concept." *Behaviour Research and Therapy* 19:157–167.

Grünbaum, A. 1984. *The Foundations of Psychoanalysis: A Philosophical Critique*. Berkeley: University of California Press.

Kazdin, A. E., and G. T. Wilson. 1978. *Evaluation of Behavior Therapy*. Cambridge, Mass.: Ballinger.

Klein, D. V. 1980. *Diagnosis and Drug Treatment of Psychiatric Disorders*, 2nd ed. Baltimore: Williams and Wilkins.

Kolata, G. B. 1979. "New Drugs and the Brain." *Science* 205:774–776.

Levine, J. D., N. C. Gordon, J. C. Bornstein, and H. L. Fields. 1979. "Role of Pain in Placebo Analgesia." *Proceedings of the National Academy of Sciences USA* 76:3528–3531.

Levine, J. D., N. C. Gordon, and H. L. Fields. 1978. "The Mechanism of Placebo Analgesia." *Lancet* 2:654–657.

Liberman, R. 1964. "An Experimental Study of the Placebo Response under Three Different Situations of Pain." *Journal of Psychiatric Research* 2:233–246.

Miller, N. E. 1980. "Applications of Learning and Biofeedback to Psychiatry and Medicine." In *Comprehensive Textbook of Psychiatry*, vol. 1, 3rd ed., ed. A. M. Freedman, H. T. Kaplan, and B. J. Sadock, pp. 468–484. Baltimore: Williams and Wilkins.

Möller, H. J. 1978. *Psychoanalyse.* Munich: Wilhelm Fink.

O'Leary, K. D., and T. D. Borkovec. 1978. "Conceptual, Methodological and Ethical Problems of Placebo Groups in Psychotherapy Research." *American Psychologist* 33:821–830.

Park, L. C., and L. Covi. 1965. "Nonblind Placebo Trial." *Archives of General Psychiatry* 12:336–345.

Piechowiak, H. 1982. "Die namenlose Pille: Über Wirkungen und Nebenwirkungen im therapeutischen Umgang mit Plazebopräparaten." *Internistische Praxis* 22:759–772.

Piechowiak, H. 1983. "Die Schein-Heilung: Welche Rolle spielt das Placebo in der ärztlichen Praxis?" *Deutsches Ärzteblatt* 4 (March): 39–50.

Schwartz, G. E. 1978. "Psychobiological Foundations of Psychotherapy and Behavior Change." In *Handbook of Psychotherapy and Behavior Change*, 2nd ed., ed. S. L. Garfield and A. E. Bergin, pp. 63–99. New York: Wiley.

Shapiro, A. K. 1960. "A Contribution to a History of the Placebo Effect." *Behavioral Science* 5:109–135.

Shapiro, A. K. 1968. "Semantics of the Placebo." *Psychiatric Quarterly* 42:653–696.

Shapiro, A. K., and L. A. Morris. 1978. "The Placebo Effect in Medical and Psychological Therapies." In *Handbook of Psychotherapy and Behavior Change*, 2nd ed., ed. S. L. Garfield and A. E. Bergin, pp. 369–410. New York: Wiley.

Shapiro, A. P., G. E. Schwartz, and D. C. Ferguson. 1977. "Behavioral Methods in the Treatment of Hypertension." *Annals of Internal Medicine* 86:626–636.

Shepherd, M. 1961. "Specific and Non-specific Factors in Psychopharmacology." In *Neuropsychopharmacology*, vol. 2, ed. E. Rothlin, pp. 117–129. Amsterdam: Elsevier.

Suedfeld, Γ. 1984. "The Subtractive Expectancy Placebo Procedure: A Measure of Non-specific Factors in Behavioural Interventions." *Behaviour Research and Therapy* 22:159–164.

Wheatley, D. 1967. "Influence of Doctors' and Patients' Attitudes in the Treatment of Neurotic Illness." *Lancet* 2:1133–1135.

Wilkins, W. 1985. "Therapy Credibility Is Not a Non-specific Event." *Cognitive Therapy and Research* 9:119–125.

Contributors

Kent Bach is professor of philosophy at San Francisco State University and was educated at Harvard College and the University of California at Berkeley. He has written in philosophy of language, theory of knowledge, and philosophy of mind. His books include *Thought and Reference* (1987) and, with Robert Harnish, *Linguistic Communication and Speech Acts* (1979).

John A. Barker is professor of philosophy at Southern Illinois University in Edwardsville and was educated at Tulane University. He has written on epistemology, logic, philosophy of language, and philosophy of mind. His book *A Formal Analysis of Conditionals* appeared in 1969. His recent research focuses on the construction of computational models of mental processes.

Edward Erwin studied at Johns Hopkins University and is currently a professor of philosophy at the University of Miami. He has been involved in research on epistemological issues pertaining to clinical psychology and psychiatry and is the author of *Behavior Therapy: Scientific, Philosophical, and Moral Foundations* (1978) and editor-in-chief of the forthcoming *Freud Encyclopedia*.

Owen Flanagan taught for sixteen years at Wellesley College and is now a professor of philosophy at Duke University. He is the author of *The Science of Mind* (2nd ed., 1991), *Varieties of Moral Personality: Ethics and Psychological Realism* (1991), and *Consciousness Reconsidered* (1992).

K. W. M. Fulford, a practicing psychiatrist turned part philosopher, is a research fellow at Green College in the University of Oxford and directs an experimental course in medical ethics at the Medical School of that university. He has published on psychopathology, medical ethics, and concepts of illness and disease and is the author of *Moral Theory and Medical Practice* (1989).

Richard Garrett has degrees from the University of Western Ontario and Boston University and is currently an associate professor of philosophy at Bentley College in Massachusetts. He is the author of *Dialogues Concerning the Foundations of Ethics* (1990). His current research focuses on the epistemology of wisdom.

Robert M. Gordon teaches at the University of Missouri at Saint Louis. The author of papers in philosophy of mind and a book entitled *The Structure of the Emotions* (1987), his current research aims to defend the "mental simulation" theory of our commonsense understanding of minds.

George Graham studied at Brandeis University and has taught for eighteen years at the University of Alabama at Birmingham. He writes about philosophy of mind and behavioral and cognitive science and is author of *Philosophy of Mind* (1993) and former editor of *Behavior and Philosophy*.

Adolf Grünbaum is Andrew Mellon Professor of Philosophy, Research Professor of Psychiatry, and Chairman of the Center for Philosophy of Science at the University of Pittsburgh. He is the author of over 250 articles. His books include *Philosophical Problems of Space and Time* (2nd ed., 1973), *The Foundations of Psychoanalysis: A Philosophical Critique* (1984), and *Validation in the Clinical Theory of Psychoanalysis: A Study in the Philosophy of Psychoanalysis* (1993).

John Heil is professor of philosophy at Davidson College. His books include *Perception and Cognition* (1983) and *The Nature of True Minds* (1992). He has recently become the North American editor of the *Philosophical Quarterly*.

Jeffrey Poland received his doctorate from the Massachusetts Institute of Technology and is currently an adjunct assistant professor of philosophy at the University of Nebraska at Lincoln. He is author of *Physicalism: The Philosophical Foundations* (1994) and has written papers on such topics as classification in psychopathology and the experimental study of pathological cognitive processes.

Ferdinand Schoeman taught philosophy since 1975 at the University of South Carolina at Columbia before dying of leukemia in 1992. His interests were in philosophy of law, ethics, and social and political philosophy, and his writings include *Privacy and Social Freedom* (1992).

Will Spaulding is psychology professor at the University of Nebraska at Lincoln. A specialist in the experimental and clinical psychopathology of schizophrenia, he is the editor of *Cognitive Technology in Psychiatric Rehabilitation* (1994).

G. Lynn Stephens studied at Harvard College and the University of Massachusetts and then taught at the University of Notre Dame before joining the philosophy faculty at the University of Alabama at Birmingham. In addition

to philosophy of mind, he has published on the history of American philosophy and on world religions.

Robert Van Gulick directs the cognitive science program at Syracuse University, where he is also associate professor of philosophy. He has published on
a variety of topics in philosophy of mind and, with Ernest LePore, has edited
a book entitled *John Searle and His Critics* (1991).

Barbara Von Eckardt is associate professor in the philosophy department of
the University of Nebraska at Lincoln. She has published *What Is Cognitive
Science?* (1993), a study of the assumptions of and controversies in cognitive
science. Among her research interests are the nature of folk psychology,
classification in psychopathology, and the use of neuroscience techniques
in the study of mind.

Index